THE BIG PICTURE
PAINTINGS
IN PARIS

Acknowledgements

The author would like to express his gratitude
to the following individuals for their kind assistance
in the realisation of this volume:

In the first place, to all the students at the Sorbonne;

To M. Jean-Jacques Aillagon, French Minister of Culture
and Communication, who had the initial idea for this book
while President of the Centre Pompidou;

To M. Henri Loyrette, President-Director of the Musée
du Louvre;
M. Serge Lemoine, Director of the Musée d'Orsay;
M. Bruno Racine, President of the Centre Pompidou;
M. Alfred Pacquement, Director of the Musée National d'Art
Moderne;

To all those who have helped in the production
of the present volume from the publications departments
of the Centre Pompidou and the Musée du Louvre
and from the cultural services of the Musée d'Orsay:
M. Philippe Bidaine, Mme Françoise Bertaux,
who has been an enthusiastic and vigilant editor;
Mme Evelyne Pomey, M. Martial Lhuillery,
Mme Violaine Bouvet-Lanselle,
Mme Monique Nonne;

And all those who, through their ideas, writings or friendly
advice, have made this 'Parisian picture album' possible:
Benedikte and Frédéric Andersson, Sébastien Allard,
Laurence des Cars, Claire and Eric de Chassey,
Béatrice de Durfort, Emmanuel Fessy, Christine Flon,
Bruno Foucart, Xavier Fourtou, Jean-Louis Gaillemin,
Annick and André Goetz, Eric Gross, Dominique Jacquot,
Barthélémy Jobert, Michel Laclotte, Laurent Le Bon,
Neil MacGregor, Alain Mérot, Jean-Christophe Mikhaïloff,
Flavie de Montgolfier, Christine Peltre,
Véronique and Arnauld Pierre, Christian Poncet,
David Radzinowicz, Bruno Roger-Vasselin, Aline Sylla,
Germain Viatte, Philippe Sage, Henri Zerner.

The author

One-time student at the Ecole Normale
Supérieure, Paris, agrégé in history,
Adrien Goetz possesses a doctorate
in art history and is currently
Maître de Conférences at the Sorbonne.
He has taught at Yale University
and has been in charge of research
at the Institut National du Patrimoine.
A contributor to various periodicals
(L'Œil, Le Journal des Arts, Zurban),
he is also Secretary-General
of a humanitarian organisation,
Patrimoine Sans Frontières.

Cover illustrations

Jean Auguste Dominique Ingres,
La Grande Odalisque, 1814 (detail)
Edouard Manet, *Olympia*, 1863 (detail)
Martial Raysse, *Made in Japan
– La Grande Odalisque*, 1964 (detail)

Musée du Louvre

Henri Loyrette, **President Director**
Didier Selles, **Chief Executive Director**
Aline Sylla, **Deputy Executive Director**

Musée d'Orsay

Serge Lemoine, **Director**

Centre national d'art et de culture Georges Pompidou

Bruno Racine, **President**
Bruno Maquart, **Director Manager**
Alfred Pacquement, **Director
of the Musée national d'art moderne-
Centre de création industrielle**

Pompidou Publications Department

Director
Philippe Bidaine
Sales Manager
Benoît Collier
Rights and Contracts Managers
Mathias Battestini, Claudine Guillon
Publications Administrator
Nicole Parmentier

Musée du Louvre

Head of Publications
Violaine Bouvet-Lanselle
Curator of the Paintings Department
Sébastien Allard

Publication

Editor
Françoise Bertaux
Author
Adrien Goetz
Translator
David Radzinowicz
Graphic Designer
Bulnes & Robaglia
Copy Editors
Les Quatre Coins (French)
Natasha Edwards (English)
Documentation
Flavie de Montgolfier (Louvre)
Dominique Lobstein, Monique Nonne
(Orsay)
Evelyne Pomey (Centre Pompidou)
Editorial Assistant
Esther Rogeau
Production Supervisor
Martial Lhuillery

French Edition
ISBN: 2-901785-38-7 Musée du Louvre
ISBN: 2-84426-151-5 Centre Pompidou
Publication number: 1204
Legal deposition: january 2003

English Edition
ISBN: 2-901785-41-7 Musée du Louvre
ISBN: 2-84426-152-3 Centre Pompidou
Publication number: 1205
Legal deposition: january 2003

Musée du Louvre, Musée d'Orsay, Centre Pompidou/Musée national d'art moderne

PERSPECTIVES ON THREE COLLECTIONS

THE BIG PICTURE PAINTINGS IN PARIS

Adrien Goetz

Translated by
David Radzinowicz

Foreword

This is the first time an attempt has been made to gather together a selection of masterpieces of painting from the Musée du Louvre, the Musée d'Orsay and the Centre Pompidou in a single, handy, reasonably priced volume. Though basically a simple idea, there is clearly a need for such a book, for art lovers and tourists, students in various disciplines, visitors from the world over, and for the young, who come in droves to understand something of art, be it with their school or on their own initiative.

In 1976, in a discussion of André Malraux's writings on art, the great cultural historian Ernst Gombrich highlighted what was for him the most important and convincing passage in *The Voice of Silence*: 'The artist conquers [forms] over other forms: the raw material for a fledgling art is not life, it is art from earlier periods.' Faced with examples of Impressionist brushwork in the Musée d'Orsay, the mind drifts back to the energy of a Fragonard or to the impulsiveness of a Rubens. And, in the opposite direction, studying some important work in the Louvre, by Giotto or Titian, one often feels the need to take a fresh look at the equally celebrated Mondrians or Matisses in the Pompidou.

This book, then, can harbour no ambitions to be a history of painting in the classic sense. Nor does it intend to be a thoroughgoing guide to all three museums, of which excellent examples already exist. It is instead an invitation to become familiar with works which, especially once they are seen side by side, etch themselves forever on the memory. Such masterworks continue to vibrate on the retina, transforming our trio of museums into a single Parisian institution, and it is to this vast entity that this book throws open the doors. The idea is not to unearth hypothetical 'inspirations', nor to hunt down 'influences' (disputable at the best of times) or to dig up from the Louvre or the Musée d'Orsay the putative 'sources' of 20th-century art. It is simply to present new horizons, far from the beaten yet intimidating track of chronology, and free of odious distinctions between national schools.

Some of these encounters have accorded me particular delight: Monet opposite Pollock rings true; Picasso is quite at home rubbing shoulders with Delacroix; the comparison between Matta and David can raise eyebrows, yet through it our attitude to both artists emerges re-energised and rejuvenated. Who would have believed that Soulages' pitch-black surfaces could hold their own next to the pale bluish sky of the *Embarkation for Cythera*? This superbly devised anthology is both rhyme and reason, consonance and dissonance: Manet's *Olympia* does not, as might be supposed, lounge opposite Ingres' *Odalisque*, and Courbet's *Studio* does not gaze across at his *Burial*, but all appear, somewhere, in an album that is as satisfying to leaf through as to read from first page to last. It is astonishing to see old friends, who one did not think were even acquainted, spend time together. To spot Ingres with Robert Delaunay, to see Veronese join battle with Thomas Couture (though it is true that the French painter claimed artistic descent from the Venetian), or, contrariwise, to contrast the painter of the *Wedding Feast at Cana* with Fernand Léger's *Noces*, is to transform raw knowledge into 'culture': works one was more or less sure of knowing in the three museums at last, together, 'paint a picture'.

I have had the renewed pleasure of meeting in these pages pictures that have figured in the collections of France since Louis XIV, alongside others that have only recently entered the national collection, such as Dalí's *William Tell*, acquired in 2002. As is their right, living artists, Aurélie Nemours, Georges Mathieu and François Morellet, to mention but three, take their place among their elders. Between these covers (it is to be hoped that this is just the first volume in an ongoing series), the three joint flagships of the French museum fleet sail forth in convoy.

I would like to thank Henri Loyrette, President Director of the Musée du Louvre, Serge Lemoine, Director of the Musée d'Orsay, Bruno Racine, President of the Centre Pompidou, and Alfred Pacquement, Director of the Musée National d'Art Moderne, for displaying instant enthusiasm for a book designed to assemble in one place the three collections they curate — three collections which are, in truth, just one: the French national collection as exhibited in Paris. They chose to entrust the concept and realisation of this synthesis to an academic, Adrien Goetz, who teaches history of art at the Université de Paris-Sorbonne. It is my opinion that this type of collaboration between museums and universities foreshadows the future development of art history in France.

On closing this book, I recalled the at once unaffected yet scholarly tone of Salomon Reinach's *Apollo*, a diminutive, green and gold volume published in 1904 that was lent to me by one of my first professors. This once renowned text, which was still being avidly devoured even in the 1960s, proved a spur to several generations of novices to the arts, and even to a few who therein acquired the necessary culture to become painters, sculptors or architects in their turn. Almost one hundred years later, I warmly wish that this innovative book has a similar effect on present-day readers.

Jean-Jacques Aillagon
French Minister of Culture and Communication

Contents

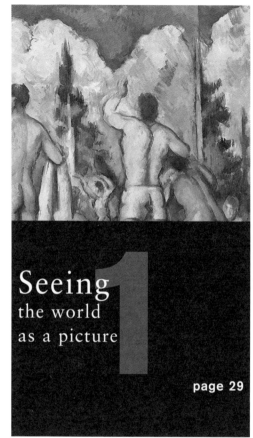

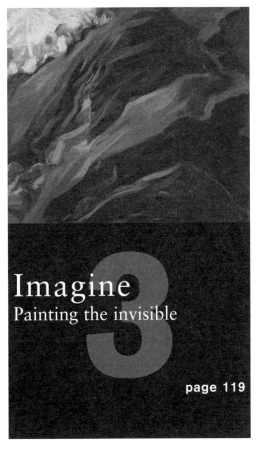

Brief History

of the three Museums and of the Growth
of the French National Collections

'The sun sets on a heaving
mass of crimes'
Henry J.-M. Levet, *Cartes postales, Sonnets torrides,
Les Voyages*, 1900.

Three collections in one book: neither an ideal nor even an 'imaginary' museum, this illustrated panorama presents more than two hundred paintings from the three most important art museums in Paris. The idea is that it should serve as a keepsake, rather like the golden casket containing Homer's poems that Ingres paints in Alexander the Great's hands, and which the conquering hero used to keep by him in all his battles.

Jean Auguste Dominique Ingres

The Apotheosis of Homer

1827

386 x 512 cm - ML

It is inevitable that literary anthologies and miscellanies reflect the taste of their time: André Gide's or Georges Pompidou's anthologies of French verse and Palgrave's *Golden Treasury*, for example, appear to us today like 'bouquets of poesy' that teach us as much about the understanding of literary history and the idea of poetry in their various eras as about the master-pieces the compilers pinned like butterflies to a card. Not all the flowers have withered, of course, but the ribbon that held them together certainly looks the worse for wear — indeed it is in this that most of their interest resides today.

The Louvre in which Théophile Gautier, with his guide's hat on, proffered commentaries on 'his pictures' (by Andrea del Sarto, Bachelier and Prud'hon, but also by Veronese and Watteau), in 1849, is no longer the one we visit today, even though none of the paintings he referred to has left the building. On the occasion of the 1867 World Fair, the critic Paul de Saint-Victor strenuously recommended visitors to the Musée du Luxembourg (the equivalent at the time of a gallery of living artists, a sort of museum of contemporary art)

not to miss Horace Vernet, Camille Roqueplan and Robert-Fleury, painters he vaunted immediately after Delacroix. Museums mirror the predominant taste of the time when their collections were amassed, enriched or their various rooms arranged.

It is even diverting to 'date' the selections chosen for the present book: Lubin Baugin (p. 154) became a great 17th-century painter only around 1960, at a time when his work was enthusiastically compared to the Cubists who themselves had only recently joined the august ranks of the 'classics'. The Dutchman Pieter Saenredam (p. 152) is now considered an artist of the first rank, thanks to our recent sensitivity to geometric abstraction and to the now almost unanimous admiration for Mondrian. Thomas Couture (p. 87), much deprecated in the past, came into his own with the opening of the Musée d'Orsay in 1986, while Puvis de Chavannes has been rehabilitated only as recently as 2001; the present volume allots him a space alongside other major painters, whereas until now, despite a splendid exhibition in 1976, art lovers showed little enthusiasm for his oeuvre.

This album of illustrations has but one ambition: to present a snapshot of what is looked at in Paris today, at the onset of the 21st century, in the realm of painting and, above all, to show, through a process of comparing and contrasting, *how* painting is looked at today, by placing works side by side in triptychs or families, or by juxtaposing polar opposites and watching the sparks fly. After these trips back and forth between the Louvre, the Musée d'Orsay and the Centre Pompidou, chronology and geography find their rightful place at the end of the volume, where the reader is invited to a crash course on the history of art. This album provides a picture of all three museums; and, just as, whether on one bank of the Seine or another, it is always the same river, so the collections are here presented as one.

Originally, the collections of the Louvre were those of the French monarchy in which painting predominated. The lion's share was made up of royal commissions and purchases from artists, together with donations. At the time of François I (1494-1547), the fortress of Philippe Auguste (1165-1223), which Charles V the Wise (1338-1380) had already converted into a well-appointed residence complete with library, was replaced by a new palace designed by Pierre Lescot (1510-1578), the starting-point for what is today the Cour Carrée. It was only in the reign of Louis XIV that Louis Le Vau (1612-1670) quadrupled the surface area of the courtyard around which the halls now containing French painting are arranged and laid out a long riverside gallery towards the Tuileries. The monumental colonnade by Claude Perrault (1613-1688) bestowed new-found grandeur on a palace that the court was to abandon for Versailles in 1682. Prior to the Revolution, artists dwelt in some of the buildings that housed a considerable proportion of the royal collections. The decision to open what became the first large-scale public museum in all Europe for the purposes of study and pleasure was taken during the reign of Louis XVI: it was a tragic irony that it unlocked its doors only after the king himself had perished on the guillotine.

Jean-Jacques Lagrenée the Younger
Allegory Regarding
the Establishment
of the Museum, 1783
52 x 68 cm - ML

It was the Revolution in 1793 that turned the Louvre into a public museum, open to all for free. Subsequently Napoleon I (1769-1821), with the guidance of Dominique Vivant Denon (1747-1825), cherished a dream of making a vast, centralised museum for the Europe he had conquered. Denon, though also interested in sculpture, drawing and printmaking, gave pride of place to painting. After 1815, France sent back almost everything of note from the Imperial Louvre to Italy, Belgium and Holland, with a few notable exceptions, such as the Giotto (p. 58), in which there was scant interest in Italy at the time, and the Veronese (p. 86), which was thought too large to safely undergo the return journey. To line the now deserted walls, the monumental cycle commissioned by Marie de' Medici from Rubens (p. 138) that then graced the Luxembourg Palace was moved to the Louvre. Hanging a painting is never an innocent act: if the Musée Napoléon recounted the glories of Empire, then the Louvre of the Restoration turned the spotlight on Henri IV, a king whose Italian marriage had so enhanced the grandeur of France. The fledgling museum was already a political space: a nation's collections give tangible reality to its history.

The modern Louvre truly emerged in the 19th and 20th centuries, when Ingres, Delacroix and Braque received commissions for ceilings, while the allocation of the rooms between seven 'departments', including one for painting, gradually evolved. The museum was expanded in 1989 with a grand new entrance, the transparent pyramid by Ieoh Ming Pei (born 1917), the architect already responsible for the new wing of the National Gallery at Washington D.C. Since 1986 the museum has cheerfully let a certain number of masterworks from the 19th century escape to the Musée d'Orsay on the opposite bank of the Seine.

Thanks to the late President of the Republic, François Mitterrand, the whole Louvre palace, for long partly occupied by the Finance Ministry, has become a museum with enlarged public spaces and state-of-the-art transit facilities. Together with the department of Egyptian antiquities, the painting galleries of the 'Grand Louvre' remain the most visited. Today, the Grande Galerie and its extension, the Salon Carré, show collections of Italian painting, with the so-called 'seven-metre room' annex serving as a sanctuary for the Primitives. The reopening of the renovated and re-hung Salle des Etats provides the opportunity to appreciate the majesty of *The Wedding Feast at Cana* (p. 86) and render obeisance before the *Mona Lisa* (p. 17). French painting from David to Delacroix is triumphantly arrayed against the red backdrop of the Salles Daru and Mollien, supplemented by a chronological presentation around the Cour Carrée that runs from the portrait of Jean le Bon (p. 92) to landscapes by the Barbizon School.

It was on the initiative of another former President of the Republic, Valéry Giscard d'Estaing, that a museum dedicated to the years 1848-1914 was to see the light of day in a disused railway station constructed by Victor Laloux (1850-1937) for the 1900 World Fair. The building had been earmarked for demolition in the 1970s and was only listed as an historic monument and so saved by the skin of its teeth in 1978. With a handful of exceptions, it is the date of birth of the artist that determines the collection into which he or she enters, those born between 1820 and 1870 being allotted to the Musée d'Orsay. This chronological split (special cases aside) means that Ingres is exhibited on both banks (*La Source*, begun in 1820 and finished in 1856, is at the Musée d'Orsay, while *Le Bain turc* (p. 55) of 1863 hangs in the Louvre), some Delacroix and Corot are in the Louvre and others in the Musée d'Orsay, while Puvis de Chavannes hangs in the Musée d'Orsay, hard by the Nabis and Matisse's *Luxe, calme et volupté*. In this manner, 'modernity' kicks off with the Cubists in the galleries of the Centre Pompidou, in which one can also find the sublime late Bonnards, whereas his early career, when he was 'the most "Japonising" Nabi', appears over in the Musée d'Orsay. The outcome of such arrangements is an imperative need to treat their museums in parallel and to visit all three collections, as it were, 'in one fell swoop'.

Pierre Puvis de Chavannes
Hope, 1872
70.5 x 82 cm - MO

The Centre Pompidou, as conceived by Georges Pompidou (1911-1974), a President of the Republic who truly loved contemporary art, was opened officially only in late 1977. It comprises holdings from the Musée National d'Art Moderne that had been formed from the collections of the Musée du Luxembourg and from the Musée du Jeu de Paume, which housed the so-called 'Foreign Schools Museum'. Since 1947, succeeding conservators at the museum have pursued an impressive acquisitions policy. On unveiling the model for the building designed by Richard Rogers and Renzo Piano, Pompidou is supposed to have murmured: 'This'll put the cat among the pigeons!' In fact the construction, all horizontal lines and transparency, has become extremely popular, and a wide public, that might previously have considered 20th-century art and the creations of the younger generation to be the preserve of an elite, has discovered that painting survived beyond Impressionism. Two floors of the Centre, that also comprises numerous cultural services, among them a much-frequented library, house the collections of the Musée National d'Art Moderne. On the fifth floor, the evolution of art from 1905 to 1960 is devoted in considerable part to painting. On the fourth floor, however, the contemporary art collections, including many works by younger artists, are evidence of the reduced dominance of painting, to just one media among others, such as sculpture, installation, photography and video art.

Three museums, one collection

The names of the three museums give no clue as to what they contain, nor straitjacket them into a single, unalterable purpose: the Louvre is the title of a former royal residence, the Musée d'Orsay reverts to the name of the erstwhile station, while the Centre Pompidou pays homage to the head of state who was the driving force behind its creation. So the collections in all three institutions can remain fluid — hopefully, forever.

In the 1970s, the Louvre offered the possibility of comparing David's *Consecration* (p. 74) with Courbet's *Burial* (p. 76). The two paintings resonate and overlap in the memory, perhaps creating between them a *guten Nachbarschaft*, that 'good neighbourliness' which Aby Warburg delighted in discovering between the books on his library shelves. Understanding painting means striving to take in everything at once. In the Louvre, the young Géricault copied Titian as well as Rigaud and Rubens to assemble his own private museum, contrasting and comparing and thus learning how to see.

Georges Braque
Le Guéridon, 1911
116.5 x 81.5 cm - CP

This book is definitely not a history of art, however brief. Though it remains true that painting generally occupies pride of place within art history, how can its history be divorced from that of architecture, sculpture, engraving and the so-called applied arts, not to mention the history of music or literature?

It was Henri Zerner who pointed out that the relatively minor status of painting in 16th-century France (he termed it the 'empty centre') might explain why the French Renaissance so long played second fiddle to its Italian counterpart whose painters had already been widely acclaimed in the 1550s, not least by the inventor of art history itself, the Florentine Giorgio Vasari. Neither is this book a history of painting, since it omits some pivotal artists, Masaccio to name but one. Much mural painting as well as book decoration is missing: the *St Louis Psalter* is not in the Louvre, nor are the illuminated manuscripts surviving from Charles V's library (the only paintings known to have been preserved in the Louvre Palace in the Middle Ages). Though a valuable key to the understanding of the development of easel painting these examples of book art, formerly in the library of the French kings, are today in the manuscript department of the Bibliothèque Nationale de France. This 'Parisian' choice — incomplete (one could just as well start with the Fayum portraits) and imperfect (especially for periods such as the end of the 20th century, by which painting is a less-commanding presence) — also unjustly privileges a few artists and a number of well-known paintings. But art history is not made up of masterpieces alone: minor masters aid in the comprehension of countless factors, while secondary works can be as enthralling as the first-rate. This selection, in addition to being exclusively Western in scope, is deliberately modest in scale: it is designed as an introduction, an invitation, an overview, but one that it is hoped will encourage its readers to venture further.

Prelude

Echoes

Only Dibutade, the mythical Corinthian maiden, who invented picture-making in ancient legend by supposedly drawing a line around the shadow of her lover's profile on a wall, created a painting without ever having seen one before. No picture is ever conceived independently of a constellation of images interacting with it — though one does not always have to employ the misleading as well as reductive term of 'influence'. In *The Pont du Gard*, Hubert Robert, painter of ruins and expansive landscapes, does more than simply depict one of the 'Principal Monuments of Provence', in the words of the original title of the series of four large canvases commissioned by Louis XVI to which this picture belongs. He also forges a synthesis between three artists with whom he had been in contact during his stay in Rome: the brilliant, extempore landscapes of Fragonard, Piranesi's way of magnifying and dramatising architecture in his engravings, and Giovanni Paolo Panini's palette and sense of space. In accordance with the conventions of his time, Robert executed the vast landscape in his studio, surely with these pictorial memories uppermost in his mind, like links to other works from his visual culture, rather more than the actual banks of the Gardon as seen from the village of Remoulins.

Monet paints his garden at Giverny. Here too, in spite of the Impressionist credo that advocated working in the open air and under natural light, one can talk of a landscape invented 'after' earlier images. In his garden facing the studio, Monet had erected a Japanese-style bridge, thereby creating the very landscape he was to depict, made by him to be

painted. The white arc of the bridge transports the ageing master back to the time when Far Eastern prints were first being discovered in Europe, an event significant for his generation in that it revealed another way of seeing, a new representational code. The bridge is thus no unpremeditated landscape, no mere sublime specimen of painting: it exemplifies Monet's interest in an alien pictorial culture.

In Estaque in June and July 1908, Georges Braque, who conceivably had seen Hubert Robert's *The Pont du Gard* in the Louvre, was absorbing Cézanne's idiom. It is this viaduct that leads from Fauvism to Cubism; we even know that in the autumn, as it hang in Kahnweiler's gallery (the preface to the catalogue was penned by Guillaume Apollinaire), this very landscape was seen by Picasso. All three bridges illustrate how interrelationships arise within and between our three museums, and how the works they contain reflect on one another, setting up mutually illuminating correspondences that one first has to sense before one can 'decipher' the paintings.

Jacques Louis David

The Oath of the Horatii, 1785 Salon

331 x 425 cm - ML

Baron Antoine-Jean Gros

Napoleon Bonaparte Visiting the Plague-Stricken at Jaffa, 1799, 1804

523 x 715 cm - ML

A shared space

A similar way of perceiving space: the division of the pictorial surface into three corresponding zones is a time-honoured practice, going back to the triptychs of the Middle Ages, and allows for comparisons on a formal level between compositions from different time-frames and with different meanings. In what is the first major statement of French Neoclassicism that the artist painted in Rome, where he had gone to steep himself in the atmosphere of the antique, David, by a tripartite division of space, instils balance and harmony, giving meaning to an image of heroism and noble feeling. The three brothers act as counterweights to the three women, while the focus of the action lies in the centre, beneath the three glinting swords brandished by the aged Horatius as he dispatches his sons against the Curiatii. At the onset of French Romanticism, such ancient world grandeur had a counterpart in the bravura of young General Bonaparte. The painting, completed the year the latter became Emperor, was intended to give a positive gloss to a much-discussed event during the Egyptian campaign.

Martin Barré
92B-124 X 128-A, 1992
124 x 128 cm - CP

Martin Barré
92B-124 X 128-B, 1992
124 x 128 cm - CP

Martin Barré
92B-124 X 128-C, 1992
124 x 128 cm - CP

Gros's work is diametrically opposed to that of his teacher David: the composition is deliberately involved, with much secondary action, the groups draped in shadow. But Gros remains close to his master in that he places the heroic act in the middle, where Bonaparte displays bravery in the face of contamination, and sets the action beneath three arcades (including, to the left, an Eastern-style one, an already 'Orientalist', Moorish arch): it is this backdrop, as well as the subject itself, that makes the scene so original. A triptych scheme imparts a majestic,

classical air to one of the earliest examples of French Romanticism, whose swirl of bodies and colours remains profoundly 'anti-classical'.

Martin Barré's equally grand triptych is not really one at all. In the 20th century, opting for a tripartite structure carries implications that require decoding. Part of a series of eight works, these three, large-sized 'false squares', spuriously white, present an indistinct, grey surface over which are arranged rectangles with a subtly graded colour scheme, whose outlines on closer inspection appear slightly

fuzzy. Barré plays here with yet more variations on the figure three, with the age-old code of the triptych as well as with the concept of the series (the *Waterlily Pond*, Monet's harmony in pink, also belongs to a 'series'). He reinvents an austere classicism which refers, in an understated and allusive way, both Minimalist and 'reductionist', to the entire history of painting, from which there emerge perhaps, in subliminal form, David's and Gros's masterpieces — so close yet so at odds — standing almost face to face in the Louvre.

Paintings on paintings: why bother 'redoing' the Mona Lisa?

Today, as in the day of Hubert Robert (p. 176), the Louvre teems with copyists, while students continue to draw in the Musée d'Orsay and take notes in the Centre Pompidou. As was already the case under Louis XVI, when the Comte d'Angiviller had the idea of creating the first public museum (before the collections opened after the Revolution), museums are crucial to artistic education. Whether consciously or not, many paintings take as their model renowned masterpieces by other hands.

Though starting out as a landscapist, Corot, in this likeness of a young woman, seeks to make his mark as a portraitist and to rival the Italian masters. As his starting-point for the position of the hands, Corot went back to the *Mona Lisa* ('illustrious if misunderstood', as André Chastel describes her), a painting which was not yet as ubiquitous in 1842 as it is today. For the strange ornament adorning the model's forehead, where no 'pearl' whatsoever can be seen (the title of the picture is as inaccurate and apocryphal as that of 'La Gioconda' herself), Corot quotes from another Leonardo in the Louvre, *La Belle Ferronnière* (p. 62). The character of the face may also bring Raphael's portraits to mind. The *Woman with a Pearl* is thus not an ironic or disrespectful transposition of Mona Lisa draped in the costume of a 19th-century Italian country wife in the vein of Duchamp's famous moustachioed version, *L.H.O.O.Q.*, or Fernand Léger's 1930 *La Joconde aux clefs*. Instead she personifies the artist's fascination with the masters of the past and with the great Renaissance Italians, demonstrating his familiarity with many paintings in the museum. Corot, who made much of being unsophisticated, whose landscapes were painted 'from nature' and whose models were taken 'from the life', is here transfixed by the spell of artistic tradition. For Corot, Leonardo functions as a 'screen memory' between painter and model. The only way to come across as original is to do nothing to conceal one's borrowings.

Leonardo da Vinci

Mona Lisa ('La Gioconda'), between 1503 and 1506

77 x 53 cm - ML

Jean-Baptise Camille Corot

Woman with a Pearl, c. 1869

70 x 55 cm - ML

17

Jean Auguste Dominique Ingres
La Grande Odalisque, 1814
91 x 162 cm - ML

Copy/create/appropriate

Martial Raysse turns his fire on the Louvre. 'Beauty is bad taste', he proclaims, just as Romantics had adopted 'beautiful is ugly' as their rallying-cry. Raysse's *Odalisque*, derisively subtitled 'made in Japan' belongs to a long series of 'hijacked' masterpieces. In its time, Ingres' picture too was a rewrite: it borrowed its blue and conventionally 'Oriental' subject matter from Boucher's *Odalisque* (p. 50), while the image of languorous beauty was lifted from prints illustrating eyewitness accounts of Constantinople. The perfectly rendered flesh, the subtly painted decor and accessories, the transparency of the smoke from the hookah, testify to a meticulous realism that seems at odds with the anatomical 'imperfections' that some contemporaries remarked on, the over-extended back in particular. Ingres transforms reality and stamps it with a 'style' to ensure it conforms to his personal canon and equates the young woman with his image of ideal beauty.

As for Martial Raysse, he pours Ingres' picture into a mould of his own devising, and he too imposes his particular strictures on a purely pictorial model. For the viewer, the picture simultaneously makes reference to Ingres (i.e. to 'Grand Painting') and to Pop Art, an art form intended as part of an everyday world teeming with adverts and billboards, neon lights and acid colours. The plastic fly Raysse sticks on his composition alludes — with the same distance — to the code of the 'painted fly', the *musca depicta*, an iconographical motif dating back to the Renaissance, which was designed to demonstrate the artist's skill at imitating nature and

Martial Raysse
Made in Japan - La Grande Odalisque, 1964
130 x 97 cm - CP

outwitting the eye. Here, by sticking a novelty store fly on an Odalisque, Raysse suggests that mimetic perfection, the flawless reproduction of reality, has today yielded the field to collage and to the readymade, as if all painting in every museum, including Ingres' ever so perfect and ever so unreal *Odalisque*, is but a storehouse of disguises from which the artist must have the courage to pilfer whatever he needs.

Titian
Concert Champêtre, c. 1509
105 x 136.5 cm - ML

Edouard Manet
Déjeuner sur l'herbe, 1863
208 x 264.5 cm - MO

'Quotations'

Certain chains of images in the history of painting have attained especial renown. In Manet's time, the *Concert Champêtre*, an enigmatic picture whose true subject has yet to be identified, was ascribed to Giorgione. The two musicians seem to belong to a separate world from that of the two women, divinities — perhaps invisible — or else figures conjured up by the music. In *Le Bain* (to give it the title as it originally appeared at the 1863 Salon des Refusés, but which Manet transformed into *Déjeuner sur l'herbe* so as to pose as a precursor of *plein air* painting vis-a-vis Monet who used the same title, p. 45), Manet's goal was to transpose the subject into modern costume, arousing a related sensation of the uncanny. Manet countered the golden tone and airy contours of the *Concert Champêtre* with splashes of bold colour, while in arranging the figures he was inspired by a Raimondi

Alain Jacquet
Le Déjeuner sur l'herbe, 1964
172.5 x 196 cm - CP

engraving after Raphael. Thus it is not the observation of Nature that underlies the *Déjeuner sur l'herbe*; it is the reworking of illustrious artistic predecessors from a history stretching back centuries.

Alain Jacquet puts his impressive knowledge of this history to good use. To a group of figures posing at the edge of a swimming pool, he assigns roles lifted from the art world: critic, artist, picture dealer and viewer (the latter two both women), who 'replay' the Manet. He signs the photograph, even though it was taken by someone else, if on his instructions as regards setting and scene, and adds to the cellophane-wrapped picnic that stands in for a still life a packet of toast baked by the 'Jacquet' company: biscuit, *bis cuit* i.e. 'twice baked'. Once screen-printed, the photograph becomes an artwork, a 'mechanical picture' with visible screen lines: the 95 copies of the work printed fit into a great cycle that opens with Raimondi's Renaissance masterworks. Walter Benjamin's celebrated essay on *The Work of Art in the Era of Mechanical Reproduction* here underpins a contemporary 'museum' piece that records the process of its own physical and intellectual genesis.

21

Tributes

For Cézanne to salute Manet's *Olympia* as a masterpiece amounted to staking a claim to an inheritance: for the then-obscure artist from Aix-en-Provence, who was having a hard time gaining a reputation, it was like swearing allegiance to a spiritual godfather of the Impressionist group who had given new impetus to painting. He positions the model at a distance and adds a spectator in evening dress, thus exacerbating the immodesty of the subject. Picking up where Manet's call to arms leaves off, he reaffirms an ambition to keep 'being modern'. Manet, who dreamed of one day entering the Louvre (in 1907, his *Olympia* was at last to rub shoulders with Ingres' *Grande Odalisque*) had posed not only his favourite model, Victorine Meurent, but also Titian's *Venus of Urbino*, which he had once copied in Florence. By adding a maidservant clasping a bouquet, and smatterings of realism such as the black bow, the bracelet and the mules, Manet sets his mythological scene against a contemporary backdrop. As Françoise Cachin wrote in the catalogue for the retrospective devoted to Manet in 1983: 'It was obvious that Manet had painted, crudely and without symbols, a prostitute on her bed dressed up and waiting for a client.'

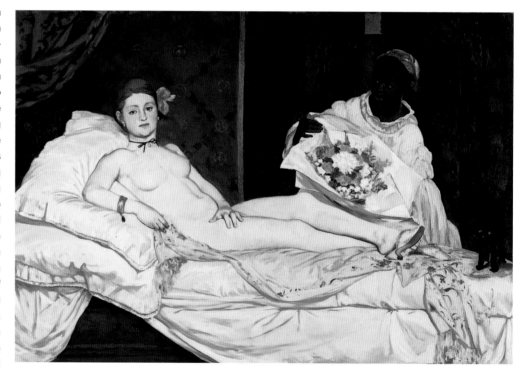

Paul Cézanne
A Modern Olympia (sketch), c. 1873-1874
46 x 55.5 cm - MO

Defending the author of his portrait (p. 180), Emile Zola contended that the picture of 1863, shown for the first time at the Salon of 1865, marked a watershed in art, opening an era of painting in which, however 'scandalous' the subject is, it remains of secondary importance: '[...] for you [Zola is addressing the painter] a picture is a pretext for analysis. You needed a naked woman, and you chose Olympia, the nearest to hand; you needed patches of brightness, of light, so you provided a bouquet; you needed patches of black, so you placed a Negress and a cat in a corner.' Thus it is that Manet joins the tradition of Titian: the 'scandal' is a sideshow. The crucial thing is to be convinced of creating a masterpiece, of adding to a history that started in the Renaissance and continues with Velázquez and Ingres, of completing that ideal museum devoted to the female body.

Cézanne was not the only painter fascinated by this work: in 1970, the American artist Larry Rivers, in an installation entitled *I Like Olympia in Black Face* (Centre Pompidou) co-opts the image for political purposes and switches the roles allotted to the white and black women. Olympia is an artistic myth understood all the better by keeping an eye on all three museums.

Circling...

The Virgin of the Host reutilises a form of which Ingres was especially fond (see *Le Bain turc*, p. 55): the circular shape known as a *tondo* borrowed from the Italian tradition and used by Renaissance masters, in particular Raphael, whom Ingres so revered. A tribute through which he might assert his continuity with the Old Masters, this formal constraint allows Ingres to contrast curves such as those of the blue dress, the candelabras, the aureoles in deep perspective, and the corollas of the flowers in the half-light at the bottom. Circles within a circle, the round face of the Virgin, her lowered eyes, and more especially the white disc of the Host which is, for Catholics, the very body of Christ, son of the Virgin and God made Man, build up into variations on a geometrical theme. Perfect circles evoke the Creation, the spinning Earth, the Creator, and the mystery of the Incarnation of the Divine in human guise; a 'squaring of the circle' evoked by the perspective view of the white, rectangular altar cloth.

Robert Delaunay places a series of circles — staggered this time — within a square space. Featuring what was Delaunay's favourite shape in the years 1912-13. It harks back to the scientist Eugène Chevreul's colour wheels, which had been of such significance for the Impressionists. No connection with Ingres, one might say? Yet both works evince the same desire to impart rhythm and make visual correspondences and, more especially, to construct a cosmogony, mystical in one case and abstract in the other — which is perhaps not so different after all, since the purpose of painting is always to materialise a world other than the real. Robert Delaunay himself noted: 'The coloured areas provide the picture's structure. Nature is no longer a subject for description, but a pretext [...]. Their orchestration gives rise to architectures that unfold [...] that lead to a new type of painterly expression, to pure painting [...].'

Inspired by the uncompromising aesthetics of the Bauhaus School, Kenneth Noland's concentric circles, a hundred years after those of Ingres, are targets, like those of another American artist of the same period, Jasper Johns. They channel the spectator's gaze towards pure zones of colour, transforming the viewer's tension into a kind of mental arrow — although he or she may simply perceive them as a sly and knowing variation on an ancient, and highly charged, symbolic artistic form.

Robert Delaunay
Circular Forms, Sun, n° 2, 1912-1913
100 x 68.5 cm - CP

Kenneth Noland
First, 1958
149.5 x 150.5 cm - CP

25

Abstractions

Delacroix here illustrates a poem by Lord Byron: besieged and vanquished, the Eastern potentate Sardanapalus, before committing ritual suicide, desired that nothing that had served his pleasure while alive should survive him, and gathered round him one final bonfire of the vanities that would destroy his wives, his slaves, his horses and all his vast wealth. At the apex of this pyramid, in the languid pose of a figure from an Etruscan sarcophagus awaiting the funeral banquet, Sardanapalus himself peers out blankly. The potentate is merely a pretext, however. Beyond its Romantic sensibility, Delacroix's dynamic, swirling composition was truly novel for 1827: a broad diagonal structures the whole — no floor, no walls, no horizon. The objects and figures exist solely in relation to one another, as if propelled by some inner mechanism, in a world that seems unreal. The picture functions as an enclosed and coherent space, eschewing genuine perspective, self-sufficient; a world in itself, all the richness and beauty of the universe fuse in a 'composition' destined for the flames, for annihilation. In a matter of seconds, Sardanapalus's pyre will blaze, complete with figures and fragments from the history of painting: its still lifes, its portraits and nudes...

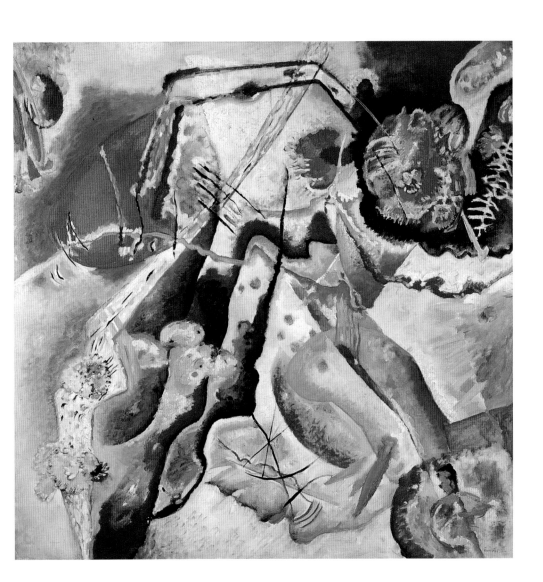

Kandinsky's picture, too, is a world that has jettisoned all reference to reality. Following his earliest abstract watercolour in 1910 (Centre Pompidou), Kandinsky was to conceive of spaces where coloured zones exist solely by dint of their interrelationships, alive (like Delacroix's clusters of figures and objects) with movements, pulsations and internal forces. The juxtaposed coloured hatching harks back to a time-honoured technique known as *flochetage*, used by Delacroix at the end of his life, which paved the way for Degas and Cézanne. The only more or less flat tint of pure, strong tone is the red-orange spot that gives the composition its title; it plays a role comparable to that of Sardanapalus's unmoving face, which supplied meaning and title to the avalanche of colour unleashed by Delacroix. As the off-centre 'centre' of the picture, the red spot constitutes neither its subject nor its primary polarity but provides one key among many others, a possible entrance to a universe created by an artist who here demonstrates total independence from reality, from pretexts and from subjects. In his novel *The Unknown Masterpiece* written in the heyday of Romanticism, Balzac described an imaginary picture, quite inconceivable in his own time: 'a riot of colour, of tones, of equivocal nuances, a kind of formless mist'. 'The mission of art is not to copy nature, but to express it.'

1

Seeing
the world
as a picture

'And the great skies stir dreams of eternity'
Charles Baudelaire, *The Flowers of Evil, Parisian Pictures,*
LXXXVI, 'Landscape', 1857

Gerhard Richter
1024 Colours, n° 350-3, 1973
254 x 478 cm - CP

The sun-kissed brush

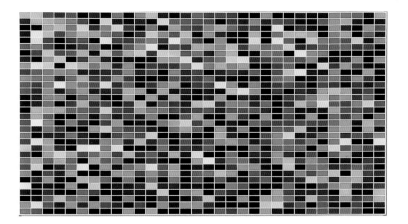

For German artist Gerhard Richter, the pleasure of painting is wedded to a desire to represent the Creation, to sweep the world with colour: in his landscapes, where he allusively renders the blur of outsized photographs, and in paintings depicting candles and skulls that refer to 17th-century *vanitas*, Richter stakes his claim as the living heir to an unbroken pictorial tradition. His *1024 Colours* are rectilinear blocks of colour which form an aleatory fragment of an infinite space that can be extrapolated logically and mathematically. Thanks to a well-known optical phenomenon, when viewed from a few paces away this series of monochrome cells, whose combination might generate a whole universe, engenders black squares at the intersection of the white lines separating the colours. These interstitial squares were not painted by the artist: they do not exist — or, if they do, only on the beholder's retina. Richter explains: 'Abstract pictures [...] make visible a reality that we can neither see nor describe, but which we can postulate. We denote this reality in negative terms: the unknown, the incomprehensible, the infinite. And for thousands of years, we have been depicting it through surrogate images such as heaven and hell, gods and devils.

In abstract painting we have found a better way of gaining access to the unvisualisable, the incomprehensible, because abstract painting deploys the utmost visual immediacy — all the resources of art in fact — in order to depict "nothing".'

Gerhard Richter, *The Daily Practice of Painting* (Notes 1982-83), ed. H. M. Obrist, tr. D. Britt, London: Thames & Hudson/Anthony d'Offay, 1995, p. 100.

Suns and skies

As well as being the source of the title of one of the most perfect pieces in all Dutch Golden Age painting, the accents of light that fall on the landscape in *The Ray of Sunlight* illuminate the canvas and give meaning to the composition. The emotional charge is given by the stream of light as it carves out the volumes with an inimitable simplicity, at once meticulously realistic and marvellously rendered. The painter catches a single moment, an effect, showing how light plays a key role in all landscape painting. *The Ray of Sunlight* was applied with the last few brushstrokes, though the painter had probably had the effect in mind from the outset.

Claude Gellée (also known as Claude Lorraine, or simply Claude in Anglo-Saxon countries) is purportedly the first artist to have dared to paint the sun head-on. Claude's landscapes often have an historical pretext, as with the *Le Débarquement de Cléopâtre à Tarse* (Louvre), where tiny figures animate the architecture on the quayside to compose a theatrical scene. Here, on the contrary, the sole subject is the treatment of light and the way it glistens on water. Light is essential in Monet, but from being the subject of the picture, it has *become* the picture, even the artist's brush. Monet paints his series in morning or evening light (he indicates the time of day in the titles) or, rather, like Ruisdael, though without the same realism, he pursues an effect. Painstakingly worked up at an open window, week after week, always at the same hour of the day, it is a paradox that the canvas mimics the impression of a fleeting instant, as if thrown off in a matter of minutes. Impressionism, through a process of accretion, fixes a transient observation of the world.

Sunlight and wind

In the *Woman with a Parasol* (to refer to the picture by the title posterity has given it), Monet locates the greater portion of the subject, of which he was to produce a number of alternative versions in 1886, in shadow. In representing the imperceptible — wind, light moulding a dress in motion — Monet countered the critics of his time who claimed that the Impressionists could not paint, that they had no 'skill', with an impeccable technique of an apparently novel kind, even if he had already been able to study it in artists like Ruisdael and Fragonard. The woman's veiled face merges with the colours of the sky above, with the white that shapes the broad blue ribbon vanishing into the clouds. It is impossible to recognise Suzanne Hoschedé, the daughter of the woman who was to become the artist's second wife, but it matters little. The original, more conceptual title of the picture, *Study of a Figure in the Open Air*, furnished no hint of its being a portrait, nor even a portrayal of a woman carrying a parasol. The accents rendering the grass bent down in the wind continue in the strokes of blue that set the sky in motion. Not a single shadow is black. Light permeates the scene, imbuing it with an ineffable poetry.

Auguste Renoir
Study or *Torso, Sun Effect*, c. 1875-1876
81 x 65 cm – MO

Winslow Homer
Summer Night, 1890
76.7 x 102 cm - MO

Shadows cast

Light streams like water over the bust of Anna, Renoir's young model. The critic of *Le Figaro*, Albert Wolff, a dyed-in-the-wool conservative, voiced indignation: 'A woman's torso is not a heap of decomposing flesh with purplish-green spots [...]'. The interest of the canvas, which appeared in the Impressionist group's second exhibition in 1876, resides both in its virtuosity and its colour scheme. It pulses with life and with the implication that henceforth painting should be made in the open air, out in Nature, in front of the model.

Vuillard is not only a painter of interiors, of bright lamps in shadowy, wallpaper-lined drawing-rooms; as this fragment from a larger decorative ensemble shows, he, too, can handle natural light. Where Renoir dotted bright patches about a female figure in a leafy shade, Vuillard builds up blocks of dark colour, creating a garden whose arrangement is subject to change at any moment depending on the weather or the time of day.

At night, before the sea, Winslow Homer's two women dance together as moonlight sparkles over the waves. This picture was one of the first American works of note to enter a French collection. How is it possible to paint light in the night?

Edouard Vuillard
Public Parks, 1894
5 panels, H. 214 cm - MO

Georges de La Tour
The Magdalene with the Nightlight, **between 1630 and 1635**
128 x 94 cm - ML

Darkness in light

The 'dark light' of 17th-century painting — like that which 'falls from the stars' in Corneille's poetry — as in the *St Sebastian Healed by St Irene*, which Louis XIII hung in his bedroom (work lost; another version is in the Louvre) or in *The Magdalene with the Nightlight* meditating before a flame, has a constant companion, a mystical, inner light that is the reason for the painter's plunging the image into night. La Tour paints a *vanitas* with a skull, a reflection on the darkness of the world and on the black night of the tomb.
Girodet's night is a pagan one through which the moon descends to awaken the shepherd, Endymion.

Anne-Louis Girodet
Endymion. Moon Effect, 1793 Salon
198 x 261 cm – ML

Henri Rousseau
The Snake Charmer, 1907
169 x 189.5 cm – MO

This picture (so admired by Balzac that he liked to come to the museum alone to admire it the better and which inspired his famous novella, *Sarrazine*) remains totally traditional in its mythological subject and the sculpturality of a hero who resembles a marble statue. However, through the cross-currents of its chiaroscuro and the dreamy, melancholic atmosphere that reigns, it already partakes of the Romantic sensibility. Like the sun on Anna's bosom (p. 36) painted by Renoir, this nocturnal light models the flesh, imbuing it with a revitalised, velvety version of Leonardo da Vinci's *sfumato* (p. 60). Girodet's

biographer Coupin recounts how the artist liked to paint at night, by the light of torches and lamps designed specially for him. This ran contrary to a tradition that required that artists, like other craftsmen, work only in natural light, forced to conjure up the effect of moonbeams through the trees in the fullness of day, in the studio.

The Douanier Rousseau is also concerned with a Nature invented wholesale, assembling a rain forest from pictures come across in catalogues and postcards, regally unconcerned with Impressionism. In his studio, Rousseau painted a night scene entirely

divorced from reality. The space of the picture, infused by a very subtle light, merges with a dream world that is the vision of a painter who has the airs of a great traveller, but who in fact never left his excise office. From within, Rousseau patrols the frontiers of a world he has created.

Jean-Baptiste Camille Corot
The Forum seen from the Farnese Gardens, 1826
28 x 50 cm - MO

Light in Nature

Corot maintained that he had wanted to see nothing of Rome's past: when staying in the city he avoided visiting the museums and admiring Michelangelo and Raphael's frescoes in the Vatican that had so fired Ingres' enthusiasm. In its ruins, he painted a triptych, three studies 'from Nature', three different places at three times of day (the second, also in the Louvre, shows the Coliseum, and the third, in the Phillips Collection, Washington D.C., the Farnese Gardens). Later worked up in the studio, these studies convey the movement of the sun over a geometrical pattern of stones. All the same, Corot depicted the centre of the Roman world, the Forum where Cicero debated and where Caesar expired, and which had fascinated artists from the Renaissance on. Though he played at being everyman, unlettered and uncultured, Corot's naïveté should be taken with a pinch of salt. By exhibiting one of the elements at the official Salon of 1845, Corot proclaimed loud and clear that landscape could do without historical or anecdotal pretence.

Representing light at a given time of the day sufficed, even though it is a happy coincidence that the sun's rays dance over the Column of Phocas, the meeting-point of all Roman roads, the site of the Milliarium Aureum, the sacred milestone towards which all the thoroughfares of the known world converged. Through a streak of white that drapes the sun's rays over the canvas, daylight makes the ruins and remains of the ancient world gleam. More important for the artist, however, is the light on the column, a stroke of white brushed on at the last moment that immediately sets all the coloured surfaces vibrating.

40

Sam Francis
In Lovely Blueness, 1955-1957
300 x 700 cm - CP

Three colours of Nature

Camille Pissarro

Hoar Frost, 1873

65 x 93 cm - MO

Claude Monet

Poppies, 1873

50 x 65 cm - MO

Painted on the ground and placed upright only afterwards, Sam Francis's immense canvas, painted in Provence as he was getting ready for a round-the-world trip, immediately brings to mind Monet's *Waterlilies*, which Francis had probably seen in the Orangerie museum in 1953. The strange title derives from a poem by the German Romantic poet Friedrich Hölderlin: 'In lovely blueness the metal roof of the bell-tower blooms...' As if hovering unseen beneath a non-figurative work, the quotation immediately suggests a landscape and an open window. Through its chromatic harmonies, the painter invites the viewer to bathe in an animated space, in colour itself, and also succeeds in capturing time. As the artist put it, white is a timeless 'expression' of all colour, unlike hues such as blue and red that are real and momentary. Here, white percolates into blueness, shatters it, in outlines reminiscent of organic forms, of cells, of water droplets, of flowers. Sam Francis was thoroughly acquainted with the Impressionist tradition, as in the use of one overall hue, like the dominant in a piece of music: red in Monet's poppies (undoubtedly one of the most popular paintings in the Musée d'Orsay) or white in Pissarro's *Hoar Frost*. What the painter chooses is crucial: of course he paints from life, but he begins by compelling Nature to obey the laws of his own internal world. Because he wanted a red, Monet chose a poppy field; because he wanted a harmony in white, Pissarro chose the rare and fleeting instant of a morning frost over a winter landscape. Painting truth does not mean simply opening a window and depicting whatever one sees; it starts by choosing something exceptional, the exact moment, some special view. This was already the case for Ruisdael in *The Ray of Sunlight* and for Corot in front of the Forum. There's nothing new...

Nicolas Poussin
Arcadian Shepherds, c. 1640
85 x 121 cm - ML

Figures in a landscape

'Et in Arcadia ego'. Referring to the blessed realm of the Gods in Greece's heartland, the Arcadia of carefree shepherds and joyous poets, this Latin inscription can be taken in a number of ways: 'I too am in Arcadia'; 'I too knew Arcadia'; 'I can be found even in Arcadia' — the speaker being Death, unless the voice is that of the deceased in the tomb. The meaning of the picture varies accordingly, though the harmony of this most famous of all classical French landscapes never wavers. Equally famous, Monet's composition, that has come to symbolise the opening of the age of *plein air* painting, shows an elegant gathering of friends, the figures totally integrated into the surrounding space thanks to bright zones of light that pass through the trees (a compositional sketch is in the Pushkin Museum, Moscow). A comparison with Manet's *Déjeuner sur l'herbe* (p. 20) shows how the figures are quite differently incorporated into the scenery. Manet's picture, painted in the studio, is not far removed from the world of Poussin, who built boxes in which he would set up his compositions using figurines. The backdrop resembles a painted cloth before which each model might have posed in turn. The new space devised by Monet is an Arcadia for a more recent generation.

Poussin placed an inscription in his picture. Klee builds up his with pictograms. An imaginary city viewed simultaneously as ground plan and in elevation, its gardens lust with plants. The arrow visible at the centre is one of Klee's favourite symbols. It propels Nature into motion, animates a two-dimensional space that is countered by perspectival features, such as the tunnel in the middle, opening beyond three dimensions on to other universes. In the edition of his notebooks

Claude Monet
Déjeuner sur l'herbe (left section), 1865
418 x 150 cm - MO

Claude Monet
Déjeuner sur l'herbe (central section), 1865
248 x 217 cm - MO

Paul Klee
Pfeil im Garten, 1929
70 x 50.2 cm - CP

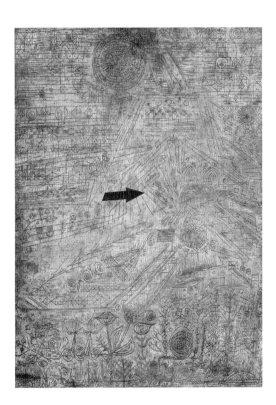

entitled *The Thinking Eye* (1921-1922), Klee engages in a veritable physics course, analysing the movement of a sling and providing a diagram of the parallelogram of forces. His picture symbolises — in the sense that mathematics and physics employ symbols — the inscription of an action in a landscape.

Daniel Spoerri
The Shower, 1961
70.2 x 96.8 x 18.5 cm - CP

Henri Matisse
Luxe, calme et volupté, 1904
98.5 x 118.5 cm - MO

The nude in Nature

The young Matisse spent much time studying works by Puvis de Chavannes, for whom everything was simply 'order and beauty'. The silent poetry of *The Girls on the Seashore*, naked or semi-naked bodies in a landscape, inspired his own picture with its Baudelairian title, perhaps to the same extent as Manet's and Monet's *Déjeuner sur l'herbe*. The hieratic appearance of the young women's physiques, the gesture of the girl snatching at her hair — there are many similarities between the two works. *Luxe, calme et volupté*, painted at Collioure in 1904 and much influenced by Paul Signac's Divisionism, was purchased by the latter

for his house in St-Tropez. Signac saw Matisse's painting as an outsized wall decoration, a speciality in which Puvis too had made a name for himself. In the Matisse, the stasis of the decoration, surfacing in the Puvis in the white, antique-style drapery over the woman seen from the rear, seems to have migrated on to the landscape. It is the massive vertical pine to the right that confers a monumentality on the whole, that the reduced-scale nudes melting into the interlocking patches of colour which link figures to ground could not supply. Nudity here is that of a new-found golden age, a tangible oneness between the beauty of the

bodies and that of their surroundings.

Spoerri, in appropriating a mediocre painting of a mountain landscape and screwing a shower rose in the middle, creates a negative version of trompe l'oeil that he terms *détrompe l'œil*. This time, a painting morphed into an installation incites the viewer to undress and melt into the 'natural' environment co-opted by the artist. The tradition of a landscape with hordes of nude figures is here 'shelved' or relegated to a storeroom for outdated backdrops and reconfigured. But, so that there is no confusion between art and reality, no jet of water spouts from Spoerri's hillside shower.

46

Pierre Puvis de Chavannes
The Girls on the Seashore, 1879
61 x 47 cm - MO

Paul Cézanne
Bathers, c. 1890-1900
22 x 33.5 cm - MO

But does a nude need a model ?

To paint a nude is both to attempt a return to the source *and* to think, as one works, about the biggest storehouse of images with which art history has ever provided artists. Hence the immense number of both involuntary and conscious quotations, borrowings and tributes that render the representation of a nude often more revealing of an artist's visual culture than of the true nature of the model. Derain's reversion to classicism, which here transports the viewer back to the great portraits of David and Ingres, stands as an unassailable and deliberate reference to the French tradition. Following the First World War, Picasso too went through an 'Ingres' period.

Renoir developed a theory of this nostalgia for a golden age, for a time of purity supposedly lost during the revolutions that the 'craft' of painting underwent in his lifetime. Painted towards the end of his life with fingers deformed by arthritis, his bathers evoke an idyllic country setting of mythological nymphs and shepherds, with, in a corner, an authentic straw hat from his Impressionist years. But what really hovered before his eighty-year-old eyes was his nostalgia for

Rubens, Boucher and Fragonard, for nudes from the era of the *douceur de vivre*. In a draft, unearthed in 2000, for a foreword to Cennino Cennini's *Craftsman's Handbook*, a landmark text from the early 15th century, Renoir wrote in 1910: 'Until that time [the end of the 18th century], everything had been beautiful, from chateau to humble thatch. There was art even in a doorknob, in a bolt. They could make gay china and tapestries, enamel, wrought iron [...]. They possessed a serenity that only a restful, simple life can bring.'

For Cézanne, on the contrary, conventional nudity (no models posed for him) served to build up and structure space, as much in the landscape as in the moving figures. A nude, an apple, the Montagne Sainte-Victoire are only props, even if, looking more closely at the leaping figure on the right or the one dancing in the background, one is also reminded of Titian's bacchanalia or of Poussin's landscapes with figures, they too shot through with rigour and geometry.

49

Jacques Louis David
The Sabine Women, 1799
385 x 522 cm - ML

François Boucher
The Odalisque, c. 1745
53.5 x 64.5 cm - ML

Heroic nudity and erotic nudity

Heroic against erotic nudity? The shield carried by David's hero, Romulus, as naked as an antique marble, bears the image of another nude from the time when he was a child with Remus, his rival brother at the foundation of Rome. Naked infants appear in the centre of the canvas, offspring of the union between the Romans and the Sabine women they had abducted by force. Intent on resolving their differences, the women, led by Hersilia in a white robe, throw themselves between their boorish husbands and virtuous brothers who are confronting each other. In this way a new Rome is founded, born of a union between peoples and bodies so that the glorious history of the most powerful city on earth can begin. The political nude can thus also be a nude of passion and a hero both lover and father; nakedness becomes a way of stripping oneself bare so as to be

reborn. In 1795, emerging from the Terror and civil war, from the most bloodthirsty and fratricidal episodes of the Revolution, the French readily recognised themselves in David's figures and in the familiar story of the Sabine women — not in the tragic episode of the Rape as treated previously by Poussin, but in one of national reconciliation. In the view of Rome in the background, nearby the Mons Tarpeius, stands the Capitol. For David, nudity has a dual nature: both historic and contemporary, it states in a language of the past what would have been less easy to admit in modern dress, creating a distance that allowed viewers to identify with the canvas and to project themselves into it. On its first exhibition, David even placed a huge mirror in front of the canvas.

In Boucher's work, the treatment of the Orient operates in a similar way. The very Parisian sensuality

of his picture can be admired without misgivings as long as he sets it in some imaginary seraglio. An Odalisque? There's nothing particularly Eastern about the interior, in spite of the silken cushions and the side table on which the painter inscribed his signature. In a genuine 'artistic transposition', Diderot, much amused with his own prose, characterises the Odalisque in a description that vies for beauty with the painting: 'A completely naked woman stretched out on pillows, one leg this way, the other that, offering the most voluptuous head, the most beautiful back, the most beautiful rump, in an invitation to pleasure, an invitation in the most easeful, the most comfortable, one might even say, the most natural, and at least the most advantageous, position...'

Rembrandt
Bathsheba at the Bath, 1654
142 x 142 cm - ML

Falling bodies

The sight of Flandrin's anatomical study hanging among the masterpieces in the Louvre would have bewildered his contemporaries. Present-day sensibilities have given new meaning (melancholy, despair, pensiveness) to what was simply an obligatory exercise for all *pensionnaires* studying at the Ecole de Rome desirous of displaying their talents for observing the body and rendering modelling: a satisfactory fourth-year piece. The pose shows the figure coiling himself into an almost perfect circle, transforming the model into a geometric hieroglyph before an horizon line. An image can thus be reduced to a circle, i.e. a man, and a line, i.e. a landscape. Flandrin's master was Ingres, a man obsessed by circles (see *The Virgin of the Host,* p. 24 and *Le Bain turc*, p. 55). Flandrin's youth, at once vulnerable yet self-contained, immured within himself, has become in the 20th century — and far beyond the intentions of the artist — an icon of the human condition, that is almost as famous as Leonardo's sketch of the ideal proportions of Man inscribed in a circle and a square. This vulnerability is shared by Bathsheba's body as

Hippolyte Flandrin
A Young Man beside the Sea, 1836
98 x 124 cm - ML

she is violated by the royal gaze. The impasto and generous pigment with which Rembrandt modelled her form are far removed from the slick translucency Flandrin inherited from Ingres. Naked, yet in a decorous attitude, Bathsheba has just learnt that she has exposed her charms to King David who spied her washing in the privacy of her bath. As her feet are dried by a servant-girl in the shade (who could be compared to Olympia's black maidservant surging forth into light, p. 22), Bathsheba is depicted holding David's letter requesting her presence. The viewer takes on a voyeuristic role. Bathsheba's disrobed body is exposed to view: the Biblical significance of the scene may elude us today, but not the troubled, resigned expression of a heroine who has become, like Flandrin's naked youth, an image of desolate loneliness.

Marie-Guillemine Benoist
Portrait of a Black Woman, 1800 Salon
82 x 65 cm - ML

Henri de Toulouse-Lautrec
La Toilette, 1896
67 x 54 cm - MO

Henri-Edmond Cross
The Head of Hair, c. 1892
61 x 46 cm - MO

The body and the decorative

A picture allows the viewer to penetrate a forbidden space, letting him see what was never meant to be shown, and hang on his wall a trapped, fictitious fragment of a world to which in reality access is prohibited. Both the intimacy of the toilet or the bath and a woman viewed from the rear unaware of being observed are frequent motifs in painting; they transform the artist into an intermediary who, for the future owner of the picture, lays the model bare, unlocking a door — to harem, brothel or bathroom — that seemed forever barred. The back of Toulouse-Lautrec's woman in black stockings sitting in apparent exhaustion is a far cry from the back of the female musician in the foreground of *Le Bain turc*; how

different is the softly modelled arm in Ingres' swansong from the scrawny, emaciated limb in *La Toilette*. *Le Bain turc* was Ingres' last will and testament in which he compounded in his mind's eye all the bathers and odalisques who had served as sources of inspiration throughout his long life. A commission from Khalil Bey, who also possessed Courbet's *Origin of the World* (p. 134), it is a cabinet picture, a closet painting, to be unveiled only before cognoscenti.

The proliferation of nudes, the diversity in adjacent poses, created an ornamental system recalled in Matisse's *Decorative Figure against an Ornamental Background*. Employing as a backcloth the interaction

between curve and counter-curve, he extracts a single, naked figure from among the rounded forms that rhythm the pictorial space. In Nice, Matisse created a complete 'Oriental' decor, discovering, in a pattern on the carpet, in the swirling background, in the juxtaposition of decorative motifs, a language able to integrate the sculptural nudity of a model in the form of an arabesque slicing across other arabesques, thereby transforming the nude into a 'decorative figure'.

If the flesh is maudlin in Toulouse-Lautrec, it is exuberant in Henri-Edmond Cross, and, in a very different, more political manner, in Marie-Guillemine Benoist. She introduced her contemporaries to the

Henri Matisse
Decorative Figure against an Ornamental Background, Winter 1925-1926
130 x 98 cm - CP

Jean Auguste Dominique Ingres
Le Bain turc, 1862
110 x 110 cm - ML

novelty of a black skin captured with all the sophistication of David's modelling technique, until then the sole preserve of the diaphanous complexions of Neoclassical heroines. The attitude of the unidentified model leaves no room for doubt: the artist deliberately chose to hail a new type of beauty that here poses majestically. This time it is a woman who paints and, without lascivious undertones, acclaims the femininity of another. With slavery only recently abolished, Benoist aimed to change how men look at things, to assert the fact of equality. And her black sitter, whose exoticism is totally at odds with that of the 'Orientals' in *Le Bain turc*, drapes herself in the three colours of the Republic.

Rembrandt
The Flayed Ox, 1655
94 x 69 cm - ML

Jean-Baptiste Siméon Chardin
The Skate, c. 1728
114.5 x 146 cm - ML

Francis Bacon
Study of the Human Body, 1981-1982
198 x 147.5 cm - CP

Flesh in and out

To see a body also means to enter its unseen interior. It means painting the flesh to the full, lifting the skin so as to understand creation: be it at the anatomy lesson or before the butcher's block, artists have always been as fascinated by the innards of the body as by its envelope. If one forgets for a moment the subject of Rembrandt's flayed ox and the silhouette of the maidservant in the background, and keeps in mind solely the 'lump' in the centre, painted in a beautifully thick, potent impasto, there surfaces an abstract geometry of a striking modernity that accounts for the work's success in our time.

Chardin's *The Skate* is more than a still life: it is an ambitious, large-size painting the artist presented as a reception piece to the Academy on his admission as a 'painter of animals and fruits'. A polemical work, it forces what was, according to a traditional hierarchy, the lowliest of the pictorial types into the inner sanctum where it competes with more 'noble' genres. Hence its compositional rigour and generous format and the dramatic power discharging from the eyes of the fish hanging in emptiness: this is still life with the ambitions of history painting.

On a table rendered in perspective, resembling a chopping block or a pedestal for an ancient statue, the being in the *Study of the Human Body* has been hacked to pieces and put together again, clad in cricketer's pads, vulnerable, yet on the move, an unbearable object held up to view. The matt red ground in pastel sets up a contrast with the modelled flesh. Bacon asked that his picture be protected under glass. Human flesh, transmuted into a cut of meat, is exhibited under a sheet of glass in which we can observe our facial expression change.

Giotto
St Francis of Assisi Receiving the Stigmata, c. 1300
313 x 163 cm - ML

Hands

A body may crystallise into a single limb, a gesture, a glance, just as a picture may be distilled into a single detail from which it acquires balance and power. Hands spread out towards other worlds. In the foreground of the Matisse, the hand attains an autonomy that transforms it into an independent figure, distinct from the dreamy face, like the content of the young woman's dream. A languid yet undeniably actual hand, somnolent and monumental: a door to some inner space.

Originally from Pisa, and entering the Louvre at the end of the First Empire, Giotto's altarpiece, which is undoubtedly the origin of an iconography later to be widely taken up, exploits the interplay between the hands of Christ and those of the blessed apostle of poverty to evoke a sacred mystery, a communion between this world and the next. Like his Saviour on the Cross, in 1224 St Francis of Assisi received the

Henri Matisse
The Dream, 1935
81 x 65 cm - CP

stigmata of the Passion on Monte Alverno, alluded to here by a rock and a few trees. The blood flowing from his hands does not come from his earthly body. Making the immaterial bond tangible, lines join his hands to those of Christ who appears in the pose of the Crucified, flanked by the wings of a divine glory. The hand becomes an offering. Within the open chapel below right, one can just make out an altar surmounted by a large crucifix. Another few centimetres and the hand of the painted Christ crucified might appear (as is often the case on this type of crucifix, the panel shows the Mater Dolorosa, St John figuring on the opposite side). Painting is already present at the origin of the saint's vision in the form of the altar picture that helps him meditate, and he would thus have first of all seen the suffering Christ 'represented', before beholding him with his own eyes and giving him his hands.

School of Fontainebleau

Gabrielle d'Estrées and one of her Sisters, c. 1595

96 x 125 cm - ML

Titian

Man with a Glove, c. 1520-1523

100 x 89 cm - ML

Leonardo da Vinci

St John the Baptist, 1513-1516

69 x 57 cm - ML

The rhetoric of gesture

The hand is also gesture, a component in a sign language that viewers contemporary with the image could decode but whose key may have been lost over the centuries. The finger of Leonardo's *St John the Baptist* points heavenwards; announcing the coming Messiah, he promises paradise to all those he baptises in the Jordan.

In the bath with her sister, the gesture made by Gabrielle d'Estrées, a mistress of Henri IV, is profane and precise, yet it remains mysterious. (Another famous portrait of two sisters painted by Chassériau is also to be seen in the Louvre.) This astonishing image, which art historians still have trouble

elucidating, is linked to a Renaissance pictorial genre that sung the praises of each part of the female body — the 'portrait of a lady bathing' is a distant forerunner of Degas' washtubs and Bonnard's baths, of Ingres' *Bain turc* (p. 55) and of Toulouse-Lautrec's *La Toilette* (p. 54). As Henri Zerner has stressed, the bath in Renaissance painting has more than one signification: the erotic bath, a purifying immersion and allusions to baptism may all be equally valid interpretations. Perhaps this double portrait of the beautiful Gabrielle and her sister commemorates the birth of a child: hence the gesture pointing to the breast, the hand indicating the ring, and also the red

curtains thrown aside as if for a theatrical revelation. Deciphering the rhetoric of the gestures at work in a picture is never straightforward.

What did the exquisite gesture of Titian's elegant if unknown sitter mean to the early admirers of the work: the scented, soft-leather glove, one of those gloves meant to be worn only once, is a mark of rank and surely provided the now lost meaning of the portrait. The title handed down by tradition makes clear that the subject of the portrait, that is, the glove, provides a meaning. Is there a text that could enlighten us?

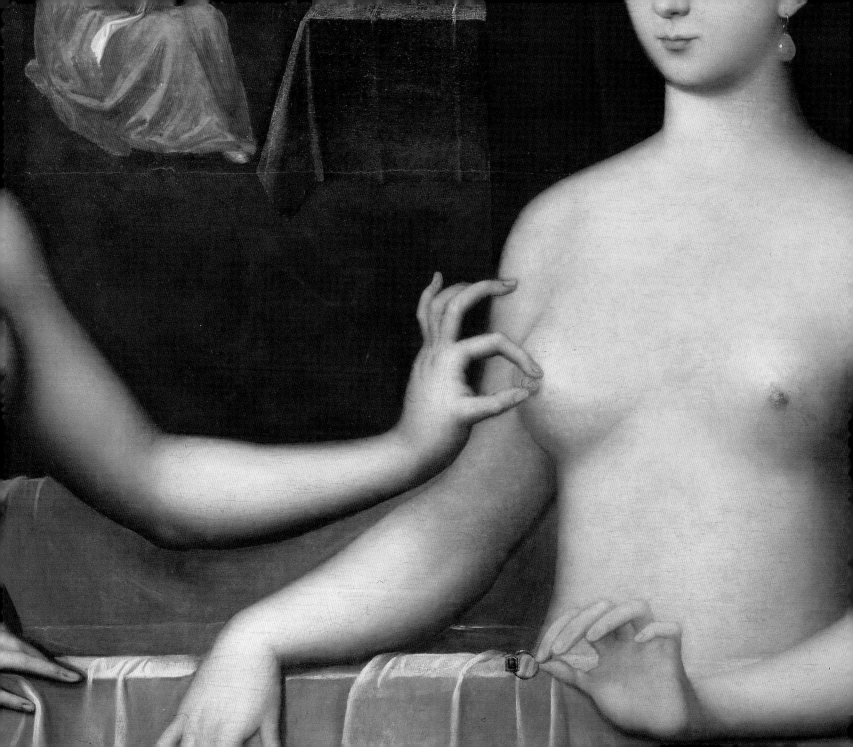

Quentin Metsys

The Moneylender and his Wife, 1514

70.5 x 67 cm - ML

Leonardo da Vinci

Portrait of a Lady of the Court at Milan, known as

La Belle Ferronnière, c. 1495-1499 63 x 45 cm - ML

Marc Chagall

Double Portrait and Wineglass, 1917-1918

235 x 137 cm - CP

Eyes

Whenever a master had help from his assistants or workshop, he would always do the face and hands himself, the two most difficult parts of the body to paint, the ones that conceal the secret of its expressiveness, its moral likeness. The eye is the window to the soul. *La Belle Ferronnière* — an apocryphal title coming from the legend that the picture shows a mistress of François I known by this sobriquet — is the portrait of a gaze. The moneylender and his wife do not see one another; they gaze only at the money, he with lowered eyes, she, forsaking her prayer book, straining to look. Neither do they see the third eye in the foreground, a convex looking-glass that reflects the sky and the exterior world, where the viewer's gaze encounters that of an unknown, red-hatted individual, perhaps the artist who elsewhere has drawn attention to his presence by leaving his signature on a sheet of parchment on the shelf above the woman.

In the Chagall, the relationship between open and closed eyes and the wineglass of Jewish wedding tradition have to do with quite another genus of portrait of a couple. The canvas dates from the early months of the Russian Revolution when the artist was residing in his birthplace Vitebsk (recognisable in the background) and had quite recently married Bella. Man and woman, fused together by poetry and dreams, advance as one in a landscape traversed by a river. While Metsys's figures are described by way of significant elements in their home, Chagall's couple forms a whole with the landscape. Their story commences. The painter just hints at its beginnings: the viewer can carry on the tale and tell the rest.

Pablo Picasso
Stage curtain for the ballet Mercure, 1924
392 x 501 cm - CP

Storytelling

'The earth recedes from me into the night,
I saw that it was beautiful, and I see that what is not the earth is beautiful.
I go from bedside to bedside
I sleep close with the other sleepers, each in turn,
I dream in my dream all the dreams of the other dreamers,
And I become the other dreamers.'

Walt Whitman, *Leaves of Grass*, 'The Sleepers', 1855

Guido Reni
The Rape of Helen, 1631
253 x 265 cm - ML

Baron Pierre Narcisse Guérin
Aeneas Relating to Dido the Disaster of Troy, 1815
292 x 390 cm - ML

Max Beckmann
The Little Fish, 1933
135 x 115 cm - CP

Mythologies

In Guido Reni's vast painting, storytelling means going back to the central episode in the story that founds the genre of narrative itself: the Homeric epic. The Rape of Helen that sparked the Trojan War here looks more like a love pageant, a choreographed dance in which the secondary episodes reverberate to a thousand echoes. Amoretti wave the firebrand that kindles the army, the ships' sails billow on the horizon, while a thronging court accompanies what is a thoroughly official abduction, right down to the two little animals in the foreground who also seem to have a tale to tell. The sea's deep blue conceals and foretells the story to come.

Guérin's account unfolds between quotation marks: the action gives no hint of what is happening. All seems concentrated in the words of Aeneas and in the eyes of fair Dido, listening attentively; the backdrop shows the building of Carthage over which the queen's funeral pyre will rise. Everyone looking at this picture at the time would have read the *Iliad*, the *Odyssey*, the *Aeneid*, and since childhood would have known stories from Homer and Virgil by heart: the Trojan War, the victory of the Greeks as retold by the warrior, and the tragic end of the unfortunate Dido, Aeneas's jilted lover. Beckmann's narrative is of a third type. It possesses all the trappings of a legend, but one about which we

know nothing. What is the significance of the fish — some commentators have seen it as sexual object — and what *captivating* story is the fisherman telling these two women who could be, as in a classical tragedy, lady and lady's maid? They will surely be ensnared in his 'net', for this is narrative defying representation, narrative as trap. All three cases here are variations: to paint a story, to paint someone telling a story or to suggest that some mysterious narrative, some play whose script we do not possess, is about to be staged, is to demonstrate that it is always the act of painting which is to be narrated first.

Dado
The Massacre of the Innocents, 1958-1959
194 x 259.5 cm - CP

Raphael
The Virgin with the Veil, c. 1518
68 x 48.7 cm - ML

The miraculous and the marvellous

What is the painter interested in? The familiar narrative he turns into an image, or the image itself? Raphael's aim in *The Virgin with the Veil* is not to rejuvenate the most frequent image in all Christian art but to demonstrate, in a relatively small format, the Master of Urbino's perfect control over blue monochrome and over a landscape, which, though faraway in the distance, is as vivid as a second picture within the first.

For Zurbarán to depict St Bonaventura's corpse is to pay due homage to a great exemplar of the faith but it also allows him, in a singularly novel way, to place a diagonal swathe of white across a dark ground. Excelling in still life (his masterpiece in the genre is in the Norton Simon Museum, Los Angeles), Zurbarán was an undemonstrative artist who extolled purity of feeling and simplicity of line, paying especial attention to the positioning of his figures.

Dado's babies were created by a painter with a head chock-full of images from museums. First and foremost, they are descendents of Baroque putti or of 'Boucher's children' so popular with painters during the Rococo; later, the first martyrs put to death on Herod's command in Judaea, shortly after the coming of Christ, came forcefully to mind. The memory furnished the title, just as Rubens, Boucher, Watteau and Fragonard had provided the material for a still Surrealist recomposition of space. The tangle of infant limbs is thus transmuted into a 'history picture', an ironic allusion to a genre, which, from the classical age to Impressionism, reigned supreme in the history of painting.

Sassetta

*The Blessed Ranieri Rasini Freeing the Poor
from the Prison in Florence*, 1444 43.4 x 63.3 cm – ML

Nicolas Poussin

Echo and Narcissus, c. 1630

74 x 100 cm – ML

Botticelli

*Venus and the Three Graces Offering Gifts
to a Young Woman* (detail), c. 1483

211 x 283 cm – ML

Staging myth

Painting a narrative often entails putting it on stage, and many pictures resemble theatrical productions. They can go one better, however, by portraying events beyond the means of any theatrical 'machine', events that no mystery play, such as those performed on church forecourts in the Quattrocento, could ever have presented for our admiration. The miraculous flight of the blessed Ranieri Rasini painted in Siena by Sassetta is an example. The miracle occurring on this small, tightly architectural predella panel seems all the more extraordinary since it is in defiance of a space otherwise depicted in accordance with the rules.

Just as astonishing is Poussin's account of a metamorphosis he had read in Ovid: the nymph Echo changes into a rock, her face absorbed into the colour of the stone, while the handsome, indifferent Narcissus prepares to dive into his reflection. Here, interplay between real and imaginary is pushed to the limits. They meld again in Botticelli's famous frescoes that depict, in a language of symbol and mythology, a wedding between some youthful Florentines. His figures are all close likenesses, yet each plays a role: embodying the Virtues or some other personification, they act out characters in a ballet planned according to principles that escape us today, and for an audience whose culture and expectations, in spite of much historical research, remains shadowy. We can also contemplate and try to understand these now alien faces, and ignore who they were.

Eugène Delacroix
Apollo Vanquishing the Serpent Python (détail), 1850-1851
800 x 750 cm - ML

Art against barbarity

Some paintings in the Louvre are affixed to the ceiling and so form part of the decoration, among them Braque's *The Birds* and Delacroix's *Apollo Vanquishing the Serpent Python* for the middle compartment of a ceiling painted in the 17th century by Charles Le Brun, future master of the Galerie des Glaces at Versailles. For Delacroix, this was more than just a prestigious official commission; it showed him sticking to tradition, and sounding a grand finale to French painting. In his own lifetime, as a Romantic, as the heir to classicism, he thus entered the palace-cum-museum for which his rival Ingres had painted an *Apotheosis of Homer* (p. 168), a much less—successful ceiling painting… Hence his subject, with scattered neo-baroque accents that fused the ambitions of man and artist, shows the timely assistance of Apollo, father of the nine Muses, in the victory of the arts over barbarity as personified by a marine monster worthy of the first act of Mozart's *Magic Flute*.

The serpent makes a further appearance coiled at the base of Redon's *The Chariot of Apollo*, a piece that combines oil paint with scattered highlights in luminous pastel. The chariot driver dissolves into a fiery halo, while the onward rush of the four white steeds suspended in mid-air suffices to conjure up a myth. For Gauguin, true civilisation was to be found on Tahiti, and he too chose to symbolise the triumph of Nature in a white horse. The riderless animal (the only one without a mount) is a figure from the island's age-old mythology. An integral part of the river, his coat merges with the pink, white and blue of the path on the water's edge. He embodies the force and power of a primitive world, yet Gauguin places him in a traditional attitude inspired by Phidias's horses on the Parthenon frieze, a photograph of which was one of the very few pictures he took with him to the ends of the earth, where it acted as a tutelary genius over his South Seas studio.

In Dalí's picture, influenced by his recent reading of Sigmund Freud, the horse trails behind him a grand piano on which lies the body of a decomposing ass, similar to the one in *Un chien andalou*, the film Dalí had made with Luis Buñuel in 1928. William Tell, a recurring character in the artist's oeuvre, holds out a bloodstained pair of scissors used in a horrific act of castration. The gesture he makes to his victim-cum-son recalls that of Michelangelo's Creation of Adam in the Sistine Chapel, whereas the fountain with a hole recalls Greuze's *The Broken Jug* (p. 172). Thus Dalí, who liked to borrow figures from art history (the horse and the 'amphora-woman'), devises his own private mythology.

Odilon Redon

The Chariot of Apollo, 1905-1914

91.5 x 77 cm - MO

Paul Gauguin

The White Horse, 1898

140 x 91.5 cm - MO

Salvador Dalí

William Tell, 1930

113 x 87 cm - CP

Jacques Louis David

Consecration of Emperor Napoleon I and the Coronation of the Empress Josephine
in the Cathedral of Notre-Dame de Paris, December the 2nd 1804, 1806-1807 621 x 979 cm - ML

History, reality and Surrealism

Two works with no common reference points and yet which make sense together. 'This picture is on the march,' Napoleon told David, his ego placated by this immense, radiant composition where, in sumptuous colours of a Rubens-like opulence, the austere painter of the Horatii (p. 14), that most republican of artists, who as a *deputé* had voted for the execution of Louis XVI in 1793, here exalts a new sovereign, his family and his court. Soldiers of fortune, romantic heroes who had just come through the Revolution, in all their finery and brand-new wealth, are captured at the moment when their adventure was starting to resemble a fanciful historical novel. 'Truth is sometimes improbable.' This immense memorial of a picture extols a unique destiny, the adventures of an artillery officer born in Ajaccio who attempted to wield once again the sceptre of Charlemagne over a Europe laid waste. The impact of the image is so strong that it makes one forget the total want of verisimilitude of a story that contemporaries realised was more in the way of a myth.

Matta

Xpace and the Ego, 1945

202.2 x 457.2 cm - CP

In similarly brilliant tones, Matta conceived of a space that recalls the vast panoramas and history paintings of the 19th century, which culminated so unexpectedly in Picasso's *Guernica*. As a Surrealist, Matta plays with anthropomorphic figures, with dazzling, luminous colours in a throb of obscure events. This is a canvas 'on the move', propelled like a well-oiled machine, but to no real purpose, with no narrative to account for it: just automatic writing over a broad surface that puts the individuality of the painter in contact with a surface, an 'Xpace' he saturates with his imaginings. Behind each of the portraits in David's composition brimful of figures — Talleyrand sneers, Murat struts, and the ambassador of the United States of America rubs shoulders with that of the king of Spain — the stories overlap, criss-crossing like in some adventure novel. Two works that, if taken on a desert island, would immediately fill it with people.

Gustave Courbet
Burial at Ornans, c. 1849-1850
315 x 668 cm - MO

Statements of intent

Courbet returns to and inverts the linear composition of David's *Consecration* (p. 74) dominated by a processional cross. The heroes he had pose in his village of Ornans were real people (proud of this artistic heritage, their descendents live on to this day in Franche-Comté), each with a portrait as faithful as those of the dignitaries of the imperial court. Unknown individuals here attain the status of historical personages or heroes through the artist's absolute power. But the link between them is no longer vanity, the crown or military glory, but death. The meaning of the composition is supplied by the skull before the common grave: it is a vanity (in the 17th-century acceptation of the word) which, instead of facing a solitary Mary Magdalene as with La Tour (p. 38), reminds an entire village — a microcosm sufficiently well-characterised to be of universal significance — of the Last Things.

The world of Basquiat, one of slaves in revolt against contemporary New York society, also functions through archetypes. Many years before, Courbet had borrowed some of his ideas from engravings in broadsheets and from popular imagery. In *Slave Auction*, the graffiti, fly-bills and torn posters stuck on

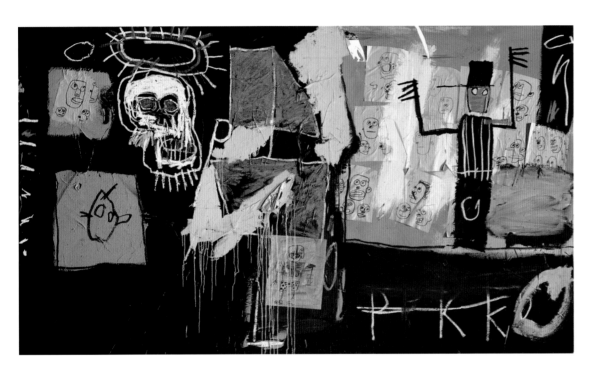

the canvas, as if on to a hoarding, present a portrait of the great American project. His tragically early death made this friend of Warhol's into a guardian angel for the cool generation, the author of messages that would only be understood much later.

In 1855, as the World Fair in its official pavilions was setting Ingres against Delacroix, Courbet launched the concept of Realism, hanging *The Burial* (p. 76) and *The Painter's Studio* (p. 178) opposite one other (as today in the Musée d'Orsay), as joint manifestos of a new painting style springing from the heart of a new society.

Théodore Géricault
The Raft of the Medusa, 1819 Salon
491 x 716 cm - ML

The militant artist

Painting can be a weapon of combat. The sheer power of certain works bears witness to the artist's commitment: the heaps of shipwrecked bodies painted by Géricault or the Resistants executed by firing squad whom Fautrier evokes in the titles of the *Hostages* series. While *The Raft of the Medusa*, painted with bitumen, delves into the night, with art restorers powerless to stop it turning blacker with each passing year, historians are still debating its political significance. A manifesto of French Romanticism, the picture was also a crypto-Republican squib against a Restoration government which, by entrusting command of the frigate *La Méduse* to an Ancien Régime officer who had not served at sea for more than fifteen years, provided satirists with a glaring example of the criminal neglect of those now at the helm of the 'Ship of State'. Engaged art, from Delacroix's barricades (p. 80) to Detaille's *The Dream* (p. 89), was perhaps born with Géricault, who a few years earlier had embodied the splendours and miseries of Empire in two great 'portraits' of officers (both now in the Louvre).

Producing his 'hostages' in Chateaubriand's former

78

Jean Fautrier
L'Ecorché, corps d'otage, 1945
80 x 115 cm - CP

residence at La Vallée aux Loups where summary executions were meted out in 1943, Fautrier's paintings commemorate the struggles of the Résistance and become weapons in the struggle. These are works of the war and post-war periods, capturing, in the subtlest tones, the sheer atrocity of execution. Is it possible to look at these two pictures without thinking about politics? Can one see *The Raft of the Medusa* as a heap of bodies, as a message of hope, since the shipwrecked men have just spotted a sail appearing on the horizon; or, as has also been proposed, does it show total despair, as with the aged father grasping the corpse of his son to his knees, as all take refuge in their interior worlds because the ship that was to be their saviour is actually sailing away? Is it possible today to see Fautrier's *Hostages* simply as abstracts, stripped of their historically datable subject with, as their sole *raison d'être*, a harmony of green, ochre and blue?

On the march

In 1830, Delacroix reintroduced allegory into painting, something thought dead and buried since David had expunged it from a sketch for his second great imperial picture, a pendant to the *Consecration* entitled *La Distribution des Aigles* (Musée de Versailles). A bare-breasted woman embodies the idea of Liberty, but the figures by her side are real enough: student, worker, street urchin. The bodies in the foreground derive from Géricault (p. 78) and Gros (p. 14). Delacroix here underscores his Romanticism, not only as regards the formal devices, which are less forward-looking than in *Sardanapalus* (p. 26), but by his heartfelt allegiance to the regime being born on the barricades.

In 1988, Chéri Samba was also campaigning for a cause. Adopting the idiom of the sign-painters of his country, the parade of figures protesting for an idea each represent a human type. The fight against disease — as with Fautrier's struggle against the barbarians and that of Basquiat against enduring servitude — endows this painstaking, stiff, faux-naïf style with a militant dimension. It incites the viewer to identify, reflect, and then act. No need of allegory here, nor of 'real allegory', to use Courbet's expression (p. 178). A picture within the picture, the image of a dying man in his bed carried in procession makes its point so forcibly that the work functions as a rallying-cry.

Antoine Caron
The Massacre of the Triumvirate, 1566
116 x 195 cm - ML

Painting: theatre of the world

On the instigation of Etienne de Beaumont, on the 17th of May 1924, at the theatre La Cigale, place Blanche in Paris, a ballet in several scenes entitled *Mercure* opened with music by Erik Satie, choreography by Léonide Massine, and stage curtain and costumes by Picasso. This curtain (the Centre Pompidou also houses the enormous curtain for the ballet *La Parade*, too large to be displayed), painted in tempera on a heavy canvas that shows its weave,

does not depict figures from this plotless 'suite of sculptural poses'. The day after the premiere, one might have read in the *Paris-Journal* a text signed by composers Francis Poulenc and Georges Auric, and the Surrealists Louis Aragon, André Breton, Robert Desnos, Max Ernst, Philippe Soupault...: 'So in *Mercure*, in displaying the full extent of his audacity and genius, [Picasso] is once again greeted by universal incomprehension: Picasso [...] appears

Jean-Baptiste Greuze

The Father's Curse : the Ungrateful Son, 1777

130 x 162 cm - ML

Pablo Picasso

Curtain for the ballet Mercure, 1924

392 x 501cm - CP

today as an eternal personification of youth [...]'.
Antoine Caron and Greuze also used 'sculptural poses' inspired by the theatre in their works. In the Greuze, the rhetorical process is simple: what is required is to arouse emotion by the representation of feelings. Here, everything contributes to the pathetic. Diderot, writing in his critic's hat, had no trouble in getting this piece, together with its companion *The Return of the Prodigal Son* (Louvre), to 'speak'. The

space of the painting resembles a stage complete with scenery and a well-drilled cast of characters.
Caron's triptych, its backcloth inspired by the monuments of Rome, fulfils a dual function. Depicting the death of Cicero during the triumvirate of Octavian, Antony and Lepidus, as recounted by the ancient historian Appian, its subtext relates to the massacres of the French Wars of Religion during the 'triumvirate' of the Connétable Montmorency, the Duc de Guise

and Jacques d'Albon de Saint-André. The picture was painted in 1566, seven years before the St Bartholomew's Day Massacre and four years after that of Vassy, the catalyst for the internecine strife that was to tear France apart. Caron uses ancient history to provoke catharsis, that effect whose mechanisms in the theatre are described in Aristotle's *Poetics*, purging contemporary passions by presenting, in painting, the passions of history.

83

Francesco Guardi

The Doge of Venice Takes Part in the Festivities..., between 1766 and 1770

67 x 100 cm - ML

Jean-Etienne Liotard

Mr Levett and Mlle Glavany in Turkish Costume, c. 1740

24.7 x 36.4 cm - ML

Disguises and masks

Carnivals, masks, disguises: why does the history of painting abound with these kinds of subject? As everyone knows by now, disguises reveal more than they hide. Liotard from Geneva disguises himself as a Turk to paint figures themselves in fancy dress. Guardi captures the moment when carousing Venice sports a costume and a mask: during Carnival in the Serenissima, disguise becomes the norm, and the social pyramid is replaced by pyramids of acrobats on the Piazza San Marco. Watteau paints travelling players, with, in majesty in the centre, a rather tubby Gilles with surprisingly big hands for an artist so fond of lean fingers and dainty features. The real subject of the canvas remains unknown, though some commentators have seen its pathos as revealing something of the true personality of the painter of *fêtes galantes*.

Well-acquainted with Watteau's masterpiece, Picasso too painted a Harlequin: perhaps he is yet another self-image. His friend Salvado, a Catalan painter like Picasso who also posed for Derain, had failed in his career: Picasso captures the despair of this pale imitation, this less-fortunate brother, dressed in the commedia dell'arte role of Arlequino, the servant of two masters in Goldoni's play. The artist who paints reality in travesty also serves two masters, one being none other than his true self. In many self-portraits, Rembrandt disguised himself as an Oriental, an actor or a soldier. No text of the time says why he did.

Jean-Antoine Watteau

Gilles, c. 1718-1720

184.5 x 149.5 cm - ML

Pablo Picasso

Harlequin, 1923

130 x 97 cm - CP

85

Paolo Veronese
The Wedding Feast at Cana, 1562-1563
666 x 990 cm - ML

The feast

Thomas Couture
The Romans of the Decadence, 1847
472 x 772 cm - MO

Fernand Léger
La Noce, 1911
257 x 206 cm - CP

Three immense canvases, full of movement, of sound and fury. Above the Romans of the Late Empire painted by Couture stand statues of notables from the Republic, in silent reproach. The feast looks more like an orgy. On the right, two spectators gaze on, reviling the morals of a time that lives in palaces that it could never build. For Couture, the picture, dating a year before the 1848 Revolution, serves as a mirror held out to contemporary society. It is also (witness the architectural perspective standing out against the sky) a tribute to Veronese whose *Wedding* had arrived in

the Musée Napoléon from Venice, remaining on the picture-rail of the Louvre following the defeat at Waterloo. In an antique palace, unrecognised but readily identifiable in the centre, the Redeemer accedes to his mother's wish, and, turning water into wine, performs his first miracle. He is the harbinger of a new era, when banquets, music and games will give way to things holy, and when the wine of men will change into the Blood of the Saviour.

Léger's canvas also shows the moment when one world succeeds another. The title nods in the direction

of Veronese, the upward spiralling composition inviting us to explore its architecture. The energy, musical rhythm and robustness of this construction poses a question that is not perhaps as incongruous as it might seem: was Léger the true 20th-century heir to Veronese, taking up a tradition that had, in spite of Couture's manifest ambition, proved beyond him in the 19th?

Paolo Uccello
The Battle of San Romano, c. 1450-1455
182 x 317 cm - ML

Dreams of battle

For Lorenzo the Magnificent's chamber in Florence, Paolo Uccello, described by Vasari as a solitary artist haunted by issues of perspective, painted three large panels, alive with reflections and glinting with weapons and helmets. Set with silvered plaques (much worn today), they were intended to give visitors the impression of being amidst the fray. The two other pictures are in the Uffizi, Florence, and the National Gallery, London. Uccello depicts combat as it would have taken place in the era of chivalry to which the merchant dynasty of the Medici were not the rightful heirs. In the Florentine panel, more modern weapons, such as crossbows, are relegated to the middle distance. The geometrical perfection of the hairstyles and the use of colour — the combatants' legs appear to move — thus serve a political purpose for the Medici who are striving to enter the old world. This they soon achieved,

providing France with two queens, Catherine, wife of Henri II, and Marie, wife of Henri IV, who was to employ Rubens for her glorification (p. 138).

Two styles of warfare also appear in Detaille's picture, long exhibited in the French Army Museum at the Invalides. Napoleon draws up his battle plans with his soldiers' dreams as they sleep. A enthusiast for vast panoramic views in which observers can feel drawn into the heat of the action, Detaille here depicts a night encampment: in the upper register, French history parades past as in dreamworld, in wars of yore and legendary victories. The conflicts of yesterday haunt the hopes of present combatants as they dream of their revenge at the next battle to be enjoined early next morning.

Charles Le Brun
The Passage of the Granicus, completed in 1665
470 x 1209 cm - ML

History at war

For the Douanier Rousseau, War is a terrifying harridan, an allegorical figure of Discord, rushing headlong on a horse that leaps over piles of corpses pecked at by crows. The majority of the possible sources of inspiration for this work hang in the Louvre and date from the Romantic era: Géricault's *The Epsom Derby* for the horse with the elongated body; the cadavres in the foreground come from *The Raft of the Medusa* or from *Napoleon Visiting the Plague-Stricken at Jaffa* by Gros, who also painted *Napoleon at the battlefield at Eylau* in 1808, which includes the most famous mass grave in the history of painting. There was nothing 'naive' then about the Douanier Rousseau.

Around 1950, Georges Mathieu was providing his pictures with carefully contrived titles taken from French history: *Louis VI détruisant la commune de Laon, La Bataille de Bouvines, La Victoire de Denain ...* Marked by the art of the Far East as much as by the paintings King Louis-Philippe commissioned for Versailles, Mathieu, without apparent contradiction, offers a theory of Lyrical Abstraction, a painting style that sets great store by gesture, on the immediate release of pigment fresh from the tube on to the surface. But for the artist, such gestures are part of 'history' and 'battle' painting, and he places himself symbolically (as his titles make abundantly clear) at the end of a long tradition.

Le Brun had allusively commemorated the noble deeds of Louis XIV even before Versailles and the ceiling of the Galerie des Glaces (1679–1684). His four immense canvases devoted to the battles of Alexander (later employed as tapestry cartoons) show the ancient conqueror with a profile reminiscent of the living monarch. *Entry to Babylon* exhibits a white elephant that recalls the one Rosso Fiorentino painted in the gallery at Fontainebleau to the greater glory of François I. *Alexander and Porus* and *The Battle of Arbela* proceed from the pages of the ancient historian Quintius Curtius, while *The Passage of the Granicus* evokes the late frescoes by Raphael and his pupils in the Vatican: warfare as shown in art is seldom real combat. Painting a battle allows the artist to rewrite history and re-stage the conflict as a hunt, a celebration, or a theatrical production.

Henri Rousseau

War, 1894

114 x 195 cm - MO

Georges Mathieu

Les Capétiens partout, 1954

295 x 600 cm - CP

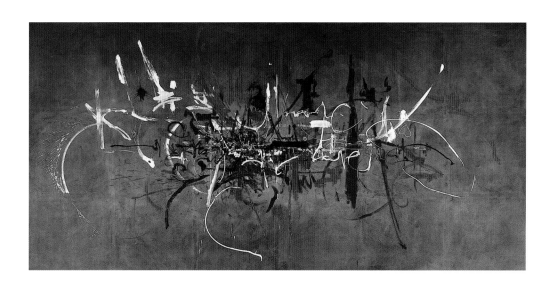

Anonymous, Paris,
Jean II the Good, King of France, vers 1360
60 x 44.5 cm - ML

Statesmen and kings

What is painting's answer to the fifth-form essay question: Do great men make history? The picture that symbolically opens the Louvre's survey of art in France, the earliest portrait in French painting, is a royal effigy. Shown in profile as on a coin (a material sign of his sovereign power), Jean II le Bon offers no attribute of monarchical majesty. His likeness, somewhat worn by time, is most probably a faithful one. Similarly the face of Georges Pompidou welcomes visitors to the Centre that bears his name, in which Vasarely pays due homage to the 20th-century French head of state who did so much for the arts and for public understanding of contemporary artists. It is a tradition France has been proud of since François I, the father of the arts who had drawn Italian artists to the French court and provided the kingdom with an initial impetus to embrace the Renaissance, as the art of Jean Clouet testifies. From this time on, in the collective imagination, the king has been engaged in a dialogue with 'his painter'. The apocryphal but symptomatic anecdote recounted by Vasari, of Leonardo da Vinci dying in the arms of François I lays the foundations of the history of the relationship between art and politics. It has a pendant in the image of Emperor Charles V picking up Titian's brush. What can a king do without his painter, François I without Jean Clouet? The genre of the royal portrait remains paramount in the history of art, so much so that artists such as Vasarely still try to subvert it. Functioning as a kinetic installation, Vasarely's aluminium sculpture nonetheless reverts to the conventions of painting, modelling the face of the president in shadow, aiming for and attaining immediate resemblance. The result, partly due to its being integrated into the architectural space of the Centre, is the nation's most recent large-scale official portrait, the face at the heart of the French hexagon.

92

Jean Clouet
François I, c. 1530
96 x 74 cm - ML

Victor Vasarely
Homage to Georges Pompidou, 1976
500 x 400 x 6 cm - CP

Power and its doppelgängers

The royal portrait is a genre with its own codes. The Marquis de Dangeau tells how at Versailles Louis XIV 'had his likeness painted by Rigaud after dinner' without pomp and ceremony in the apartments of his favourite, Mme de Maintenon. The king posed only for the face. The rest, the so-called 'Charlemagne' sword, the coronation robes, the crown of France, is assembled into an image of his status, the 'royal body' of the monarch which coexists with the traits of the real individual. Before being a man, the king embodies a centuries-old continuity, a moment in French history of which he is the trustee.

Of the bombastic Imperator invented by Alfred Jarry in his texts and plays, Max Ernst's *Ubu* keeps only the swollen body: an outsized gyrating spinning-top whose sharp tip inscribes lines on the ground that look like those automatic writings and drawings which the Surrealists, whose troop Ernst had joined at this time, recommended scribbling down daily. Resembling a robot in a film, the profile of this *Ubu*, which once belonged to the poet Paul Eluard, recalls faces by Arcimboldo (see p. 172). A 'vision of half-sleep', according to the artist, it was executed following a dream Ernst had had about his father. Rigaud's image of the king is also that of a father, a robot fine-tuning the cogs and wheels of the court, a 'king-machine', as Jean-Marie Apostolidès has termed him, a sun in perpetual rotation whose shining face is that of the paternal state and of divine right.

Philippe de Champaigne
Cardinal de Richelieu, c. 1639
222 x 155 cm - ML

Eminent men

Piero della Francesca
Portrait of Sigismondo Pandolfo Malatesta, c. 1450-1451
44 x 34 cm - ML

Raphael
Baldassare Castiglione, 1516
82 x 67 cm - ML

Jean Auguste Dominique Ingres
Portrait of Louis-François Bertin, 1832
116 x 95 cm - ML

Red: a lightly applied horizontal line on Baldassare Castiglione's doublet that breaks up the monochrome with contained violence; a patch, that of an armchair by that devotee of Raphael, Ingres; an ecclesiastical prince's robe for the 'Red Man' who governed France in the name of Louis XIII... In painting, power is not confined to kings. Piero della Francesca's Renaissance *condottiere*; the courtier (and author of a celebrated handbook to polite intercourse entitled *The Book of the Courtier*) painted by his friend Raphael; Philippe de Champaigne's all-powerful cardinal-cum-minister; or the first modern press baron, energetic,

dishevelled, portrayed ensconced in an armchair in his editor's office, are all ersatz images. They show the features of four 'doppelgängers' of absolute power — military might, *bon ton*, political acumen, progressive daring. A bizarre misreading has seen Ingres' portrait of Bertin as an icon of the ruling middle-class. Ingres' skill in painting a window reflected in the wood of the easy-chair compounds the confusion, as it immediately suggests the essentially burgher and mercantile art of the Flemish School (*The Moneylender and his Wife*, p. 62). Like Castiglione, the director of the *Journal des débats*

poses unaffectedly, his black suit replaces the cardinal's purple and the military braid. A famous organ of liberal opposition, Bertin's review had only recently, in 1830, succeeded in imposing its liberal views. From the time of King Louis-Philippe, the press reigns supreme: it is the press that creates *condottiere* by publicising their victories, that makes and breaks ministers, that enshrines a style of the day which turns us all into 'courtiers'.

The Brothers Le Nain
Peasant Family in the Home, 1642
113 x 159 cm - ML

Frédéric Bazille
Family Reunion, 1867
152 x 230 cm - MO

Real life: the family

Degas here depicts the family of an aunt with whom he lodged as a young man in Florence. The rigorous construction of this group composition, with its steplike arrangement formed by the girl's dress, the picture and the mantelpiece, is calculated to demonstrate that Degas is from the same stock as Ingres. It is similar with Bazille, a painter who died in battle before having time to become a Impressionist, and who exhibited this rather stiff, Ingres-like, group portrait, dominated by sun and sky at the Salon. Though Ingres drew many group portraits, he never painted one. The idea of co-opting the incredible skill of the greatest portraitist of the century and of applying it to a genre scene (the paragon of which is the depiction of the family) is equivalent to dropping daily life into the arena of 'great painting'. But was it as new as all that? Both Degas and Bazille could point to earlier images in museums of the sheltered, cloistered world of the family. Peasant interiors in paintings by the Brothers Le Nain show a world quite alien to those who admired them. These manifestly well-off farmers, drinking wine, laying a fire or showing off their fine linen, remain anonymous, even if they look like real portraits. *The Peasant Family* of

Jean-Baptiste Siméon Chardin
Le Bénédicité, 1740 Salon
49.5 x 38.5 cm - ML

Edgar Degas
The Bellelli Family, c. 1860-1867
200 x 250 cm - MO

1642 tells no story — unlike the Bellellis' contretemps, all too evident from their portrait. The picture offers a striking everyday image of humble folk, an image of austerity, dignity and distinction in demeanour that served, perhaps, as a moral lesson to the families of the royal court. In the same way, and with touching simplicity, Chardin paints the unremarkable life of a pious family from the Parisian lower middle-class. But the mother in *Le Bénédicité* could never have hung Chardin's picture in her home; at most she might have possessed an engraving of one of his best-known works. Buyers and collectors of Chardin's paintings were wealthy individuals or European sovereigns. Like *La Mère laborieuse*, *Le Bénédicité* belonged to the collections of Louis XV. The family life he shows is an exemplar of bourgeois simplicity and honesty that must have charmed and delighted the affluent nobles of the *parlements*. Degas and Bazille on the other hand painted solely so that their recipients could possess and contemplate pictures of themselves.

Eugène Delacroix

Algerian Women in their Apartment, 1834

180 x 229 cm - ML

Paul Gauguin

Tahitian Women, 1891

69 x 91.5 cm - MO

Confidences veiled and unveiled

Besides obvious analogies in subject matter — the depiction of the private life of women, the gyneceum, of a world surprised and pictured by a man — these three works are also linked by an interplay between materials, fabrics and decorative motifs. In Picasso, *papiers collés* and scraps of wallpaper are applied to a tempera surface: the piece is in fact a preparatory cartoon for a Beauvais tapestry woven the same year. Tapestry-making has been a mythical, feminine activity since Penelope waited for Ulysses and all the needlewomen in the history of painting (p. 124). In *Algerian Women in their Apartment*, Delacroix also introduced decorative elements. The ceramic floor and wall tiles, brightly coloured woven cushions and luxurious textiles of a lampas pattern were ornaments he had seen with his own eyes during his sojourn in 1832. Delacroix depicts the inside of a Jewish house in an Islamic land. The world which

Pablo Picasso
Confidences, 1934
194 x 170 cm - CP

men are forbidden from entering is also that of a religion from which the human figure is banned, where art is composed of 'arabesques' and lines: to paint these women's faces was thus to transgress the norm twice over and portray an absolute Other.

In the Gauguin, the red and white pattern of the pareo plays a role similar to Delacroix's geometrical tiles. The woman on the right adopts an attitude close to that of the Algerian girl seated cross-legged in the

Delacroix, while the gold interlace she gathers up in her fingers echoes the necklaces and the curve of the hookah. At the time of his first voyage to Tahiti (1891–1893), Gauguin could still recall everything he had learnt at the Louvre. His composition reverses the central motif of Delacroix's picture, the dark Algerian and the dusky Tahitian in profile, each with a flower behind her ear, enter into symmetrical dialogue. What one can hear, in an undertone, is an

interchange between these inaccessible, remote women captured in paint. The hope is that a story will begin between 'their' exotic females, a story woven between a trio of pictures, by way of a secret history of painting.

Destitution

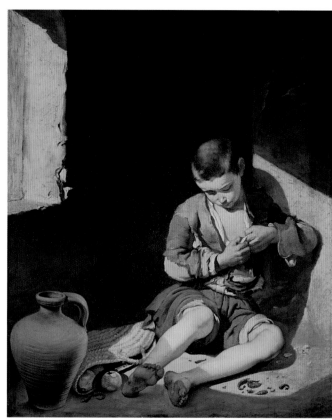

The depiction of lowly subjects is as old as art itself. Pliny the Elder, in *The Natural History*, Book XXXV, which is devoted to a history of ancient painting, mentions a certain Piraeicus who 'adopting a humble line [...] attained in that field the height of glory. He painted barbers' shops and cobblers' stalls, asses, viands, and the like, consequently receiving a Greek name [*rhyparographos*] meaning painter of sordid subjects [...the pictures] fetched bigger prices than the largest works of many masters.' Brueghel the Elder's beggars, whose significance art historians have failed to elucidate completely (what, for instance, does the tunic stuck with fox tails on the right mean?), bear a message of hope conveyed by the open door leading to the garden and an inscription on the back: 'Cripples, take heart, and may your fortunes prosper!'
Rather than a realistic likeness, Murillo's beggar boy, despite the accumulation of 'telling details' (the red shrimps he is shelling and the wall peeling in the sun), is a literary stock character, a waif from a

Pierre Puvis de Chavannes
The Poor Fisherman, 1881
155.5 x 192.5 cm - MO

picaresque novel, one of the best-known figures in Siglo de Oro Spain.

Poverty as painted by Puvis de Chavannes is sacred in nature. The picture's matt surface and the use of a limited chromatic range give it the appearance of fresco. The figure turning his back on the world and retreating into his own inner realm is possessed of Evangelical grandeur. The boat's reflection is cast crisp as a shadow. Puvis' contemporaries were struck by how he glorified destitution and by the monolithic character he bestowed on human suffering. Divested of its original mystical meaning, *The Poor Fisherman* remained a seminal piece for Seurat, Signac and Picasso, who each absorbed many of its lessons.

Parlour games

Playing cards, little rectangles of an almost pure white stand out in both the Cézanne and the La Tour. One tiny white oblong, contrasting with the modelling of the hand that grasps it, presents a reduced-scale image of the blank canvas. The playing card serves as a model of figurative representation, the least complex of all the symbolic, ludic and abstract uses to which the art of drawing in colour is put. No influence here though, in spite of some disconcerting similarities: the table draped with cloth, Cézanne's bottle and the wicker-wrapped flask in the La Tour, the poses, the profiles and the positioning of the hands. Cézanne would never have

seen this picture by a 17th-century master little known in his time. On the other hand, thanks to the museum in Aix-en-Provence, he did know the art of the Brothers Le Nain, and group portraits showing card players are not infrequent in French classical age painting. La Tour painted two versions of *The Card Cheat*: a card sharp with an ace of clubs, the near-twin of the picture in the Louvre, is in the Kimbell Art Museum, Fort Worth. Cézanne also produced other *Card Players*: alternative versions of the small work in the Orsay, some more elaborate, with four or five figures, are today scattered far and wide (Barnes Foundation, Merion; the Metropolitan

Museum, New York; the Courtauld Institute Galleries, London, etc). Cézanne compresses the action into symmetry, into a duel. In La Tour's work, three players face one another, while a maidservant holding out a wine glass observes the game. Perhaps the elegant youth on the right is the Prodigal Son of the Gospel squandering his father's fortune. Such inn scenes, sometimes known in Italian as Bambocci, derive from a tradition inaugurated by Caravaggio as a pretext for grouping together musicians, gamblers and immodest females.

Duchamp upends the convention, redesigning Cézanne's face-to-face placement of the two players

Paul Cézanne

The Card Players, c. 1890-1895

47.5 x 57 cm - MO

Marcel Duchamp

Chess Players, 1911

50 x 61 cm - CP

(an inescapable reference in the years when Cézanne appeared as the spiritual godfather of Cubism), he introduces movement, upsetting the new-found codes of Analytical Cubism and conceptualising the image space by adding two black bands on either side. The format thus becomes that of a real chessboard. Henceforth, the game is to be played out on a painted surface on which stand a knight, a pawn and a king; but then Duchamp went on to resign from painting altogether, changing the rules of the game forever.

105

The fleshpots

In La Tour's *The Card Cheat*, wine and lechery, gaming and deceit are marshalled in order to give the young man a lesson. Whether it is a parable or not, the realism of the scene is devoid of squalor. In the Degas, however, there is loneliness, with a glass of absinthe for company, while the juxtaposed figures (the engraver Marcellin Desboutin and an actress, Ellen Adrée) totter on the brink of an abyss. The geometrical space imprisons the two faces in a linear grid; the woman's eyes peer into the void. Imprisoned in the thick black lines that encircle their bodies, the creatures in the Rouault, a great Christian artist who nevertheless eschewed moralising, also seem to be gripped by lethargy.

One thinks of Carpaccio's *Two Venetian Women* (c. 1495, Museo Correr, Venice), traditionally identified as two courtesans, vacantly staring, their cheeks bedaubed, who inspired Louis Aragon's poem: 'Carpaccio's women, ravishingly slow and heavy...'
The significance of spatial construction in Dix's piece is totally different. Analysing the figures from various angles, the *Souvenir of the Cristal Palace in Brussels* is a humorous reformulation of Cubist codes. Like the Café de la Nouvelle-Athènes where Degas set his picture, the Cristal Palace in Brussels actually existed. A house of ill repute for officers, its walls lined with mirrors, this establishment fostered every species of voyeuristic fantasy.

Dix, ex-serviceman and a volunteer in 1914, piles up unflattering references to the recent war, down to a bottle and a tricolour ribbon. Smooth surfaces that overrun the pictorial space, his mirrors play a role comparable to the marble tables in Degas' cafe. But Dix's mirrors reflect images, casting them back and forth, and expanding the painting to reveal more, whereas in Degas' café, reflections are reduced to dull shadows, as sombre as his figures' destinies.

Georges Rouault

Filles, 1917

72 x 56 cm - CP

Otto Dix

Souvenir of the Cristal Palace in Brussels, 1920

124 x 80.4 cm - CP

Enguerrand Quarton
Pietà of Villeneuve-lès-Avignon, c. 1455
163 x 218.5 cm - ML

Death and resurrection

All stories conclude in death. In the Western painting tradition, the archetypal dead body is that of the Son of God on the Cross. That is to say, a picture of a death that every viewer knows is followed by a Resurrection and the beginning of a new narrative. The realism of the Crucifixion, the force with which the corpse is represented, only adds to the unseen yet implied miracle on which the Christian faith rests. The rents in El Greco's skies are the wounds of a Christ whose body has not yet been pierced by the centurion's spear: he yet lives. Striving with might and main for the beyond, Jesus' ligneous, slender body ascends like a carved crucifix to the Father, while the geometry of the Cross pins him firmly to earth and to suffering. And Christ prays. The elongated members are characteristic of El Greco's art and, more generally, of the Mannerist aesthetics that proved a decisive influence during his Italian sojourn. The picture was originally on an altar in the Hieronymites' convent in Toledo, and Christ's prayer finds an echo in the lower half of the canvas in the gestures of the donors who commissioned it.

Enguerrand Quarton, in the mid-15th century, placed his donor in the same pose of worship. The picture's gilt ground and the distant heavenly Jerusalem fulfils the same function as the tumultuous and dramatic sky in the El Greco. They allude to the beyond and to our passage into the next world, yet in a tranquil, abstract way, in marked contrast to the dramatic emotions felt by the Virgin in the centre, or by St John or the Magdalene, who holds the vase containing perfume with which she had anointed Christ's feet. Here, too, Christ is sculptural, face gaunt, chest collapsed, exceedingly realistic: the stream of blood follows the vertical of the Cross and Christ's arms are as stiff as the instrument of his torture. The Christ has become a Cross. An inscription running round the scene voices the thoughts of the Virgin, the Mater Dolorosa, issuing a visual appeal to the beholder: 'O, all you who pass by this way, look and see whether there is any sorrow like my sorrow.' Her pain is shared, except by the donor who belongs to a different space and time, and who can partake of the sacred scene solely through prayer.

Caravaggio
The Dormition of the Virgin, completed end of 1605-beginning of 1606
369 x 245 cm - ML

Recumbent figures

'I passed like the flower, I withered like the grass of the field.' On a cave face like a Gothic arch in 'forests of the New World' of unparalleled exoticism, Girodet inscribes a touching sentence from Chateaubriand's immensely popular *Atala*, a novel that his contemporaries could all recite by heart with tears in their eyes. The Christian Indian girl has drifted off into death, recumbent like one of the medieval tomb statues that were regaining favour at the time. Chactas, the Indian who loved her, of a statuesque beauty inspired by the antique, and Father Aubry, the good hermit, who seems to have stepped out of some troubadour ballad, bear her to the tomb, her features stamped with saintly purity. This soothing image of death, popularised by an engraving, an illustration for Chateaubriand's *Génie du christianisme*, met with unparalleled success.

Its idealisation is a far cry from the realistic corpse of Caravaggio's Virgin, with dirty, even putrefying feet that scandalised her contemporaries. Of the same colour as the Virgin's robe, a red curtain flaps open, floating off. According to Catholic tradition, the Mother of God does not suffer death: she falls asleep and is borne up to heaven to be crowned by her risen Son. The wretched model Caravaggio employed, her face bloated as if she'd drowned, has visibly experienced physical death; this time, it is the tears of the apostles that are sacrilegious. Will the miracle take place? Is this a sacred scene at all?

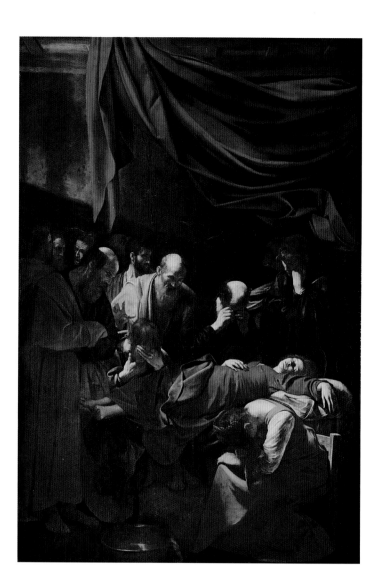

Anne-Louis Girodet
The Burial of Atala, 1808 Salon
207 x 267 cm - ML

Henri Regnault
Execution without Trial under the Moorish Kings of Granada, 1870
302 x 146 cm - MO

Executions

For Warhol the most brutal death takes the form of the inquisitorial rack. This is torture without the mess: progress has been made since Revolutionary guillotines and makeshift beheadings with broadsword. The electric chair is the ultimate instrument of democratic justice — injection was not yet the norm in the United States in 1967. The strict geometry of the apparatus photographed, reinforced by the choice of a red dominant drenching an image bloodier than if it had showed a condemned man, is very remote from the Pop Art supremo's usual output: it is a far cry from Marilyn and Liz and all the adverts, even if one were to concede that distributing a picture of an electric chair might publicise justice. The universality, the objectivity of the message is ensured by the absence of any human figure. Perhaps the monumentality of Warhol's electric chair might be compared to the towering stature of Regnault's executioner, proud of his skill and dominating a

scene in which the viewer's eyes first light on the severed head rolling at his feet? The folds in his tunic evoke the ancient statue of the *Charioteer* of Delphi. The shudder felt in 1870 by beholders of such 'fearsome picturesque' was a throwback, divorced from reality: the scene is undated and refers to no known event. Crudely rendered, the blood splashing the canvas resembles a precocious specimen of Action Painting, with which Delacroix had already experimented in *La Grèce expirant sur les ruines de Missolonghi* (Musée des Beaux-Arts, Bordeaux). The 'execution' of the picture otherwise verges on trompe-l'oeil. Death is real, yet far-off, legendary, imaginary. Painting can show democracy as well as despotism. The society that produces Mickey Mouse and Campbell's Soup is the same that resorts to the electric chair; the society that built the gardens of the Alhambra and the dazzling patios of Granada is the same in which 'summary justice' dispatched men with the sabre.

André Masson
The Labyrinth, 1938
120 x 61 cm - CP

Pierre Puvis de Chavannes
The Dream, 1883
82 x 102 cm - MO

Dream and nightmare

Sleep, brother to Death. Masson's oneiric world is a nightmarish labyrinth in Minotaur form, bristling with pitfalls, concealed staircases and dismal oubliettes. The monster is a digesting, sexualised machine, a Freudian beast possessing chambers like the Unconscious. In the fifth act of *Macbeth*, as a somnambulant Lady Macbeth enters carrying a candlestick, the Doctor observes: 'You see, her eyes are open', but the Gentlewoman counters: 'Ay, but their sense is shut.' And Lady Macbeth, in the grip of a dream more real than reality itself, staring at her hand she sees covered in blood, cries out: 'All the perfumes of Arabia will not sweeten this little hand.' In 1784, Füssli captured the Romantic character of this nocturnal dream, placing it in two distinct spaces, the heroine, in the grip of remorse and an alien world, and the horrified witnesses looking on.

Puvis de Chavannes, in 1883, works in the manner of a Primitive. Against the backdrop of an untroubled sky, Sassetta had already depicted three allegorical female figures in long, loose robes: Poverty, Chastity and Obedience, appearing to St Francis of Assisi. The picture, today in the Musée Condé, Chantilly, was purchased in 1879 at the sale of the great collector Frédéric Reiset by the Duc d'Aumale, though the painter remained unidentified. In the Puvis, the three figures address a pilgrim who has set down his staff and bundle beside him in a dream. Like Girodet's

Johann Heinrich Füssli
Lady Macbeth Sleepwalking, 1784
221 x 160 cm - ML

Endymion (p. 39), his face is caught in moonlight filtering through the branches. The golden crown in the centre of the canvas shines like a promise of the next world and contrasts with the dowdy shrubs bordering the path. On the horizon, an azure coastline symbolises all the 'shores' towards which one can set sail in one's dreams.

Setting sail

The vast, white sky, vaguely blue, vaguely green, of *The Embarkation*, worked up with the brush in accents and shifts that hint at clouds is a pure piece of painting that reveals the freedom of the artist's gesture. In the Soulages, a single colour, black, that in the light shows palpable traces of the broad brushstrokes from which it is made, becomes a space outside time, like the golden grounds of the Renaissance. 'Narrative time,' the painter declares, 'that of a line the eye follows, of a progression with a certain duration, is thus superseded.'

Watteau's most famous work (at which, at the time when Neoclassicism was all-powerful, students in the study rooms at the Academy used to throw bread pellets) remains mysterious (as much in the first version in the Louvre as in the second conserved in Berlin). Its original title, *The Pilgrimage to the Isle of Cythera*, does not allow one to decide between two different readings that imply two contradictory approaches to the scene, two conceivable narratives. Does it show a group of *galants* embarking for an unknown island where love reigns — the white mountain standing out against the blue-tinted sky? Or, on the contrary, is it the end of voyage through love — the man viewed from the rear carries a pilgrim's staff, but it could be a shepherd's crook — the moment when Cythera, the fortunate isle at which the young woman near the centre casts a nostalgic look back, must be left behind? In the gamut of poetic genres, we hesitate between hymn of love and elegy. This rapidly executed work summarises Watteau's entire career, recapturing the spirit of his earlier pieces in which ambivalence definitely plays a role. Contemporary accounts do not allow us to say on which of the two banks — on the dry land of daily life or on the enchanted isle — the painter has set his easel. The narrative evaporates in a surge of euphoria, setting off for the beyond in a golden-hued light. What will the horizon bring? Is the mountain the real world that love lets one forget for an instant and to which the lovers have to descend once more — whence the elegiac feel? Or is it the country of a love unknown towards which a boat, adorned with a shell that belongs both to Venus and to pilgrims, seems preparing to weigh anchor, while cherubs fly above brandishing Cupid's torch? Perhaps Cythera, in the distance, does not exist.

Pierre Soulages
Painting, 29 June 1979, 1979
202 x 453 cm - CP

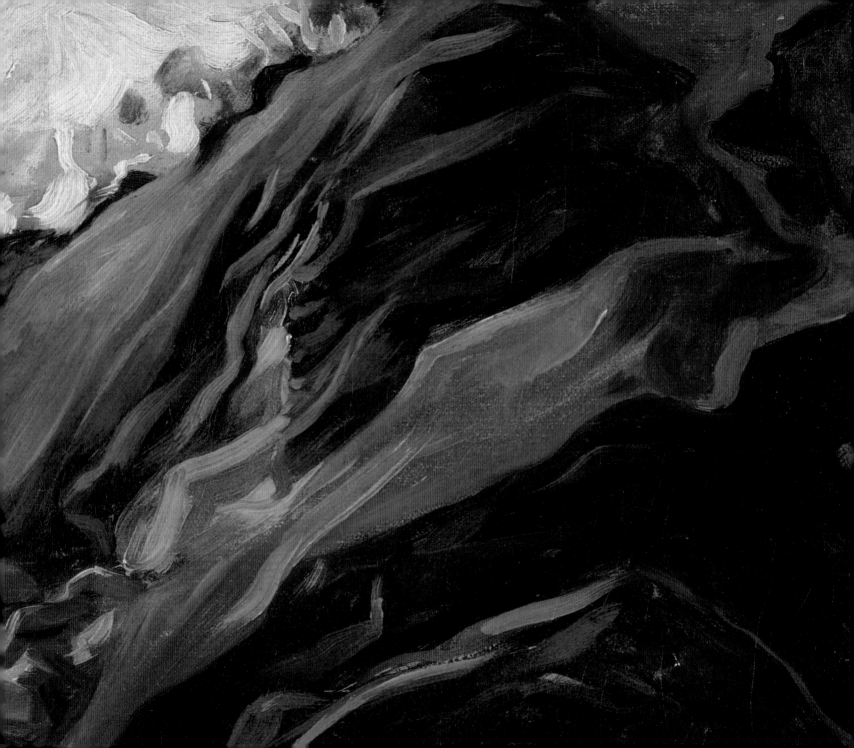

Imagine
Painting the invisible

"And Elstir's studio appeared to me like the laboratory of a sort of new creation of the world in which, from the chaos that is everything we see, he had extracted, by painting them on various rectangles of canvas that were placed at all angles, here a sea wave angrily crashing its lilac foam on to the sand, there a young man in white linen leaning on the rail of a ship. The young man's jacket and the splashing wave had acquired a new dignity from the fact that they continued to exist, even though they were deprived of those qualities in which they might be supposed to consist, the wave being no longer able to wet or the jacket to clothe anyone."

Marcel Proust, *In Search of Lost Time*, vol. II, 1918 *(Swann's Way & Within a Budding Grove)*, tr. C.K. Scott Moncrieff & T. Kilmartin, London: Chatto & Windus, 1981, pp. 892-893)

Alberto Giacometti
Jean Genet, 1954-1955
73 x 60 cm - CP

Hans Holbein
Erasmus, c. 1523
42 x 32 cm - ML

The life of the mind

Rembrandt
The Meditating Philosopher, 1632
28 x 34 cm - ML

It seemed to James Lord, the GI and man of the world who frequented Picasso's studio at the end of the Second World War and who became a friend of Giacometti, that Genet gave up sitting for his portrait because he could feel himself being transformed into an object. After many preliminary drawings and much pondering in the Louvre before *The Seated Scribe* and the Egyptian portraits from Fayum, this image of an intellectual, who had adopted theft as a precept for life, doubles as a record of the 'theft' of the sitter by the painter. Jean Genet's head, 'shrunken' in the Jivaro Indian sense of the word and enwrapped in a greenish, roseate void, boiling like plasma, no longer belongs to its model. To paint the workings of the mind equates with purloining the soul, with a Faustian pact.

Erasmus, sitting for Holbein the Younger in Basle in 1523, is condensed to his quintessence: the profile of a man writing. Later, in the portrait of Nicolas Kratzer, astronomer to Henry VIII of England (also in the Louvre, less vigorous if more sumptuous than that of Erasmus, it dates from 1528), Holbein placed numerous scientific instruments which would not have been fitting in a portrait of the famous humanist, author of *In Praise of Folly*. Rembrandt, the probable painter (in spite of recent controversy regarding its attribution) of the celebrated picture long known as *The Alchemist* distilled what is a metaphysical portrait of a philosopher deep in thought into a symbol. Besides, is it in truth a 'portrait'? The staircase conveys the ascent to knowledge, the overcoming of density, the world of books and ideas, the alchemical transmutation of matter, all of which should by rights escape the artist, but which, in a few scattered instances in the history of painting, have been captured and translated into colour and form.

121

François Boucher
Madame de Pompadour, c. 1756
60 x 45.5 cm - ML

Jacques Louis David
Madame Récamier, begun in 1800
174 x 244 cm - ML

Depicting intelligence, painting grace

Boucher's *Madame de Pompadour* is a sketch on paper remounted on canvas; David's *Madame Récamier* is an unfinished portrait in which many areas are merely hinted at in scumble; Otto Dix's *Sylvia von Harden* represents the talented journalist of the *Berliner Tageblatt* in a seemingly impromptu pose on the terrace of the Romanische Café in Berlin: three women from three eras who acquired their notoriety through the role they played in the intellectual arena

— and for whom the artist has to demonstrate that the plastic qualities highlighted for centuries in female portraiture can, in a world of literati, be wedded to intelligence. She who was to be known to posterity as the Marquise de Pompadour (in the 19th century, the brothers Goncourt even invented a 'goût Pompadour'), Jeanne Antoinette Normant d'Etioles, née Poisson, became mistress to Louis XV in 1745, then to reign over the Arts. A harpsichord, some

scores, a globe, and especially the books — as in Maurice Quentin de La Tour's superb pastel portrait (Louvre) — proclaim the sitter as a protector of artists, scientists and philosophers alike.

At the date of her portrait, 1800, Juliette Récamier, daughter and wife of a banker, was only twenty-three. Already renowned for her beauty and wit, she is not yet the woman a Platonic love affair with Chateaubriand and a friendship with Madame de Staël will make

Otto Dix
The Journalist Sylvia von Harden, 1926
121 x 89 cm - CP

famous. 'Madame, women have their whims and artists have theirs; permit me to satisfy mine, I will keep your portrait,' David confided when she complained of his snail's pace; and the painter conserved the work in his studio until his death. The gracefulness of the barefoot young woman creates an unexpected contrast with the grandeur of a setting whose furniture (preserved in the Louvre, Département des Objets d'Art) is in the latest style. David used this type of large format only once elsewhere, for the celebrated Lavoisier couple (Metropolitan Museum, New York).

Otto Dix, who in 1918 advocated 'truth, fervent, virile and profound, like that of Grünewald', had Sylvia von Harden, sporting a gamine haircut and a provocative-looking monocle, revert to an aristocratic pose, with the expressive hands of Cranach and Dürer, in the tradition of the masterly portraits of the German Renaissance. As centuries ago, the name of the sitter is written next to her, though now in her cigarette case. This new aristocracy, which portrayed itself in the Germany of Expressionism, is that of wit and scandal.

Johannes Vermeer
The Lacemaker, c. 1670
24 x 21 cm - ML

Mary Cassatt
Girl in a Garden, or *Young Woman Sewing*, c. 1880-1882
92 x 63 cm - MO

Fernand Léger
Woman Sewing, 1909-1910
73 x 54 cm - CP

The soul of the silent seamstress

In contradistinction to Mary, the woman who attended to the words of Jesus, the Gospel places the figure of Martha, who instead busied herself with the household chores. Commentators encounter difficulties explaining why Christ said: 'Mary hath chosen that good part which shall not be taken from her'. Will a woman who works manually find it harder to enter the kingdom of heaven than an intellectual? The theme of a woman sewing is a classic one, already appearing in the background of the double portrait of Gabrielle d'Estrées and her sister (p. 60). In Ancien Régime Europe, needlework was the female occupation par excellence — the highly intelligent Madame de Pompadour did not disdain it, though she preferred printmaking and gemstone engraving. The quality of concentration, care and taciturnity emanating from these sitters explains the large number of portraits of women embroidering and lacemaking. One should also remember how hard it is to 'hold the pose' for a portrait: a woman plying her needle in the light constitutes an ideal model for a painter; she keeps still, while the position emphasises her face and hands. But such constraints have an obvious corollary: as she sews, a woman lives an experience of introspection, a retreat into the ego, a self-hypnosis, that allows the painter to delve deeper into a perception of interiority, into the ineffable domain of the heart.

A close associate of Degas, author of a picture famous in its day called *Modern Woman* (whereabouts unknown), the American Mary Cassatt revelled in portraying the traditional occupations of womanhood: *Maternity*, *The Cup of Tea*, *The Boating Party*... Léger's *Woman Sewing*, a work from the very beginning of his career, is symptomatic in that it is an almost sculptural transposition of a theme frequent in the Old Masters, of which Vermeer's *Lacemaker* constitutes, with its uncomplicated, pyramidal structure, the most accomplished example and a consummate demonstration of how the humblest activity can embrace the universal.

Giovanni Paolo Panini
Musical Performance Given by Cardinal de La Rochefoucauld..., c. 1750
204 x 247 cm - ML

Can music be painted?

Music is perhaps still more intractable to paint than silence, despite the terminology it shares with painting: 'chromatic range' or 'key', or those 'chords', which we will now try out between the following three pictures. In the Panini, the musical dimension is conveyed by the architecture of the capacious auditorium. The room is itself the spectacle, the music accompanies a society ballet, a highly pictorial excuse for scintillating colours and for layer upon layer of figures, listening, watching and parading about.

Degas' portrait of bassoon player Désiré Dihau is as if caught on the wing. Naturally, the composition was reworked in the studio: Degas had some companions pose for the musicians' faces, with a cavalier disregard for the traditional arrangement of string and wind sections in an orchestra. Degas' viewpoint zeroes in on the essentials, while the composition is strongly structured by the diagonal of the instrument, by the horizontal lines bordering the orchestra pit, by the vertical accents of the bows, and by the rectangle of the chair oddly resembling a stretcher on the back of a canvas. Degas shows the opera 'behind the scenes', whereas Panini displays its outward splendour. The balustrade in the foreground suggests

Edgar Degas

The Orchestra of the Paris Opera, vers 1870

56.5 x 46 cm - MO

Nicolas de Staël

The Musicians. Souvenir of Sidney Bechet, 1953

161.9 x 114.2 cm - CP

the unseen audience, or rather it transforms the viewer into a listener at the concert. The ballet itself, the future source of such inspiration for Degas, is only hinted at, interest concentrating on the musicians, on those to whom the public is not supposed to pay any attention. The dancers have neither head nor pumps and the dark scroll of the double bass is superimposed rather brutally over the pale tones of their tutus; the black and white mass of the male group attracts the eye more than the shards of pink and blue. To the right, underscored by a streak of red velvet, is the minute head of the composer Emmanuel Chabrier, gazing, listening — perhaps he wrote what we cannot hear.

The bands of colour at the base of Nicolas de Staël's canvas render visible the rhythms of jazz, sound vibrations invading a space. His orchestra is as geometrical as that of Degas and as carefully rehearsed as Panini's *Teatro*. Left unfinished at the time of his suicide, Nicolas de Staël's last picture was entitled, *The Concert*.

Rogier van der Weyden
The Annunciation, c. 1435
86 x 93 cm - ML

Vittore Carpaccio
St Stephen Preaching in Jerusalem, c. 1514
148 x 194 cm - ML

Conveying the power of words

Words act. They are not limited to causing actions or to recounting them, they are active, they produce effects. The archetype of words that do what they say is the Annunciation, one of the most widespread subjects in all iconography. The moment when the words of the Angel saluting the Virgin are enough in that very instant to make her the Mother of God is absolutely beyond representation. The Angel's greeting (angel means 'messenger') is the crux of the miracle. This pictorial marvel which, to be understood, requires adherence to the faith, led painters such as Van der Weyden to devise a symbolic system: the immaterial action of God, creator of matter, has to be made visible. A madonna lily signifies the purity of the Virgin, the vase, childbirth, the holy book recalls the Gospels and the prophets who foretold of the Messiah, the landscape by the window, the Garden of Eden, lost at the beginning of time, which the birth of Jesus will make it possible to regain. A saint's mission is a human version of the Divine Word transmitted by the angel. The absolute, inexplicable miracle gives way to the wonder of rhetoric, to those visible gestures that reinforce an orator's eloquence that Cicero calls his *actio*. In a fantasy Oriental city, Carpaccio shows St Stephen preaching and converting his listeners. All that remained was to push this idea to its limits and to let the written word take complete possession of the pictorial space.

In 1921, Picabia was treating an eye infection with soda 'cacodylate' — the Greek root of the word indicates a substance emitting a foul odour — and invited a few Dada colleagues to write something around a picture of an eye. One eye to the bad, the painter renounced use of the paintbrush and let his friends compose him a picture that is nonetheless all his own work, a kind of ex-voto vouchsafing the artist's return to health, a canvas to look at and to read. Here too, the word is an act, and paint merges with action.

Francis Picabia

L'Œil cacodylate, 1921

148.6 x 117.4 cm - CP

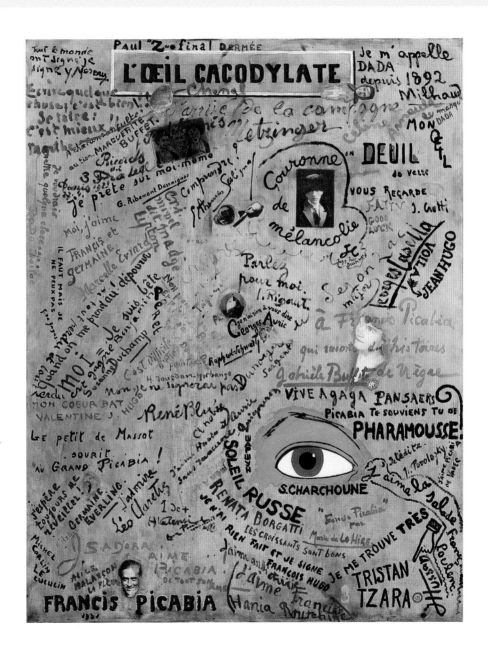

Can madness be painted?

Is it easier for painting to portray reason, intelligence, the persuasive force of an argument or some marvellous event than to convey folly? The earliest representations of insanity, a subject that became current towards the end of the Middle Ages, derive from the convention of the 'world upside-down', in an aesthetic similar to that of the carnival. Bosch's *Ship of Fools*, the title of a immensely successful book by Strasbourg moralist Sebastian Brant (1458-1521) published in Basle in 1494, shows a becalmed ship teeming with little figures, each embodying an aspect of common sense 'stood on its head'. The voyage described by Brant to the fools' paradise of Narragonia is undertaken on a paradoxical craft whose mast is a tree rooted to the spot. A monk and a nun join in a serenade, each trying to unhook food from the mast as if from a maypole: does not the human condition make us all, especially ungodly sinners, passengers on the Ship of Fools that is our world?

As delineated by Géricault, insanity has nothing symbolic about it, it is no longer a systematic inversion

Théodore Géricault
Madwoman with Gambling Mania, c. 1822
77 x 64.5 cm - ML

of reason, but a modern disease with recognisable clinical signs. Perhaps these pictures (museums in Lyon and Ghent possess other paintings from a series unique in the history of portraiture) were used by his friend, Dr Georget, a physician at the Salpêtrière madhouse, to expound on his diagnoses. Georget, a disciple of the psychiatrist Esquirol, believed in 'monomania', a well-defined condition, as opposed to 'madness', which is an absolute. The 'monomaniac' sitters were undoubtedly genuine patients, though their names are not recorded: each stands for a specific ailment, be it theft or desire, gambling or 'military command' — the latter condition being endemic in France following the collapse of the Empire. Traditional iconography places the instruments of their martyrdom in the hands of the saints; on the faces of his lunatics, Géricault etched the symptoms of what makes them suffer, what corrodes them and cuts them off from their fellow man, and thus, in spite of their anonymity, makes them individual.

131

Sexe, amour et peinture

Like in Racine's play, before visiting King Ahasuerus, Chassériau's Esther adorns herself. Flanked by a maidservant and a eunuch, she does not represent love, but its trappings. Painting halts on the threshold of what can be shown; the concept of decorum, paramount in classical French tragedy, provides a fulcrum for many paintings of a love which is rarely carnal — unlike in drawing, a bolder, more clandestine art form. The power of these three images stems from how they capture a moment 'before' — unlike, for example, Greuze's *The Broken Jug* (p. 172) which concentrates on the emotions that follow 'after'. Gérard's decorous *Amor and Psyche*, as frail as a Tanagra statuette, prepares herself to receive a first kiss from love, a young god painted in profile as on a Greek vase. Above them flutters a butterfly (the same Greek word designates the heroine Psyche, the butterfly and the soul) so that the image is read as a spirit as well as bodily union. In his time, the classicism of Gérard's composition felt like a riposte to the audacious maelstrom of Fragonard's *The Bolt*. Here too, several meanings are possible, and the scene is perhaps not quite as clear as it might appear. Its companion piece is a religious scene, an *Adoration*

of the Shepherds (also in the Louvre): is this an irreverent joke on the part of some libertine patron or a clue as how to read both works jointly? With hindsight perhaps, the apple placed in full view and the upset jug in the shadows connect with the forbidden fruit of original sin and the mystic vase of the Annunciation. On one side, Sin, immutable since Adam and Eve, shooting the bolt of the pearly gates shut; on the other, the birth of Christ who throws them open again?

Sacred against profane love, as in the mysterious allegory by Titian (1515-1516, Galleria Borghese, Rome)? The innocent Jewess Esther sacrifices herself to save her persecuted people. In the Gérard, the soul hovers above the alabaster body. Profane love is inextricably linked to the mysteries of spiritual love.

Yet one can just as well see nothing of this and delight instead in the most obvious meaning (one apparent before any analysis) of three pictures that celebrate the triumph of love.

133

Gustave Courbet
The Origin of the World, 1866
46 x 55 cm - MO

Painting = rape?

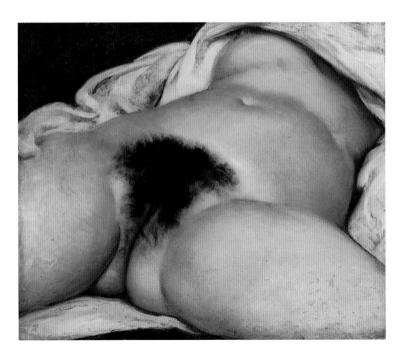

Painting can show what society conceals. The most infamous and legendary picture in the history of art, for long hidden in the home of psychoanalyst Jacques Lacan behind a crypto-erotic landscape by André Masson, can today be seen by all. In the Musée d'Orsay, the orifice of our origin lies opposite the pit dug by the gravedigger in the middle of the *Burial at Ornans* (p. 76). Painted for the Eastern collector we have already referred to, Khalil Bey, a famous figure in Parisian society during the Second Empire who also possessed Ingres' *Bain turc* (p. 55), Courbet's observation of woman disregards her individuality, her face, her identity.

In the Magritte too, the face disappears, confined to the fair hair that frames it and transformed into a torso and a sex. Balthus shows a woman who shows herself. In the *Nouvelle Revue française* in 1934, Antonin Artaud wrote: 'It is by the light from a wall, a parquet floor, a chair and from the epidermis that we are invited to enter the mysteries of a body, its genitals exposed and jagged. This nude [...] is an invitation to love that does nothing to dissimulate its dangers.' The writer Pierre-Jean Jouve who 'possessed' *Alice* in his bedroom for twenty years, commented: 'This strange companion was naturally that of my nights, by which I mean that she watched over me in sleep, capable of slipping inside it.' Might this be a painting that rapes the person who looks at it?

Balthus
Alice, 1933
162.3 x 112 cm - **CP**

René Magritte
The Rape, 1945
63.3 x 50.4 cm - **CP**

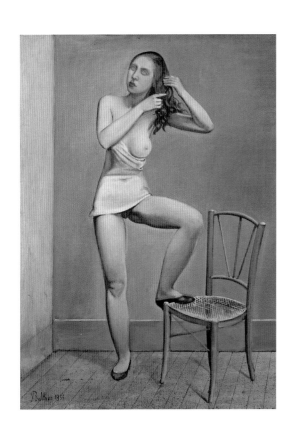

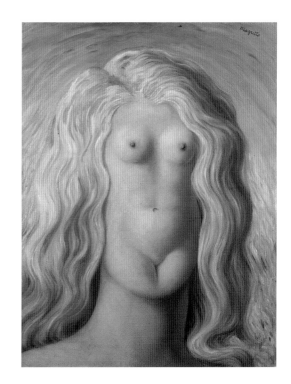

Frans Hals
The Gipsy Girl, c. 1628-1630
58 x 52 cm - ML

Georges Seurat
Model, Frontal View, c. 1886-1887
25 x 16 cm - MO

Antoni Tàpies
Grand Blanc horizontal, 1962
195 x 310 cm - CP

Closely observed pictures?

 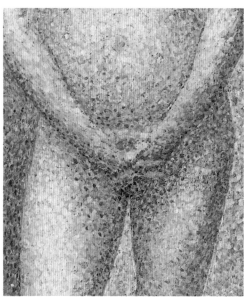 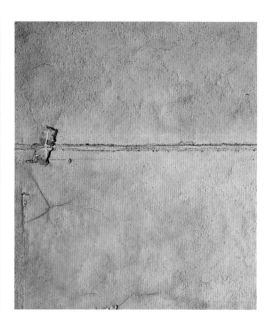

136

Standing before a picture, one should lose oneself in the paint surface and identify or compare, not so much the subjects and their meanings, nor even the construction or composition, but the touch, the movements of the brush, if brush it was. This is a different way of looking, of taking a few steps closer — nose to paint layer, at the risk of sounding the museum's alarm or of feeling a warden finger one's collar, it gives one access to a second, imperceptible dimension of painting. The secret is also the craft, the tricks of the painter's trade, which the artist might display with pride or else masks as an enigma essential to his art. Hals is known to posterity as the master of a debonair style, of vibrant canvases executed in a few, precise gestures, the brushstrokes clearly visible. This sketch-like facture, much admired in Fragonard, Goya and Delacroix, was long neglected, appreciated only by connoisseurs. The officially exhibited, highly 'finished' picture should bear no trace of its making, and sketches remained behind in the workshop. Hals' attention to substance contrasts with Seurat's intricate combinations where the brushstroke shatters into tiny tesserae of paint. A quite different way of painting, a different rhythm and time scale transpire when we examine these marks. Close observation of the surface allows the painter's attitude vis-a-vis his work to be gauged: Tàpies tackles his materials like a bricklayer erecting a cob wall. The rich impasto turns the picture into a slice of reality, a re-creation of the soil, wood and water that have proved such a constant inspiration in his work.

Peter Paul Rubens

Marie de' Medici Landing at Marseille,

between 1621 and 1625 394 x 295 cm - ML

Jean-Honoré Fragonard

Abbé de Saint-Non, c. 1769

80 x 65 cm - ML

Simon Hantaï

Peinture (Écriture rose), 1958-1959

329.5 x 424.5 cm - CP

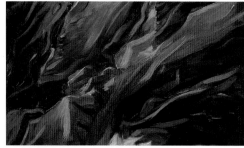
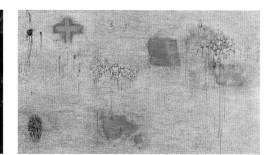

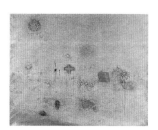

Freedom in the details

Rubens and Fragonard belong to that group of artists who dare lift the veil on their craft. Géricault painting *The Raft of the Medusa*, the young Delacroix preparing for his first polemical piece, *Dante's Barge* (Louvre), for the Salon, and Courbet, creator of *La Femme à la vague* (1868, Metropolitan Museum, New York), must surely have inspected the water droplets striking the white skin of Rubens' Nereides as the marine divinities accompany Marie de' Medici off her ship. Rubens shows himself less uninhibited here than in his more compact sketches, but the spatters of white paint demonstrate a consummate skill that the public, overwhelmed by the overall effect, scarcely notices, but which has always been applauded by painters. Fragonard, whose touch can be meticulous (witness *The Bolt*), attains absolute freedom of technique in the portraits of people close to him or of patrons who were also friends, many examples of which are in the Louvre (all hang together, with the exception of one displayed in the room set aside for the Collection Beistegui). This fantasy figure was apparently executed in the absence of the sitter and in a veritable painting frenzy. An inscription on the back states: 'Painted by Fragonard in 1769 in a single hour'.

André Derain
The Two Barges, 1906
80 x 97.5 cm - CP

Derain thought long and hard over *The Two Barges*, working out how to frame the image in his sketchbook. With a touch derived from Van Gogh, Derain left some of the surface bare, occasionally letting the primer and the canvas weave beyond show through. The complex, 'Japonised' construction, the calculated contrast between the colours lain side by side — the sail is red and blue — still allow for total freedom and a quick-fire, lively attack of the brush. The visible traces of its execution give little inkling of the lengthy meditation that preceded it.

For Hantaï, until his career took a decisive turn with this work — soon after which he began crumpling up and folding his canvases — the act of painting merged with that of writing (*écriture*), with a graphical language that here builds up into a pink wall comprising colours and signs, which are difficult to read but easy to see. It might be said that the movements of Fragonard's brush, laying in the folds and tucks of his friend Saint-Non's sleeve, had already given rise to such a calligraphy.

139

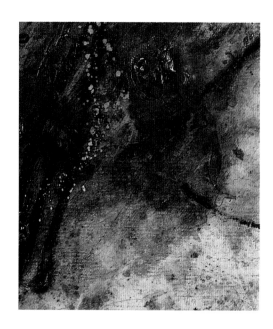

The raw materials of painting? The invisible brushstroke

In marked contrast to such dazzling sketches, authoritative critics of the 19th century considered that the acme of the painter's craft was a translucent touch, a dematerialisation of the artistic craft that thus became as unfathomable to the non-professional as the workings of the Creator. The eye should not be able to tell 'how it was painted'. For this reason Flemish techniques were envied and parroted throughout Europe. Their virtuosity had culminated in *The Madonna of Chancellor Rolin*, since it was applied as much to the textiles, gems, and flesh as to a landscape represented with all the precision of an illuminated manuscript. The mimetic dimension, which lies at the epicentre of all discussion of painting in the classical era — a picture must mirror reality to the point of deceiving the eye — demands the touch remain unseen and the artist to absent himself from the painting. Antonello da Messina practised its principles in Italy in a few works whose qualities were already trumpeted by Vasari, while Ingres raised the skill he had learned from David to an unprecedented level. Modelling the face and allowing the eye to travel from a zone of light to one of shadow is to be assured without the viewer sensing any dividing line. For Ingres, painting is a process of accretion: to attain perfection in modelling, the master has to superpose layer upon layer of transparent glaze, giving the illusion that he has carved cheeks and arms out of solid flesh.

The transparency effects in Wols have nothing to do with this tradition, neither in technique nor in spirit. Bonnard admired these 'butterfly wings' as the most natural, fragile painting conceivable. Wols scrutinised Nature 'under the magnifying glass': stones, crystals, the sea. His tiny, superimposed flecks, his liking for watercolour, are part of a mysticism born out of Surrealism, but which spurred him on a search for a visual equivalent of the unrepresentable.

Jan van Eyck

The Madonna of Chancellor Rolin, c. 1434

66 x 62 cm - ML

Antonello da Messina

Christ at the Column, c. 1476-1478

29 x 21 cm - ML

Jean Auguste Dominique Ingres

Mademoiselle Caroline Rivière, 1806 Salon

100 x 70 cm - ML

141

Nicolas de Staël
Roofs, 1952
200 x 150 cm - CP

Henri-Edmond Cross
Les Iles d'or, c. 1891-1892
59 x 54 cm - MO

Gustav Klimt
Roses under the Trees, c. 1905
110 x 110 cm - MO

The living surface of the canvas

In great, clear canvases, turning darker in his later period (*Browns over Dark* being an example), Rothko is undoubtedly the most intrepid explorer of the properties of pictorial substance. In the 'Rothko Room' at the Phillips Collection, Washington, in other museums with rooms devoted to him, or in the chapel he designed at the Menil Foundation in Houston, it is not rare to see visitors deep in meditation, lost for hours in his works. Rothko's canvases call for close examination, one enters them like a stationary traveller into a universe of brushstrokes and marks. But from a distance, they irradiate with a density to which no photographic reproduction can do justice. This at once tactile and spiritual dimension is met with in other works, apparently unrelated to Rothko's by art history's tentacles. Cross, in *Les Îles d'or*, advances imperceptibly towards abstraction, as does Klimt, when he fills a space with leaves of gold-green decor. Discerning harbingers of abstraction in these works is not to relegate Rothko's work to the 'decorative', nor to betray the ornamental essence of Klimt's art. Contrariwise, Nicolas de Staël gives a figurative title to a work that at first sight is not. Initially, the viewer discerns only geometry, power and construction. 'A museum work', the painter remarked to art historian Bernard Dorival before donating it to the Musée National d'Art Moderne.

In 1949, Rothko said: 'The progression of a painter's work, as it travels in time from point to point, will be toward clarity: toward the elimination of all obstacles between the painter and the idea, and between the idea and the observer. As examples of

Mark Rothko
N° 14 (Browns over Dark), 1963
228.5 x 176 cm - CP

such obstacles, I give (among others) memory,
history or geometry […]. To achieve this clarity is,
inevitably, to be understood.'

Jackson Pollock

Number 26 A, Black and White, 1948

205 x 121.7 cm - CP

Paul Rebeyrolle

Nude, 1971

190 x 275 cm - CP

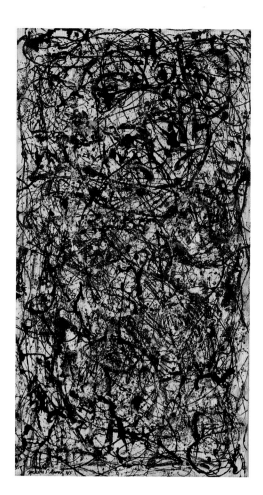

The act of painting

If one goes back to the source, one always finds Monet's *Waterlilies* — Monet, the 20th-century artist. Unshackled from Impressionism, Monet invented a species of painting simultaneously decorative and abstract, elaborate in detailing, but which can only be judged by taking in its vast clumps of colour. Monet breathed new life into the workings of the brush, into those gestures he found increasingly difficult towards the end of his life that turned every large format work into a struggle.

Pollock's drippings (the technique dates back to 1947, the works being numbered sequentially only from 1948) proceed from the same drive to appropriate space, to fill an entire surface with rhythmical gestures, subscribing to a ritual that saw the canvas laid on the ground and subjugated by the artist. Pollock's Action Painting was no trite formula; developing over the following years through 'series' in a Monet-like vein, it proved to be a new way of binding matter to style, ground to colour, the broad surface of the canvas to the painter's necessarily restricted movements. Rebeyrolle also occupies vast areas; invading entire walls, he interlards human life with abstraction, nudes with matter. It is the surface that is naked and palpitating, taller and wider than reality. Beneath one of Pollock drippings, there might shelter the palest of female bodies, becoming almost visible if one gazes at the canvas for long enough…

With or without a brush?

Raymond Hains and Jacques Mahé de La Villeglé
Ach Alma Manetro, 1949
58 x 256 cm - CP

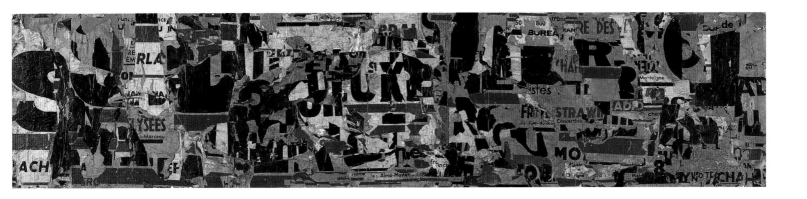

In Divisionism as practised by Signac, every brushstroke is individualised. The loaded brush, the principal actor, no longer sweeps across the canvas surface; instead, it is positioned exactly at the place where a dot of paint can resonate with its neighbour. A painstaking business, it requires prolonged contemplation of the landscape and much scrutinising of the canvas as it builds up, finally attaining total equilibrium. Into the port of St-Tropez, Signac immerses a geometrical form that contrasts with the cubes of the houses and their reflections: the red buoy that gives the work its title also serves as its centre of gravity. It floats on the surface of the rectangle of the port, an ultimate dot of colour on the surface of the canvas. Made out of minuscule squares of paint, it is the discordant note, the link between sea and earth, between landscape and reflection. With Raymond Hains and Jacques de la Villeglé, as with Yves Klein, there is no longer any brush. A four-hander produced by the friends in 1949, the title of this *arrachage* (or 'ripping'), derives from scraps of writing that can still be deciphered; it is also intended to bring to mind several cantatas by J. S. Bach that begin *attacco* with the word 'Ach!', a breath. The music of the picture thus derives from removing strips of poster from a wall; painting, if it is still painting, is created in the same way as a 'direct carving' sculpture, by removing instead of adding material, making a brush superfluous. In his *anthropométries* of the 1960s, Yves Klein also eliminated the brush. This example refers to a 1959 film by Joseph Mankiewicz after a story by Tennessee Williams, *Suddenly Last Summer* that had impressed the artist. The canvas devours bodies dripping paint like brushes. During an art ceremony that is also a spectacular public performance, these bodies are deprived of their volume by being crushed on the canvas. The artist devised the 'choreography' and the method, but he relinquished control of the physical gestures, of the action — that was the sole responsibility of the naked models whom he daubed in paint. 'The picture is only a witness, a sensitive plate that observes what has occurred.'

147

Eustache Le Sueur
Dedication of a Carthusian Church, c. 1645-1648
191 x 287 cm - ML

Drawing, geometry, perspective

'I love the rigour of geometry; but I love even more making shit happen. It is a bit like I'd entered orders to expose myself at Mass,' François Morellet declared in a 1988 issue of the Toulouse journal, *Pressing*. In Morellet, geometric rigour and an obsession with purity go hand in hand with iconoclasm and a wicked sense of humour. This painting installation whose title provides an initial descriptive key was presented by Morellet to the Centre Pompidou. The flip-flop effect between its pair of white squares could be as cold as ice. The artist aims at a monumentality that resonates in the place where the piece or 'machine' is shown, but also with what he has termed 'a geometry in spasms'.

Le Sueur's perfectly geometric painting also has something of the 'machine' about it. Part of a series of eight pictures hung in the corners of a small cloister that completes a twenty-two painting cycle of the life of St Bruno (Louvre), the shape of this panel was

148

François Morellet

Superposition and Transparency, Square behind 0°90° B-Square in front, 20° B-110°, 1980

256.5 x 363 cm - CP

adapted to the basket arches at the Carthusian convent in Paris, but the pegging of the boards can clearly be seen, introducing, beneath the geometry of the painting, a geometry of the support. On the ground, the vast perspective of an X delimits a space as pure as in the paintings of the Dutchman Saenredam (p. 152). The crosses reappear on the pillars, on the book, in a subtle chromatic interplay that sets up visual echoes in the broad nave. The same blue links the book, the eye of the monk holding the crozier and the columns of the church whose masonry is consecrated during the ceremony depicted. The 'rigour of geometry' makes it possible here to comprehend an unrepresentable event: the 'dedication' of a church that transforms lines and elementary forms into an earthly image of the house of God.

Patrick Saytour
Untitled, 1968
354 x 136.5 cm - CP

Folds, shadows

In a comparison of these two works, art historian Arnauld Pierre remarks: 'Saytour dematerialises painting, ridicules it.' Responding to the geometry of Champaigne's picture, Pierre re-reads the tablecloth in the foreground as a series of 'folds' similar to those in the Saytour. (Daniel Dezeuze does the opposite, covering the wooden stretcher with transparent plastic film, thereby eliminating the materiality of the 'canvas' [1967, Centre Pompidou]). Champaigne, who from 1640 came under the influence of the severe, Jansenist spirituality of Port-Royal, depicts the austerity of the table at the Last Supper draped in a white cloth that reminds visitors to the Louvre today of the winding-sheet in the same painter's *Dead Christ*, a dramatic instance of raw realism. If the tablecloth 'already represents' Christ's shroud, why did the painter highlight the folds? A preoccupation with realism, to bestow greater nobility and geometrical rigidity on the composition or as an image of predestination? The folds visible on the tablecloth are the consequence of a humble, practical process of

folding, each stage of which can be reconstituted from the painting. Human life also has its folds and its shadows: it is left for Man to read what the hand that made the lines intended to do

'To ridicule painting' and its symbols is also to reflect on the relationship between support and surface, between the suspended stretcherless canvas and the visible side over which shadows dance in the light. Probably in spite of himself, Patrick Saytour has invented a Minimalist, Jansenist installation of wry austerity: the logic of Port-Royal applied to contemporary art. A canvas in a museum does not necessarily mean that there was a painter, nor even a woman from Jerusalem wielding an iron as the 17th century imagined her, to starch it: there is simply an artist, who carefully folded it, then opened it up, so as to see.

Pieter Jansz Saenredam
Interior of the Church of St Bavo in Haarlem, 1630
41 x 37 cm - ML

Architectures

Was Mondrian an architect? He had started out painting reality and nature — Holland, her mills and trees: 'I always felt that I worked like an Impressionist expressing specific sensations, and not reality as it is.' After a conventional training at the fine arts school in Amsterdam, over the years Mondrian invented his own art of balance and purity — hence its juxtaposition (unburdened of religious dimensions) with the church interior of another Dutchman, Saenredam. In both paintings the picture space is divided into sections, monochrome surfaces with lines of force. 'In architecture,' Mondrian wrote in 1926 in the review *Vouloir*, 'empty space counts as non-colour. Matter can count as colour'. Primary colours, almost white surfaces, black lines arranged in a lattice with blue and red insets like a stained-glass window: this *Composition* belongs to a series begun in 1935 that reconfigures space as a geometric

Piet Mondrian
Composition in Red, Blue and White II, 1937
75 x 60.5 cm - CP

system, an optical 'construction'. The interiors of Saenredam's churches (sparser and less anecdotal than those of his contemporary Emmanuel de Witte) also deploy a restricted range of colours and exploit perspective and planar effects. Scarcely more than fifty works are known by this master; all are marked by an architectural sternness, a rigour relying on pale ochre and beige or a slightly off-white and grey so as to enter the muffled atmosphere of the nave of a church. Saenredam's preparatory sketches resemble architectural plans or elevations. The present-day eye hesitates before such clarity of vision: meticulous realism — or the unconscious precursor of abstraction?

Georges Braque
Le Guéridon, 1911
116.5 x 81.5 cm - CP

Lubin Baugin
The Wafers, c. 1630 or 1635
41 x 52 cm - ML

The construction of space and the line

In the 1960s, the comparison of Baugin's still lifes with Braque's Cubist works sent artistic circles into ecstasies. Forty years on, the experience is worth repeating. A parallel between Braque's side-table and Baugin's tray, jutting out slightly over the tabletop, can still provide a basis for examining how two artists analyse space. In 1911, Braque, attached to Picasso, as he said, 'like mountaineers roped together', wrote from Céret to the art dealer Daniel-Henry Kahnweiler: 'I've discovered an imperishable white, like velvet beneath the brush which I'm overusing.' Meanwhile, Matisse, nearby in Collioure, was painting *Interior with Aubergines* (Musée de Grenoble). Kahnweiler reacted with enthusiasm to Braque's paintings: an 'erudite', highly constructed, deeply pondered art that calls for long examination to understand how it functions. Scattered about in the fragmented space one can make out a roll of paper, a violin scroll (a recurring motif in canvases from this series), notes of music, all allusions to reality and to the traditional genre of the still life as recalibrated by Braque. A pupil of Simon

Vouet, Baugin stresses the interactions between simple geometrical forms — here, the ellipse of the tin dish, the oval of the bottle — and more virtuoso visual tricks, such as the frangible, overlapping cylinders of the waffles, like in the game of spillikins in which whoever picks up a stick but moves another loses. Is it an image of our fragile human destiny suggested by the crystal wineglass and the crumbling biscuits? There is no way of telling, even if, at that period, still lifes often masked a *vanitas*. Things are not so clear here; there is no skull, no hourglass to corroborate an arguably symbolic approach to the work. The pure, 'geometric' reading remains, permissible today since our eyes have grown accustomed to the discoveries of Braque and Picasso. Stendhal claimed that he wrote novels to be read in the 20th century: perhaps Baugin, though active under Louis XIII, painted to be seen and understood only after Analytical Cubism?

Squared-up

Monet builds a space of the utmost rigour, a spatial box opening to the front in which classical symmetry reigns, like in a Giotto predella. Monet, who painted landscapes, a genre unreceptive to symmetry and who preferred to place his figures off-centre, gives proof here of the kind of precision he would return to in the Rouen Cathedral series. Were not railway stations the cathedrals of the 19th century? 'Our artists must discover the poetry of stations,' Zola wrote in 1877. At the third Impressionist exhibition, Monet exhibited seven of the twelve canvases he had painted on site (with the railway authority's go-ahead) beneath the glass vault of St-Lazare. He reinvents the cityscape through the industrial, 'tubular' dimension on which modernity is founded: from this great 'nave' trains left for the Normandy coast, for the sea, for the land with its poppy fields and beaches — subjects that were the painter's enduring love. Impressionism in *St-Lazare* has nothing to do with the conventional image perpetuated by official histories of the movement. The neat metal armature is interrupted solely by smoke.

Pierre Bonnard
L'Atelier au mimosa, 1939-1946
127.5 x 127.5 cm - CP

Horizontal in Monet, a grid also structures the canvas in the Bonnard, but vertical and in perspective. At St-Lazare, smoke wafts across the lines; in Bonnard, light dances through the mimosa, passing over the geometrical array of lines, flooding the foreground. Bonnard's canvas is square, but the space is divided into parallel rectangles. He too assembles a 'box', opening this time on to a landscape. In the left-hand corner appears the face of a woman; Marthe, one of his favourite models who died in 1942. The picture, begun before the war, in 1939, was retouched after the Liberation, in 1946, and several critics have read it as an image of happiness regained. This is surely misguided, since Bonnard's very private image is free of political connotations. The heights of Cannes, seen from the painter's studio in Le Cannet, are darker in the distance than the rest of the canvas: but this is perhaps merely to offer a foil to the thick, yellow colour of the blossoming trees.

Line by line

With her 'polychrome monochrome' surfaces, Aurélie Nemours creates rhythm and sets colour vibrating. For her, a work's success stems from a single consideration: 'A picture has to blaze — and that's it.' In this work, Nemours has assembled nine squares measuring 80 cm along each side. Fascinated by the architectural compositions of the stained-glass window makers who worked at the Gothic cathedral of Chartres, she thinks of herself as a medieval artist. Less well-known to the general public than Daniel Buren, with whom he founded the group BMPT (the name comes from the initials of its four founder members, the others being Mosset and Toroni), Michel Parmentier's canvases are delimited into parallel stripes. Buren's most famous work is the *Deux Plateaux* installation in the courtyard of the Palais Royal, with its uneven striped columns; his bands are always vertical, whereas Parmentier's are horizontal. From 1965 to 1968, Parmentier spray-gunned 38 cm-wide bands on a canvas folded accordion-wise in accordance with an invariable formula that, over the years, only modifies only the colours. The artist leaves instructions on how his works are to be exhibited: 'As to conservation: before every hanging, time should be allowed for [the work] to be folded up following the original creases so that, on unfolding, they are once again visible.' This note, which appears in a file of material accompanying the piece in the documentation centre at the Pompidou, concludes with the sentence: 'This description says everything about the product-painting of which I was the author.' Geometry then is simply an outcome. What counts for the artist is the idea, the formula, the 'description'.

159

Kasimir Malevich
Black Cross, 1915
80 x 79.5 cm - CP

Crosses

His whole life long, Malevich lived his art as did the icon painters of old: *the Running Man* (1933–1934, Centre Pompidou), a work from the period of his return to figuration, shows a vast red cross against a blue sky. In 1915, he had broken with figuration in a work that laid the foundations of 20th-century art. Should it be seen as a sacred image or as a purely geometrical element or else as an icon of the death of painting? In December 1915, Malevich exhibited thirty-eight canvases he called Suprematist, a

movement he defined as 'new pictorial realism, non-objective creation', using as its 'geometrical units' squares, circles, crosses, black on a white ground. Crosses and squares lie at the centre of Malevich's vision: for him, the basic shape is a square that can be hung in a corner of a room, like the icons of the Orthodox Church.

Champaigne here puts himself forward as a maker of ex-votos, a form of popular art hung in chapels as a sign of gratitude: like Malevich, the court painter

sought to participate in a more modest painting tradition. His two daughters had become nuns in the severe Jansenist community at Port-Royal des Champs. A year before this picture was painted, Louis XIV had begun persecuting the Jansenists. It depicts a miracle at once personal and political: against all expectations, the artist's daughter recovered from an illness, proof positive that God was indeed at work among the persecuted. A lengthy Latin dedication stresses the presence at

160

Philippe de Champaigne
Ex-Voto de 1662, 1662
165 x 229 cm - ML

the scene of God and of the painter-father: 'As she was joining Mother Catherine Arnauld in prayer, in an instant [sister Catherine Suzanne de Champaigne] regained perfect health. Philippe de Champaigne presented this image in 1662, in testimony to a great miracle and to his joy.' Champaigne's image, in which the power of God is exalted in an abstract manner, through light, through the small reliquary his daughter holds, the book and the letters of the inscription, inside an interior of unsurpassed austerity, invites us to see painting as a miracle. Louis Marin comments on how it shows the links between 'making the invisible presence visible on the one hand, and the effective actuation of the signs of discourse on the other.' Malevich's minimal cross, also an efficacious sign, connects with the red fabric crosses on the robes worn by Champaigne's nuns. 'Joy' is expressed in both images, a spiritual joy translated into geometrical language. In 1919, Malevich wrote in *Suprematism*: 'I have emerged into whiteness, comrade aviators […] infinity lies before us.'

Painting the cosmos

Three landscapes which are far more than views of the 'countryside': visions of the infinite, microcosms with the whole world in a scrap of canvas, encapsulating the universal, representing it in a single, isolated fragment. The Louvre possesses a characteristic painting from Turner's last period, in all likelihood left deliberately unfinished by the artist, which contemporary sensitivities thus enjoy all the more. Freed from illustrative constraints, the landscape acquires a panoramic breadth, an abstract-like value. Conceived in the studio, it is no longer a representation of reality nor of anything exterior to the artist's world. Millet's landscape also allows one to apprehend a private world. The colour contrasts, the violent irruption of spring in a Nature still gripped by winter, the red branches of the great tree, the white flowers, everything is lit after the storm by a rainbow that professes the painter's faith. Does the colour spectrum belong to Nature or to the artist's palette? Friedrich conveys the shift from one world to another, from the real world to one of dreams, from Neo-classicism to Romanticism, from one season to the next. Jutting out in the foreground, the tree occupies a huge amount of space in what is a small-format picture. As always in Friedrich's landscapes, natural elements take on symbolic meaning, features in an image that talks of desolation and death. Only crows haunt this shattered hulk of Nature — ready to fly off to other climes.

162

Johannes Vermeer
The Astronomer, c. 1668-1670
51 x 45 cm - ML

Natalia Goncharova
Space, 1958
55 x 46 cm - CP

On through space

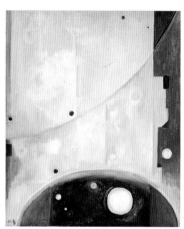

To represent what cannot be represented is also to try to elucidate the indistinct. The attempt to convey the inexplicable cosmos in pictorial space has led painters to reflect on the links between their art and the sciences. To aid him in laying out his perspectives, Vermeer utilised some kind of optical chamber. His designs emerge from within a scientific system he pressed into the service of art — the 'blurred' effects are 'photographic' *ante litteram* in the etymological sense of the word, since it is the light itself that draws, creating an interaction between a near-invisible finer grain and a more consistent one materialised by visible pinpricks of white. An image of an esoteric world, a celestial sphere sprinkled with dots that are stars, it collects light as it passes through the window. The

hypothesis of a self-portrait of the 'artist as scientist' should not be rejected out of hand. The astronomer, too, knows how to unravel ambiguities and to interpret the most obscure phenomena, how to establish a logic of things and demonstrate it to mere mortals, such as painters. Likely also an astrologer on the side, the astronomer peers into present and future, reading on the surface of things what is hidden from the unenlightened. In Holland, where medicine, chemistry and astronomy as well as the humanities flourished, the artist's knowledge can compete with the scientist's. The space that opens up to beholders of a Vermeer is not only that of constellations and stellar bodies; it also takes in those far-flung coasts from which fleets of merchantmen returned to the United Provinces

laden with that 'embarrassment of riches' which financed its wonderful collections of paintings.

In 1957, the first Soviet satellite filled the Eastern bloc with wonder and the United States with consternation. The subject was addressed in twenty canvases by Goncharova, including *Space* that dives headlong into a painted infinity. The horizon of painting has just been moved back; such a new world had never been depicted before. Abstraction is a good medium for capturing infinite space and the interstellar vacuum with a paintbrush. Humankind has crossed a new frontier which the act of painting reflects with a poetical enchantment that equals Vermeer's masterly technique in *The Astronomer*, when he portrayed he who can explain the stars and the mysteries of the cosmos.

Fra Angelico
Coronation of the Virgin, c. 1430-1432
209 x 206 cm - ML

The whole world in a picture

A picture, be it encumbered with halos or straw hats, is a microcosm. Its borders encompass a whole world. In Fra Angelico's *Coronation of the Virgin*, the celestial host arranges itself around the divine throne. A Gothic dais surmounts a stone staircase standing for the steps or stages of the Creation, while on the ground appears the modernistic tour de force of an artist who impresses most by his control of perspective. At the summit, Christ in Majesty and the Holy Mother, surrounded by the orders of angels and saints, are readily identifiable. Viewed from the rear, the Magdalene, bearing the casket of perfume, has loosened her long, wavy locks; St Catherine holds the wheel of her martyrdom; wearing a historiated chasuble, St Nicolas carries his mitre and crozier. In Paradise, the figures lie outside time, in Eternity. Only in the predella's panels does narrative time subsist. Running from left to right, they show the major episodes of the life of St Dominic, from Pope Innocent III's dream of a monk in black and white shoring up the walls of the Church, to the death of the saint amid his companions. The retable was exposed to the faithful in the convent of San Domenico at Fiesole in the hills over Florence where the artist lived. Already in the Quattrocento, the dazzling lapis lazuli and gold made the painting hugely valuable, worthy in a merchant and trading city like Florence of the sublime, the 'priceless' subject it depicts. To the cost of materials involved, the artist added both his talent (whose value cannot be easily gauged) and — something beyond the values of this world — the saintly reputation the friar enjoyed while alive. To

Auguste Renoir
Bal du Moulin de la Galette, 1876
131 x 175 cm - MO

represent the celestial court so gloriously, perhaps one has to have glimpsed it?

For the *Bal du Moulin de la Galette*, Renoir worked on the spot, using a few friends as sitters; indeed this vivid spontaneity is one reason for the painting's enduring popularity. A group portrait of quite normal people, in motion, in daylight that plays over the curved lines, it pulls the viewer into the heart of the subject. Early depictions of Paradise often show the elect dancing in mystical roundelays. The harmony of the *bal populaire* has ambitions similar to the more daunting *Coronation of the Virgin*: to squeeze the universe, earthly or heavenly, into a single image. Renoir's world is a quotidian one: we may recognise Norbert Goeneutte, the painter, or Georges Rivière, who was to write a biography of the artist. For Renoir, this human pyramid is 'his world', vibrant, harmonious, alive with music. Some figures are cropped by the edge of the canvas, as in a photograph; the technique is no modernist statement, it proves simply that life extends beyond the confines of the image. Fra Angelico had used it previously; paradise is not limited to the elect few huddling into his altarpiece, all those who gaze on it should hope to appear in heaven in their turn. The sacred and the secular paintings are open worlds because in both the viewer wants to believe wholeheartedly in what the painter shows him.

Jean Auguste Dominique Ingres
The Apotheosis of Homer, 1827
386 x 512 cm - ML

Jean Dubuffet
Rue passagère, 1961
129.3 x 161.7 cm - CP

The whole world in a picture (continued)

After years concentrating on materials, on *sols* or 'grounds', cutting out sections of earth or tarmac to create spaces he called 'texturologies' or 'matériologies', in 1961 Dubuffet opted to return to figuration and the figure. He filled the surface of the canvas with colour and with tiny people, cells of the human species: his streets teemed with passers-by, storefronts and comic shop signs which are worth deciphering one by one. Thenceforth, matter became social, human, dense, the 'paving-stone' in the street became a subject for a canvas that shows, in festive, good-humoured colours, normal, everyday life.

Ingres aimed for higher things and his paradise overflowing with the great and the good has no real 'ground': a ceiling-painting for the Louvre now hung on the wall like an easel work, it is replaced in situ by a copy by the Brothers Balze and Michel Dumas. Surrounding the blind poet Homer, two allegories represent the Iliad and the Odyssey, the former

carrying a sword, the latter an oar, allusions to the Trojan War and to Ulysses' meandering voyage home. The canvas swarms with portraits, exercises in admiration in which, with scant respect for chronology, great figures from the humanities and the arts rub shoulders: Sappho, Aeschylus, Sophocles and Euripides, Socrates and Plato, Phidias and Anacreon, but also classical French artists such as Poussin and Corneille, Molière, Boileau and Racine, together with figures who inspired Romanticism, Dante — accompanied by Virgil as in Delacroix's *Dante's Barge* (1822, Louvre), Shakespeare and Camoëns. The piece is a statement, a pictorial and intellectual affirmation. Fra Angelico's altar panel (p. 166) and Raphael's Vatican frescoes that Ingres so admired (*The School of Athens*, *La Disputa*, *Parnassus*) already juxtaposed figures that never coexisted in reality. They are players in a secular version of the Sacre Conversazione of the

Renaissance, in which figures belonging to various periods and places gathered in a conventional locale (an Ionic temple on this occasion) and in a time that abolishes Time. All carry within them a world; the group constitutes Ingres' inner world, a fractured self-portrait. In 1973, in *Les Cahiers de l'Herne*, Joseph Delteil wrote: 'Jean Dubuffet's great discovery, his supreme vision, is the atom. That matter is the origin and mystery of all art, its Alpha and Omega. We now know that every cell in the body, every atom of matter, is itself a universe, the entire universe. A complete universe with its stalks of grass and Hannibal's elephants, with its Socrates and stars. Every atom is a Noah's Ark.' Perhaps Ingres, exasperated with the effusions of Romanticism, was trying to construct a Noah's Ark of 'classic' geniuses?

Domenico Ghirlandaio
Old Man and a Child, c. 1488
62.7 x 46.3 cm - ML

James Abbott McNeill Whistler
Arrangement in Grey and Black, also known as *The Mother of the Artist*, 1871
144.3 x 162.5 cm - MO

The workings of time

Like Rigaud (Louvre), like Léger (p. 124) and many others, Whistler too had his mother sit for him. Joris Karl Huysmans describes the portrait in *Certains*: 'The profile of an elderly lady dressed in black stands out against a grey wall that flows into a black curtain flecked with white. It is disturbing, of a colour different from those we usually see. Moreover the canvas is sparsely painted, almost betraying its weave. The concord between the grey and the Indian ink black was a treat for eyes surprised by such supple, such profound chords; it was a realistic art, intimate, but deployed in the dreamland beyond.'

Ghirlandaio's *Old Man and a Child* is an astonishing piece. The relationship between the models, even their identity, is totally unknown: is it a posthumous portrait of a grandfather with his grandson commissioned to consolidate a family tree; a portrait of a child and a precocious depiction of tenderness; an allegory of youth and old age; a tangible image of passing time? The difference between the child's profile, treated in an almost antiquated manner, and the naturalistic face of the old man, singularly modern for its time, makes it seem likely that only the elder head is by Ghirlandaio's hand and that perhaps the

painting was finished by a pupil. Or perhaps this stylistic discrepancy has its own meaning: experience harrows the face; life leaves a wound; the purity of the child's profile has features that time has not yet remodelled. The old man is 'better painted'. Old age, for which the artist appears to feel genuine sympathy, has not only brought scars and ugliness; it also provides the painter with experience, with a chance to perfect his imitations of reality. Time passes for the artist, promoting him from pupil to master.

Giuseppe Arcimboldo
Summer, after 1573
76 x 63.5 cm - ML

Jean-Baptiste Greuze
The Broken Jug, 1772 or 1773
108.5 x 86.5 cm - ML

Yves Tanguy
Jour de lenteur, 1937
92 x 73 cm - CP

Moment and duration

The Surrealist Yves Tanguy speaks of slowness. This landscape peopled by anthropomorphic outlines is a realistically treated vision of a non-existent planet. Through spatial distortion, it allows one to sense how the nature of time might be modified, how it might pass differently. The representation of time is a challenge; to represent a time that is not our own is a Surrealist exercise.

For Arcimboldo, a painter venerated by Breton and his friends, time has many faces that can be divided into seasons: each face is composed of natural elements that seem to have been harvested from the landscape. Their combination is not the outcome of Surrealist 'objective chance', but is explained by a desire to build a kind of temporary *Wunderkammer* containing whatever Time, in each successive season,

brings, before it dies and is replaced by the next picture with the features of autumn, winter or summer — faces one has to guess, like in a parlour game. Arcimboldo was the inventor of a playful kind of painting that started out as courtly entertainment, but which became a philosophical disquisition on the transient nature of earthly things and on the foreseeable return of that which is past.

Confronted with the sense of time's irreversibility, there is no way Greuze's young heroine can turn the clock back. The startled innocence in the eyes of this theatre ingénue, who had gone to draw water from the fountain, contrasts with the sensuality of her mouth. In a blatant allusion to the loss of virginity, the title of the work supplies the reason: at that time (as in La Fontaine) the French word *cruche* ('jug') already

had the colloquial meaning it conserves today of 'clot' or 'dolt'. Beaumarchais provides a witty moral for the story: 'If the jug goes to the water often enough, it'll eventually fill up!' The armfuls of flowers overflowing from the dress, the broken vessel, the ruffled clothing — everything points to the denouement of a libertine tale, after which the author signs off with a 'moral': *Comment l'esprit vient aux filles*, or 'How a girl learns "what's what"', 'the "facts of life".' The instant Greuze depicts makes it possible to deduce what has just befallen her. New life gushes from the fountain, a future commences. Initiation has taken place; the penetration of a surface that breaks like an earthenware jug. Here begins the journey to the other side.

Lucio Fontana

La Fine di Dio, 1963-1964

178 x 123 cm - CP

Rogier van der Weyden

The Braque Triptych, before 1452

Closed and open. Central panel, 41 x 68 cm. Side panels, 41 x 34 cm - ML

A journey to the beyond

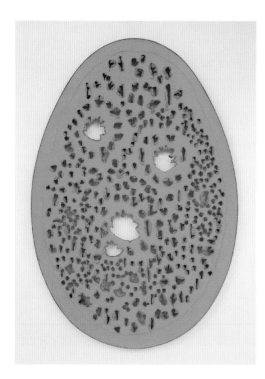

'I come from South America and we have the Pampas! Which is twice the size of [your] Arizona! I am not interested in the kind of space you are talking about, mine is a different dimension. The hole is this dimension. I say dimension because I cannot think what other word to use. I make a hole in the canvas in order to leave behind me the old pictorial formulae, painting and the traditional view of art — and I escape symbolically, but also materially, from the prison of the flat surface.' The invention of Spatial Art as acclaimed by Lucio Fontana in his *Manifesto blanco* of 1946 ('neither painting nor sculpture, but forms, colours, and sounds in space') bears witness to a desire to create a radically different type of art, but one still dependent on stretched canvas and oil paint.

Open or shut, an age-old triptych, such as Van der Weyden's painted about 1452 for Catherine of Brabant, also conveys a sense of space, a process of mystic revelation. When open, we see all the colours of the world; closed, there is Death and the armorial bearings of the family of the patron's husband, Jehan Braque. An inscription evokes the vanity of life and of sublunary things.

Do Fontana's 'celestial' eggs, like his famous slashed canvases, really express a 'philosophy of nothing', as the artist himself maintained?

Painting for Miró is a manner of going beyond appearances, of conquering a world of the absolute, into which the viewer, following the painter, can plunge in a voyage towards a realm alien to the world of the senses, shackled to poetic reminiscences, such as Victor Hugo's 'field of stars' and Mallarmé's *Azur*, that are surely irrelevant here. The three pictures entitled *Blue* that Miró regarded as the culmination of his oeuvre (now reunited in the Centre Pompidou) express the universality of the physical act of painting encapsulated in a few signs, the outcome of a long process of meditation, of a titanic struggle, armed with paint and brush, over the vast surface.

Joan Miró
Bleu II, 1961
270 x 355 cm - CP

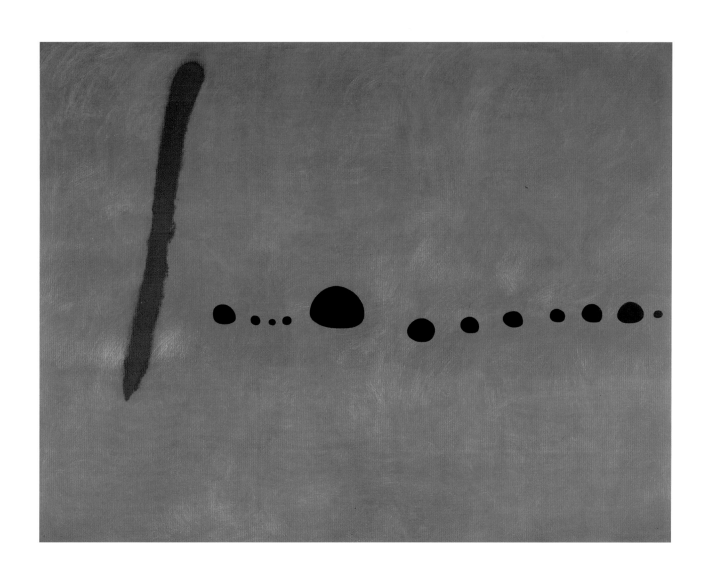

Hubert Robert

Project for the Grande Galerie of the Louvre, 1796 Salon

114.5 x 146 cm - ML

Conclusion

Elements for a history of painting

Art history is written first in the museum. The copyists and wanderers who frequent Hubert Robert's Louvre — an ideal gallery, lit from directly above by pyramidal sections of glass (that might become, as the artist, a contemporary of the French Revolution, sees it, the Louvre of the future) — *animate* the museum in the strongest sense of the term: they give it a soul. A pendant to this canvas (also in the museum) shows an imaginary view of the Grande Galerie of the Louvre in ruins: all the paintings have disappeared with only a few dilapidated antiquities upon which to meditate.

Opening up what are now the national collections gave new impetus to the art of the French School, as well as allowing an educated public to acquire the rudiments of art history. Aesthetic emotion was to be accompanied by increased historical understanding. Museology and the hanging of paintings are never without implications: they give the collections meaning and tell a story that runs from work to work, weaving a tapestry of themes and figures, just as we have seen them parade past here, in these few pages, as if in a kaleidoscope. Now it is time to leave and look at everything these pages have omitted: all the things that allow one to go from one page to another, what has had to be erased from the margins or what separates — or unites — any two works treated together here.

Poet:
To th' dumbness of the gesture
One might interpret.

Painter:
It is a pretty mocking of the life.
Here is a touch; is't good?

Poet:
I will say of it
It tutors nature. Artificial strife
Lives in these touches, livelier than life.

Shakespeare, *Timon of Athens*, I, 1, c. 1604 and 1607, published in 1623

Depicting the conditions for art

To allow the viewer into the painter's studio and, thus, to let him into one or two secrets of creativity, is a frequent theme in the history of painting. It culminates in Courbet's 1855 manifesto, the vast 'Real Allegory' that demonstrates the extraordinary scope of the painter's talents: nude, still life, landscape, portrait and group portrait, animal painting... The outcome is, of course, improbable, a declaration of intent by the inventor of 'Realism' in painting in which a model poses nude for a landscape... In the centre, the artist ushers everyone to their places, as if for some Last Judgement, his friends, to the right of the picture (Baudelaire is easily recognisable engrossed in a book on the far right), then social figures like the huntsman and the bourgeois who can be read as caricatures of Napoleon III and of Finance Minister Achille Fould seated in the same pose as M. Bertin (qv. p. 97). The painter finds his inspiration in the real world.

Picasso harks back to the Muse, to the one who inspired the poet in the celebrated picture by Poussin presently in the Louvre. The painter's house is like no other: it is visited by the Muse, a supernatural being of flesh and blood. A green curtain shields the window.

Vincent van Gogh
Van Gogh's Room at Arles, 1889
57,5 x 74 cm - MO

Pablo Picasso
La Muse, 1935
130 x 162 cm - CP

Once a model, the young woman has become an artist, and it is she who draws before the mirror. Curved forms reflected in the gilded frame contrast with the angular lines on the page of the drawing-book — Picasso made countless preparatory sketches for the Muse. In the background, another, violet-tinged young woman slumbers, her arms folded: is she perhaps the female artist's Muse?

Vincent's little room in Arles did not perhaps double up as a studio. It is more an 'inside-out' self-portrait: his clothes hang on a hook, family portraits can be seen on the wall, yet the white rectangle of the mirror fails to reflect his image. The artist spoke of an 'interior with nothing'. The Orsay picture was painted from memory after leaving Arles; it is a self-portrait from which he has oddly absconded. This 'interior

view' drove him out into Nature: there he was to work alone, with none of the onlookers Courbet had orchestrated in a dazzling and carefully stage-managed demonstration of his powers.

Edouard Manet

Emile Zola, 1868

146 x 114 cm - MO

Vincent van Gogh

Doctor Paul Gachet (1828-1909), 1890

68 x 57 cm - MO

For the love of art

Many lovers of painting appear in the portraits lining the walls of our three museums. Manet thanks Zola for his defence of *Olympia*, who gazes down on Zola from a little reproduction among pictures decorating the writer's study. Zola's brochure entitled *Manet* figures among the writer's papers: once painted, it changes meaning, half dedication and half signature. Doctor Gachet adored art: he supported Van Gogh and gave him fresh hope. The portrait is thus a homage to an obscure art lover who has become a household name in the wake of the Van Gogh legend. Cézanne came to paint in the library of the critic Gustave Geffroy at least sixty times before fleeing and leaving both his art materials and an unfinished canvas: it was all 'rather confused,' as he explained to Monet, 'the result obtained was slender [...] especially considering all the sittings, all the enthusiasm and encouragement.' Cézanne seems to have finished the accessories on the desk, established the lines and the colours of the books, but the left hand and the face remain in a state of indecision that today serves as overwhelming evidence of how the painter worked, of his feelings, hesitation and incertitude.

Paul Cézanne

Gustave Geffroy, 1895-1896

110 x 89 cm - MO

Giorgio De Chirico

Premonitory portrait of Guillaume Apollinaire, 1914

81,5 x 65 cm - CP

The extremely famous portrait of Guillaume Apollinaire painted in 1914 by Giorgio de Chirico prefigures the war wound the poet was to receive in March 1916. Initially christened *L'Homme-cible*, this picture was considered by the author of *Alcools* as a 'self-portrait', a 'singular, profound piece', as if the poet and the painter, the artist and his model, had swapped masks. The reliefs stamped on the baking moulds make a Surrealistic impact, while the poet, like the bard Homer (see Ingres' depiction [p. 168]), is blind, a plaster bust, a sombre silhouette, like a dummy in a shooting gallery. If he has no eyes to see, it is because he is a 'visionary', as were in their time Zola, Gachet and Geffroy. What does he see? The future, the one the soothsayers of ancient Greece could predict by examining a portrait.

Living in painting

Works of art do not speak only of themselves or of what they represent; they also bear witness to all those who lived with the painting, who loved and exhibited it, understood and possessed it. In a museum catalogue, the provenance — the list of past owners of a piece — is rarely without interest. It is important, for instance, to know that Robert Delaunay got his mother to buy him Douanier Rousseau's *The Snake Charmer* (p. 39), and that Louis XV owned

Chardin's *Bénédicité* (p. 99). The history of each painting gives clues as to the history of the art generally.

The French State did not accept every item in Gustave Caillebotte's estate, although through him the national collections acquired Monet's *Gare St-Lazare* (p. 156) and Renoir's *Bal du Moulin de la Galette* (p. 167). Caillebotte's pictures in the Musée d'Orsay are precious in more than one respect. They are

examples of an elegant idiom that marries Impressionism and Realism; the creation of an art lover who was, as his collection grew, to become a painter himself, and thus able to dialogue with the works he purchased. Caillebotte's collection was exceptional, incorporating as it did only pieces that were (to oversimplify somewhat) 'ahead of their time'. The artist-collector's eye was acute and, by no means short of money, he bought from his painter friends,

above all, those pictures that they were otherwise unable to sell, those that corresponded least to prevailing taste at the time.

When Fantin-Latour painted his *Homage to Delacroix*, the painter of *Sardanapalus* had been in his grave just one year. Delacroix's likeness in the centre is taken from a photograph. Painted in a different palette, a brownish monochrome, it vehicles the distancing effect introduced by a 'picture within a picture', and there is no confusion between the portrait of the great man and the real people gathered together to pay him homage. Among this mix of painters and writers, one can identify, from left to right, Louis Cordier, the critic Edmond Duranty, Alphonse Legros, Fantin-Latour himself in the white shirt-sleeves he would wear when in his studio, Whistler, Champfleury, Manet with a golden halo, the artist-engraver Félix Bracquemond, Baudelaire who had written so much on Delacroix whom he admired above all others, and finally Albert de Balleroy, a friend of Degas. Like Frans Hals' *The Regents* in the 17th century, the art world poses for a group portrait, underlining the fundamental solidarity between theoreticians, commentators and critics. The bouquet of flowers beneath the portrait refers to Fantin-Latour's forte as a painter of still life: the flowers are at once a funerary offering and the artist's signature.

Pierre Bonnard
Self-portrait in Bathroom Mirror, 1939-1945
73 x 51 cm - CP

Portrait of the artist as a creator

In one of his last self-portraits, Bonnard depicts himself as a vulnerable Man of Sorrows, reflected in the bathroom mirror that he had often used in earlier works. Like Rembrandt before him, Bonnard produced a great many analyses of his own countenance. Though he once portrayed himself in the guise of Christ (1500, Alte Pinakothek, Munich), here Dürer is spruce and youthful, in the pose of a *gentiluomo*. A self-portrait allows the artist to depict himself as he is, to display something of his style, to show his ambitions realised: painting himself, the resemblance resides as much as the evocation of his features as they really were as in the deployment of that 'style' which allows his work to be recognised at first glance.

Yves Klein commented: 'I love in myself all that doesn't belong to me, that is to say, my life; and I loathe everything that belongs to me: my education, my psychological background, that inculcated, conventional viewpoint [...], everything that leads me, day by day, irredeemably, to my physical and emotional death.'

For Van Gogh, whose self-image with cut ear presents even his physical integrity compromised, self-portraiture is an exercise in the radical appropriation of the pictorial surface, in the painter's identification with painting. The 'living' blue ground covered with lines in motion, is neither a photographer's backcloth nor a landscape, but a 'hinterland': it continues 'outside' the lines, the flames, in which the face is drawn to create the likeness, and prolongs, beyond the limits of the human body, a man's life. Self-portraits are often created by artists for themselves alone, to be kept by their side, a silent witness, a vestige of their struggle with materials, with ambition, with Time. Except perhaps young Dürer's *Self-portrait*, painted most probably on the occasion of his marriage to the shadowy Agnes Frey, who became his wife in 1494. Artistic effort culminates in these moments of total concentration, of hypnotic focus, peering into the mirror so as to leave behind a self-image to which he might assent without reserve. In 1435, the humanist Leon Battista Alberti (1404-1472) wrote in his seminal theoretical treatise *On Painting*: 'The aim of painting: to give pleasure, good will and fame to the painter more than riches. If painters will follow this, their painting will hold the eyes and the soul of the observer.'

Albrecht Dürer
Self-portrait, 1493
56.5 x 44.5 cm - ML

Vincent van Gogh
Portrait of the Artist, 1889
65 x 54.5 cm - MO

Dürer's thistle

It remains to be explained (at least the question is worth asking) why Dürer, ambitious, triumphant, at the outset of his artistic career, chose to portray himself holding a thistle of complex shape, delineating it with the exactness of a botanist. Saint-Simon, whose memoirs unpick the intricate rituals of court life under Louis XIV and in the Regency, wrote, he states, 'to prove to himself, unflinchingly, the nullity of the world'. The thistle in Dürer's hand — an equivalent of the Crown of Thorns crammed on Christ's head during his Passion — is also a metaphor in plant form of the Creation, an involved ornamental shape, spiny, intertwined. The youthful painter shows himself in his best light, sporting the elegant, slashed costume of a well-heeled Nüremburg citizen with subtle cross-currents of colour effects and striking that contrived casualness the Italians call *sprezzatura*. But in his fingers stands this bizarre plant, the actual subject of the painting, the object of the artist's contemplation. The same hand created the picture as holds the thistle, an explication, perhaps, of the inscription written next to the date: 'Things happened to me as they are written about above.' The universe the artist creates, over which, within the limits of his work, he is the supreme overlord, is a reflection of the world as he sees it, in its glory as in its nothingness, in all its folds and with all its thorns…

Leonardo da Vinci expressed the power of the painter's as creator of worlds in the following words :
'[…] the painter is lord of every kind of person and of all things.
If the painter wishes to see beauties that would enrapture him, he is master of their production, and if he wishes to see monstrous things which might terrify him or which would be buffoonish and laughable or truly pitiable, he is their lord and god. And if he wishes to produce places or deserts, or shady and cools spots in hot weather, he can depict them, and similarly warm places in cold weather. If he seeks valleys, if he wants to disclose great expanses of countryside from the summits of high mountains, and if he subsequently wishes to see the horizon of the sea, he is lord of them. Or if from low valleys he wishes to see high mountains, or from high mountains low valleys and beaches. In fact, therefore, whatever there is in the universe through essence, presence or imagination, he has it first in his mind and then in his hands, and these are of such excellence that they can generate a proportional harmony in the time equivalent to a single glance, just as real things do.' *Leonardo on Painting*, ed. M. Kemp, Yale University Press, 1989.
'He has it first in his mind and then in his hands' : this perhaps provides the key to Dürer's thistle.

Biographical notes
from Angelico
to Zurbarán

Anonymous
Paris, 14th century

ML - *Jean II le Bon [Portrait of Jean the Good, King of France]*, c. 1360
Wood. 60 x 44.5 cm / Cabinet des Estampes of the Bibliothèque Nationale, on deposit at the Louvre, 1925 / R.F. 2490

Who was the painter of the portrait of King Jean le Bon (1319-1364) that symbolically opens the rooms in the Louvre devoted to the survey of painting in France? Though the portrait's purpose is unknown, it was the first to be executed on a separate panel after the model since those of the ancient world. The king's profile stands out against a gold ground — though much repainted over the centuries: his attire was originally less sumptuous. The likeness is more that of a man than that of a king and Jean carries no royal attribute, so a date before 1350 (the year of his accession to the throne) has been proposed. The profile is derived from portraits on coins and from illuminations. It does not show an idealised prince; for the first time, a whole panel is used to both glorify and perpetuate a face.

Anonymous,
School of Fontainebleau, late 16th century

ML - *Gabrielle d'Estrées et une de ses sœurs [Gabrielle d'Estrées and One of her Sisters]*, c. 1595
Wood. 96 cm x 125 cm / Acquired in 1937 / R.F. 1937-1

Probably representing on the right Gabrielle d'Estrées, mistress of King Henri IV of France, with at her side her sister, the Duchesse de Villars, the exact theme of this picture has been the object of lengthy controversy. The carefully calculated gestures each performs may be interpreted as paying tribute to the beautiful Gabrielle's status as mother of the king's bastard son, César de Vendôme. The smoothly delineated flesh, accessories, such as the ring, and the mystery of the mirror clear of any reflection, hanging in the background, are all characteristic of an intellectualised court art, which prolonged the first School of Fontainebleau that had emerged in the reign of François I, following the arrival in France of several Italian artists.

Angelico, Fra
the Blessed Giovanni da Fiesole
(Guido di Pietro, *by his lay name*), *known as*
Vicchio di Mugello, Florence, c. 1395/1400 - Rome, 1455

ML - *Le Couronnement de la Vierge [Coronation of the Virgin]* c. 1430-1432
Wood. 209 x 206 cm / Entered the Louvre in 1812 / Inv. 314

Solemnly beatified by Pope John Paul II, Angelico is no longer seen today by art historians as an industrious and solitary monk who passed his life shut away in the convent of San Marco, Florence (decorated by himself and his pupils). The *Coronation of the Virgin*, painted for one of the altars of the church of San Domenico in Fiesole on the hills above Florence, shows that the greatest religious painter of the Renaissance, far from being on the margins of his period and city, had absorbed Masaccio's innovations in the field of perspective and spatial construction.

Antonello da Messina
Reggio di Calabria, c. 1430 - Messina, 1479

ML - *Le Christ à la colonne [Christ at the Column]*, vers 1476-1478
Wood. 29 x 21 cm / Acquired in 1992 / R.F. 1992-10

Following Vasari's vividly coloured account, Antonello is supposed to have learned his art in Flanders and brought the secret of oil-based paint to Italy. Though there is no evidence for this legend, it does testify to the artist's dual character, since he was successful in synthesising the influence of Flemings, such as Jan van Eyck and Petrus Christus, whose works he had surely got to know in Southern Italy, with the heritage of the Tuscan Renaissance and Piero della Francesca, in particular. Like the *Portrait of a Condottiere*, also preserved in the Louvre, *Christ at the Column* demonstrates the studied realism of the art of Antonello that was to have repercussions in Venice where the artist spent some time, most particularly on Mantegna and Carpaccio.

Arcimboldo, Giuseppe
Milan, 1527 - *ibid.*, 1593

ML - *L'Eté [Summer]*, 1573
Canvas. 76 x 63.5 cm / Acquired in 1964 / R.F. 1964-31

It was first at the court of Ferdinand I, and then at those of the Holy Roman Emperors Maximilian II and aesthete collector Rudolf II, that Arcimboldo distinguished himself, with his readily recognisable style — the four pictures of the seasons in the Louvre being typical. An *ornemaniste* with a fondness for the strange compositions and *capricci* of the Mannerists, this Italian, who moved to Prague in 1562, retained the typical Mannerist taste for technical *tours de force*, unusual themes, and surprise effects. His constructions of flowers, fruit, shells and books — a reflection of the spirit of contemporary *Wunderkammer* — were rediscovered in the 20th century by the Surrealists whom they greatly impressed.

Bacon, Francis
Dublin, 1909 - Madrid, 1992

CP - *Study of the Human Body*, 1981-1982
Oil and pastel on canvas. 198 x 147.5 cm / Purchase, 1983 / AM 1982-433

Fascinated by ancient forms, such as the triptych, and by the grandeur of the portrait of Pope Innocent X by Velázquez, Bacon's art seems to distort models taken from museums and to fragment the figure. Imprisoned within a geometrically confined space over a ground of an array of lines or bars, the bodies are as if tortured on the rack — here, a table that reminds one of a postmortem. Standing before a canvas by Bacon, one thinks not only of Otto Dix and Max Beckmann, but also of the films of Luis Buñuel.

Balthus
Balthasar Klossowski de Rola, *known as*
Paris, 1908 - Rossinière, Canton de Vaud, Switzerland, 2001

CP - *Alice*, 1933
Oil on canvas. 162.3 x 112 cm / Purchased with the aid of the Fonds du
Patrimoine, 1995 / AM 1995-205

Throughout his long life, Balthus played the part of an inaccessible recluse, though it would be truer to say that, from his post as director of the Villa Médicis in Rome to his chalet at Rossinière near Gstaad where he died, he was the last of the great *mondains* of painting. Strongly influenced by Puvis de Chavannes and Maurice Denis, the only masters he would admit having were Piero della Francesca, Masaccio and Courbet. Though his output was more abundant than he felt he could admit, there are a handful of undoubted masterpieces, including this hieratic and sculptural nude that once belonged to the writer Pierre-Jean Jouve. Balthus's sulphurous period, when his main theme was very young female models in provocative poses, remains the most famous facet of his output.

Barré, Martin
Nantes, 1924 - Paris, 1993

CP - *92B-124 X 128-A*, 1992 / *92B-124 X 128-B*, 1992 /
92B-124 X 128-C, 1992
Acrylic on canvas. 124 x 128 cm / AM 1995-158 / 159 / 160

As solid and as coherent as any 17th-century adherent to the classical tradition and a firm believer in the rules of serialism, Martin Barré's art is one of mathematically programmed spaces, sobriety and rigour in saturated colours. His superficially simple canvases (in fact the squares are not true quadrilaterals, and on closer examination the lines appear slightly fuzzy) have to be approached as a series — just like Monet's *Waterlilies*. Each individual work makes sense only within the larger grouping that it echoes. These series often break down into triptychs, such as that in the Centre Pompidou. A discreet, even neglected artist, Barré remains one of the most fascinating personalities in French geometric abstract art.

Basquiat, Jean-Michel
Brooklyn, 1960 - New York, 1988

CP - *Slave Auction*, 1982
Acrylic, pastel, collage. 183 x 305.5 cm / Gift of the Société des Amis du Musée
National d'Art Moderne, 1993 / AM 1993-99

As with Caravaggio, Géricault and Van Gogh, Basquiat's premature death turned the existence of a tormented young man, who strove to fuse life and art, into a fated destiny. Dying of an overdose, and already a legend in 1980s New York, Basquiat embodied the lost youth of a generation. Taken up by Warhol, Basquiat hung out in The Factory, the elder artist's painting, cinema and photography studio. A view of consumer society through ethnically mixed eyes, a painting, a collage, a scribble of graffiti-like signs, this huge canvas presents figures from American society (a football player, a financier in an undertaker's hat) as if in some violent video game. The *Slave Auction* can be seen as a requiem for the American Empire, then at the height of its power.

Baugin, Lubin
Pithiviers, c. 1612 - Paris, 1663

ML - *Le Dessert de gaufrettes [The Wafers]*, c. 1630 or 1635
Wood. 41 x 52 cm / Acquired in 1954 / R.F. 1954-23

Four still lifes (two in the Louvre, one in the Musée des Beaux-Arts at Rennes and one in the Galleria Spada, Rome) — and perhaps a fifth discovered more recently — have been enough to make the taciturn, meditative and secretive Baugin into one of the greatest French masters of the 17th century. According to Jacques Thuillier by whom he was rediscovered, he is the same artist who produced religious subjects, in particular for Notre-Dame in Paris. A journey to Italy, clearly a turning-point in his career, might explain these two very different manners, though one might have been inclined to believe in the existence of two artists, perhaps belonging to the same family, who both signed works 'Baugin'.

Bazille, Frédéric
Montpellier, 1841 - Beaune-la-Rolande, Loiret, 1870

MO - *Réunion de famille [Family Reunion]*, 1867
Oil on canvas. 152 x 230 cm / Acquired in 1905 with the participation of Marc
Bazille, the artist's brother / R.F. 2749

The *Family Reunion* is an evocation of the middle-class milieu of Montpellier in which this elegant and wealthy artist moved. Méric, his own family estate, served as the backdrop to several canvases. A friend of Renoir, Monet and Sisley, and admirer of Delacroix, Courbet and Manet, Bazille completed only about sixty pictures before dying on the battlefield during the Franco-Prussian War of 1870. He had intended to support a group exhibition of the young artists who were then striving to renew the art of painting; in 1874, this wish was realised, if posthumously, when his friends organised what would go down in history as the first Impressionist exhibition.

Beckmann, Max
Leipzig, 1884 - New York, 1950

CP - *Der kleine Fisch [The Little Fish]*, 1933
Oil on canvas. 135 x 115 cm / Purchase, 1933 / JP 679 P

In Berlin from 1907 to 1915, Beckmann taught at the fine art school in Frankfurt between 1915 and 1933, the year he was forced to leave Nazi Germany. Under the influence initially of Otto Dix and Expressionism, his art evolved into large narrative pictures, rediscovering Gothic masters, such as Dürer and Schongauer, and affirming the continuity of German culture above and beyond the hammer blows of the two World Wars. The two women listening to the fisherman also bring to mind Picasso's 'Ingrist' period and the widespread return to classicism that marked Europe in the years 1920-1930.

Benoist, Marie-Guillemine
Paris, 1768 - *ibid.*, 1826

ML - *Portrait d'une femme noire [Portrait of a Black Woman]*,
1800 Salon
Canvas. 82 x 65 cm / Acquired in 1818 / Inv. 2508

In the wake of Marie-Antoinette's favourite artist, Elisabeth Vigée-Lebrun,
several women were to become painters in France during the last years of
the 18th and the beginning of the 19th centuries. Marie-Guillemine Benoist
inherited her craft from David, possessing a mastery of portraiture that shows
she had studied in the studio of the artist who revived French painting. Her
novel if fashionable subject — at the same period, Girodet was painting the
Indian Chactas and the black deputy from Santo Domingo, Jean-Baptiste
Belley (Musée National des Châteaux de Versailles et de Trianon, Versailles)
— provided her with the opportunity of bringing out her model's complexion,
contrasting it with the snow-white fabrics. Of unknown identity, the young
woman poses with an elegance worthy of the finest portraits of the
Renaissance.

Bonnard, Pierre
Fontenay-aux-Roses, 1867 - Le Cannet, 1947

CP - *Autoportrait dans la glace du cabinet de toilette [Self-
portrait in Bathroom Mirror]*, 1939-1945
Oil on canvas. 73 x 51 cm / Allocated in lieu of death duties, 1984 / AM 1984-698

CP - *L'Atelier au mimosa*, 1939-1946
Oil on canvas. 127.5 x 127.5 cm / Purchase, 1979 / AM 1978-732

Unfairly perceived as persisting in the Impressionist idiom during the Cubist
era, Bonnard owed more to the Nabis, Paul Sérusier, Maurice Denis and
Gauguin, though without their Symbolist ideas. With a predilection for
interiors, his spaces incorporate cleverly calculated apertures (the mirror on
the bathroom cabinet visible in this self-portrait was often returned to), the
surfaces being geometrically divided and saturated in bright colours. A
painter of a superficially happy and quotidian existence, as his many female
nudes testify, this self-portrait, in which he resembles an elderly Oriental
sage, shows him as the pathetic and broken hero of his last period.

Bosch, Hieronymus
Jeoren Anthoniszoon van Aecken, *known as*
Den Bosch, c. 1450 - *ibid.*, 1516

ML - *La Nef des fous [The Ship of Fools]*, vers 1500
Wood. 58 x 32.5 cm / Gift of Camille Benoit, 1918 / R.F. 2218

Little is known of the life of Hieronymus Bosch. In great works such as *The
Garden of Earthly Delights* (Prado, Madrid), he invented a world full of
symbolic, often humorous figures, whose religious import frequently escapes
us. *The Ship of Fools* perhaps depicts pilgrims who have deserted the path
of Christ. They are all illustrations of the *topos* of a nonsensical, upside-down
world from which edifying lessons may be drawn. This may be a work from
the master's early period, before his larger, more ambitious compositions in
which the number of figures increases.

Botticelli
Sandro di Mariano Filipepi, *known as*
Florence, c. 1445 - *ibid.*, 1510

ML - *Vénus et les Grâces offrant des présents à une jeune fille
[Venus and the Three Graces Offering Gifts to a Young Woman]*
(detail), vers 1483
Fresco. 211 x 283 cm / Originally from the Villa Lemmi, near Florence / Acquired
in 1882 / R.F. 321

A pupil of Filippo Lippi, the inventor of a fluent, musical style who placed his
figures in the attitudes of dancers in contemporary court ballet, Botticelli was
a major force in the humanist, erudite Florence of Lorenzo the Magnificent.
La Primavera, the *Birth of Venus* (c. 1477-1478 and 1484, Uffizi, Florence)
testify to this early manner, as do the frescoes painted in 1481-1482 on the
walls of the Sistine Chapel. Under the influence of the fire-and-brimstone
preacher Savonarola, Botticelli's later subjects turned to morality and
mysticism, and his symbols and allegories were placed uniquely in the service
of the faith.

Boucher, François
Paris, 1703 - *ibid.*, 1770

ML - *L'Odalisque*, c. 1745
Canvas. 53.5 x 64.5 cm / Baron Basile de Schlichting bequest, 1914 / R.F. 2140

ML - *Madame de Pompadour*, c. 1756
Paper on canvas. 60 x 45.5 cm / Baron Basile de Schlichting bequest, 1914 /
R.F. 2142

In the eyes of his most inspired biographer Georges Brunel, Boucher was as
great as Chardin, Fragonard and David. Long thought of as simply too
talented, a painter who as Diderot put it misused his incredible facility and
whose art degenerated into the decorative, Boucher still suffers from the
Davidian reaction that arose in the final years of the 18th century.
Academician, court painter to the king, showered with commissions and
honours, and collected in his own lifetime throughout Europe, Boucher is very
well represented in the Louvre collections, from *Le Déjeuner* to the famous
Venus and Vulcan that Louis XV had hung in his chamber at Marly. For how
long will Boucher's decorative grace and his taste for ornament blind the
public to his brilliant, provocative, even violent grandeur?

Braque, Georges
Argenteuil-sur-Seine, 1882 - Paris, 1963

CP - *Viaduc à l'Estaque [Viaduct at l'Estaque]*, 1908
Oil on canvas. 72.5 x 59 cm / Allocated in lieu of death duties, 1984 / AM 1984-353

CP - *Le Guéridon*, 1911
Oil on canvas. 116.5 x 81.5 cm / Gift of Raoul La Roche, 1952 / AM 3168 P

A craftsman, Braque loved materials, solidity, humble reality. Starting out as a Fauvist with the young Matisse and Derain, he was bewitched by the Cézanne retrospective at the 1907 Salon d'Automne, from which *The Viaduct at l'Estaque* stems. In 1908, he worked with Picasso on a new language, Cubism, in its 'Analytical' phase, where objects are broken up and viewed from different angles. After the First World War, he kept faith with a number of themes, such as fruit, mandolins and fabrics, before tackling an increasingly austere, testamentary series of 'studios'. In the Louvre in 1952-1953, Braque painted *The Birds*, a ceiling that opens out to the sky — an innovation in a career that had up to that point explored the secret intimacy of everyday things.

Bruegel the Elder, Pieter
Brueghel, c. 1525/1530 - Brussels, 1569

ML - *Les Mendiants [The Beggars]*, 1568
Wood. 18.5 x 21.5 cm / Gift of Paul Mantz, 1892 / R.F. 730

Founding father of a prolific dynasty in which his two sons Pieter the Younger, known as 'Hell' Bruegel (1564-1638), and Jan, known as 'Velvet' Bruegel (1568-1625), particularly distinguished themselves, Bruegel the Elder produced no more than forty-five paintings of certain attribution, the finest collection being in the Kunsthistorisches Museum, Vienna. With despair doused in humour, Bruegel's theme was everyday life, often with a moral, political or philosophical dimension. The artists of his lineage did much to imitate and propagate the subjects he invented.

Caillebotte, Gustave
Paris, 1848 - Gennevilliers, Hauts-de-Seine, 1894

MO - *Raboteurs de parquet [The Floor Scrapers]*, 1875
Oil on canvas. 102 x 146.5 cm / Gift of the heirs of Gustave Caillebotte with his executor Auguste Renoir acting as intermediary, 1894 / R.F. 2718

A friend to painters, who bequeathed to the national collections his Monets, Renoirs, Manets, Pissarros, Sisleys, Degas and Cézannes, Caillebotte was also a fine artist in his own right. Aged twenty-five and finding himself with a great fortune, he defended the new painting, supported the Impressionists, and himself exhibited modern scenes showing canoeing, city squares, gardens and cafés. *The Floor Scrapers* appeared at the second Impressionist exhibition in 1876. Though the scene refers to the construction of new buildings in Third Republic Paris, formally it proposes an original view of space that might be compared to Vincent's room in Arles. The sculptural backs of the workmen are imprinted upon a grid of straight lines, against which the balcony's ornamental arabesque, back-lit, stands out — a motif to which Matisse later returned.

Caravaggio
Michelangelo Merisi, Caravaggio, *known as*
Lombardy, 1570 or 1571 - Porto Ercole, 1610

ML - *La Dormition de la Vierge [The Dormition of the Virgin,* or *The Death of the Virgin]*, completed late 1605-beginning 1606
Canvas. 369 x 245 cm / Collection of Louis XIV / Inv. 54

Abandoning traditional decorum, Caravaggio, a painter of poverty-stricken and unsavoury characters, whose adventurous, scarcely believable existence is swathed in a romantic aura, treats the pages of Holy Scripture as a genre scene. Tragic figures surge forth from darkness into light, playing their parts with an identical mute grandeur whether in sacred episodes or tavern scenes. The Virgin in the Louvre is a fine example of this popular yet innovative art that at the time gave rise to heated dispute but from which was born a European trend later known as Caravaggism, which forceful personalities, such as Valentine de Boulogne, Orazio and Artemisia Gentileschi, Hendrik Ter Brugghen and Gerrit van Honthorst, made their own.

Caron, Antoine
Beauvais, c. 1521 - Paris, 1599

ML - *Les Massacres du Triumvirat [The Massacre of the Triumvirate,* or *The Massacre of the Triumvirs]*, 1566
Canvas. 116 x 195 cm / Gift of the Marquis de Jaucourt, 1939 / R.F. 1939-28

Working initially at Fontainebleau with Primaticcio and Niccolo dell'Abate, Antoine Caron set up in Paris at the end of the 1560s. As the organiser of festivals and ephemeral decorations, he displayed a taste for the theatrical arrangement of the figure in space. A court painter who delighted in complex allegories and symbols, he forged an intellectual style whose meaning is today largely a matter for hypothesis. There remains the singular charm of these immense history pictures, resounding to noise and fury, in which the viewer's eye is waylaid by an architectural marvel, an extraneous figure or some secondary action.

Carpaccio, Vittore
Venise, c. 1465 - **ibid.**, 1525/1526

ML - *La Prédication de saint Etienne à Jérusalem*
[The Sermon of St Stephen at Jerusalem or *St Stephen*
Preaching in Jerusalem], vers 1514
Canvas. 148 x 194 cm / Brera, Milan, 1812; acquired through exchange / Entered
the Louvre in 1812 / Inv. 181

Training in the Venetian milieu of Gentile Bellini, Andrea Vivarini and
Bartolomeo Montagna, Carpaccio was surely acquainted with Flemish
painting, and perhaps also with the Orient. With a marked taste for
architecture and decorative opulence, Carpaccio's history plays are staged
in contemporary costume, in the form of major narrative cycles such as the
History of St Ursula (Accademia, Venice) and the group devoted to St
Jerome, St George and St Tryphon (Scuola di San Giorgio, Venice). In
addition to the picture in the Louvre, other scenes from the life of St Stephen
are preserved in Milan, Berlin and Stuttgart.

Cassatt, Mary
Allegheny City, United-States, 1845 - Mesnil-Théribus, Oise, 1926

MO - *Jeune Fille au jardin*, ou *Femme cousant*
[Girl in a Garden or Young Woman Sewing], c. 1880-1882
Oil on canvas. 92 x 63 cm / Antonin Personnaz bequest, 1937 / R.F. 1937-20

This wealthy American joined the Impressionist group through her
acquaintance with Degas before moving more towards Renoir, particularly in
subjects showing young mothers with children. Vying with Berthe Morisot,
she too imposed her talents as a woman in the male-dominated circle of the
Impressionists. She was an advisor to many collectors and contributed
greatly to the popularity of the Impressionists in the United States.

Cézanne, Paul
Aix-en-Provence, 1839 - **ibid.**, 1906

MO - *Une moderne Olympia [A Modern Olympia]* (sketch),
c. 1873-1874
Oil on canvas. 46 x 55.5 cm / Gift of Paul Gachet, 1951 / R.F. 1951-31

MO - *Les Joueurs de cartes [The Card Players]*, c. 1890-1895
Oil on canvas. 47.5 x 57 cm / Isaac de Camondo bequest, 1911 / R.F. 1969

MO - *Baigneurs [Bathers]*, c. 1892-1894
Oil on canvas. 22 x 33 cm / Allocated in lieu of death duties, 1982 / R.F. 1982-41

MO - *Gustave Geffroy*, 1895-1896
Oil on canvas. 110 x 89 cm / Lifetime enjoyment gift of the grandaughter of
Auguste Pellerin, 1969. Entered in 2000 / R.F. 1969-29

After a period he himself called 'swaggering', Cézanne gave up his dense
black impasto and joined the Impressionist group, but early shows met with
little success. In his endeavour to paint 'Poussin after Nature', he launched
out fearlessly into ambitious series, including bathers of both sexes and card
players, returning ceaselessly to the same objects in his still lifes, and,
towards the end of his life, to the landscape around the Montagne Sainte-
Victoire, near Aix. Emile Bernard, Maurice Denis, as well as Braque and
Picasso learned much from the artist who strove to convey Nature 'through
cylinders and spheres.'

Chagall, Marc
Vitebsk, Belarus, 1887 - St-Paul-de-Vence, 1985

CP - *Double portrait au verre de vin [Double portrait and*
Wineglass], 1917-1918
Oil on canvas. 235 x 137 cm / Gift of the artist, 1949 / AM 2774 P

After a formative Parisian period (1910-1914), during which he met the artists
Delaunay, Gleizes and La Fresnaye, and the poets Apollinaire and Cendrars,
Chagall spent the years 1914-1922 at his birthplace Vitebsk and in Moscow.
This large-sized double portrait and the ornamental panels for the Jewish
Theatre of Moscow date from this time. Back in France, as a Bible illustrator
and the creator of stained-glass and paintings for the much-loved ceiling of
the Palais Garnier (1963-1965), his renown continued to increase. At one
time praised to the skies, this final period is somewhat neglected by critics
who prefer the Russian years, though a revaluation of the later works is today
much needed.

Champaigne *or* Champagne, Philippe de
Brusels, 1602 - Paris, 1674

ML - *Cardinal de Richelieu*, c. 1639
Canvas. 222 cm x 155 cm / Seized during the Revolution from the collection of the Duc de Penthièvre at the Hôtel de Toulouse, Paris / Inv. 1136

ML - *La Cène [The Last Supper]*, c. 1648
Canvas. 158 x 233 cm / Transferred to Port-Royal, Paris between 1709 and 1711. Seized during the Revolution / Inv. 1124

ML - *Ex-Voto de 1662*, 1662
Canvas. 165 x 229 cm / Donated by the artist to the Abbey of Port-Royal, Paris, 1662. Seized during the Revolution / Inv. 1138

Official painter to the court of Louis XIII, Champaigne developed into a spiritual and contemplative painter whose two supreme achievements are the *Ex-Voto* and the *Dead Christ Laid Out on his Shroud* (Louvre). Champaigne was certainly the finest portraitist of his generation and worked for the king, for Cardinal Richelieu (who commissioned the decoration for a gallery of *objets d'art* from him), and for the spiritual directors of the Jansenist community at Port-Royal-des-Champs (*The Last Supper*, which dates from the year his daughters entered the convent, came to the Louvre from the Paris Port-Royal). There are several versions of the *Richelieu*: that in the Louvre was donated, probably by the cardinal himself, to Louis Phélypeaux de la Vrillière, and provides ample evidence of the sparkle and intelligence of a prince of the Church, as captured by the brush of a painter, who was thenceforth to turn his hand to depicting puritan sparseness.

Chardin, Jean-Siméon
Paris, 1699 - *ibid.*, 1779

ML - *La Raie [The Skate or The Rayfish]*, c. 1728
(Academy reception piece) Canvas. 114.5 x 146 cm / Collection of the Academy / Inv. 3197

ML - *Le Bénédicité*, 1740 Salon
Canvas. 49.5 x 38.5 cm / Collection of Louis XV. Given by the artist to the king in 1740 / Inv. 3202

Chardin's entire career took place in Paris, where he depicted everyday life in bourgeois interiors and the silent existence of the objects that adorned his own home. A painter of feeling and of intimacy, he also endeavoured to portray childhood, in the Dutch manner. Louis XV purchased his *Serinette* (Louvre), Diderot praised him, and he was respected by his colleagues at the Academy for his wisdom and spirit of equity, but fell into an oblivion that was to be dispelled only during the second half of the 19th century. The Louvre possesses about thirty of the very numerous pictures that Chardin continued to produce even in his old age.

Chassériau, Théodore
Sainte-Barbe-de-Samana, Santo Domingo , 1819 - Paris, 1856

ML - *La Toilette d'Esther [The Toilette of Esther]*, 1841
Canvas. 45.5 x 35.5 cm / Baron Arthur Chassériau bequest, 1934 /R.F. 3900

A Romantic painter, an admirer of Delacroix, and Ingres' best pupil (he entered the master's studio while scarcely more than a child), Chassériau is a prime example of the generation that strove towards the revival in the art of painting eventually brought about by Courbet and the Realist school in the years around his death. Chassériau is very well represented in the Louvre with masterpieces from throughout his short career: *Andromeda Tied to the Rock by the Nereides* (1840), *The Two Sisters* (1843), *The Toilette of Esther*. A painter of pleasure, of the Orient (he spent time in Algeria in 1846), of mysterious, inaccessible women, his art culminates in a vast, ancient-world picture, Pompeian in style, *The Tepidarium* (Musée d'Orsay) that appeared at the World Fair of 1855.

Claude Lorraine
Claude Gellée, *known as*
Chamagne, Lorraine, c. 1602 - Rome, 1682

ML - *Port de mer au soleil couchant [Sea Port at Sunset]*, 1639
Canvas. 103 x 137 cm / Collection of Louis XIV; presented by Le Nôtre to the king in 1693 / Inv. 4715

This *Sea Port* has links with the architectural *capriccio*, a genre that — unlike Claude's 'historical landscapes' such as the *Landing of Cleopatra at Tarsus* (Louvre) — tells no story. In the foreground appear genre scenes, complete with a brawl, tradesmen, luxurious and less elaborate seacraft, and men working in the dry-dock. Only the French fleur de lys provides an historical context for the large vessel moored to the right of the picture. Claude concentrates on the atmosphere of the moment, thereby heralding the art of one of his greatest admirers, Turner.

Clouet, Jean, *known as* Janet
?, 1485/1490 - ?, 1541

ML - *François I*, c. 1530
Wood. 96 x 74 cm / Collection of François I / Inv. 3256

It was in about 1530 that Clouet depicted the king, protector of the arts, friend to the Italians, in an extremely elegant costume and holding a sword symbolising his power; his gloves posed on a ledge mark the limits of the picture. He sports the chain of the chivalric Ordre de Saint-Michel founded by Louis XI, at that time a rival of the Ordre de la Toison d'Or. Clouet, father and son, developed a rigidly stereotypical 'court portrait' that was produced in abundance by both their studio and their imitators. Henri Zerner has written: 'The very monotony of the Clouets' pictures is a condition for their operating effectively, since belonging to the close-knit world [of the Court] was more urgent than the desire to stand out from it' — an observation that might arguably be applied to portraits by Warhol, painter to a certain international class in New York with its own codes and rites.

Corot, Jean-Baptiste Camille
Paris, 1796 - *ibid.*, 1875

ML - *Le Forum vu des jardins Farnèse [The Forum Seen from the Farnese Gardens]*, March 1826
Paper on canvas. 28 x 50 cm / Artist bequest, 1875 / R.F. 153

ML - *Femme à la perle [Woman with a Pearl]*, c. 1869
Canvas. 70 x 55 cm / Acquired from the residue of the Maurice Audéoud bequest, 1912 / R.F. 2040

Modest in both speech and appearance, the prolific Corot painted landscapes after nature yet in a classical facture, shot through with a restrained lyricism and an interiorised poetry. The Louvre contains a number of masterpieces dating from his Italian sojourns, as well as some 'views' executed during his many trips through France. The museum shares with the Musée d'Orsay examples from Corot's final period that overlapped with the triumph of Realism, when he turned increasingly to historical landscape treated in misty tones and reverted to mythological subjects. Much indebted to the museum tradition, Corot's portraits, the least known part of his oeuvre, are moving and subtle.

Courbet, Gustave
Ornans, 1819 - La Tour de Peilz, Switzerland, 1877

MO - *Un enterrement à Ornans [Burial at Ornans]*, c. 1849-1850
Oil on canvas. 315 x 668 cm / Gift of Mlle Juliette Courbet, the artist's sister, 1881 / R.F. 325

MO - *L'Atelier du peintre [The Painter's Studio: A Real Allegory]*, 1855
Oil on canvas. 361x 598 cm / Acquired in 1920 with the aid of a public subscription and of the Société des Amis du Louvre / R.F. 2257

MO - *L'Origine du monde [The Origin of the World]*, 1866
Oil on canvas. 46 x 55 cm / Allocated in lieu of death duties, 1995 / R.F. 1995-10

In the years around 1855, this inventor and promoter of Realism — a provincial much attached to his home village of Ornans in Franche-Comté who was nonetheless a friend of Baudelaire in Paris — revolutionised painting. A democrat and a republican, convinced that modern life was worthy to be enshrined in art, the saviour of the Louvre when the Commune set fire to the Tuileries in 1871, Courbet was nonetheless forced into exile in Switzerland where his last works were produced. Under the cover of Realism, he devised a metaphysical reality, filled with complex symbols and reminiscences of Romanticism. Courbet is the prototype of the innovative painter overflowing with energy in whose work the desire to shock fuses with the desire to please. For artists later in the century, from Manet to Degas, Courbet was to become at once talisman and father figure.

Couture, Thomas
Senlis, 1815 - Villiers-le-Bel, 1879

MO - *Les Romains de la décadence [The Romans of the Decadence]*, 1847
Oil on canvas. 472 x 772 cm / Acquired in 1847 / Inv. 3451

To remind oneself of the often forgotten fact that Couture was the master of Manet, teaching him how to paint with loaded brush and with muscular contrasts, one only has to inspect the quality of paint and brush technique of *The Romans of the Decadence*. The work's meaning was expounded in a booklet published at the Salon of 1847 with a quotation from the Latin poet Juvenal: 'Crueller than war, vice swooped down on Rome and avenged a vanquished world.' In the eclecticism of his sources and manner, permeated by echoes of other works, Couture is a highly characteristic Second Empire painter.

Cross, Henri-Edmond
Henri-Edmond Delacroix, *known as*
Douai, 1856 - Saint-Clair, 1910

MO - *Les Iles d'Or* (Iles d'Hyères, Var, France), c. 1891-1892 / Oil on canvas. 59 x 54 cm / Acquired in 1947 / R.F. 1977-126

MO - *La Chevelure [The Head of Hair]*, c. 1892
Oil on canvas. 61x 46 cm / Acquired in 1969 / R.F. 1977-128

It must have been hard for a painter born in 1856 to be called Delacroix! Starting out as a Realist and an admirer of Manet and the Italian Macchiaioli, Cross converted to Seurat's Divisionism in 1891 (*Portrait of Mme Cross*, Musée d'Orsay). Close to Puvis de Chavannes and the Nabis, he sometimes succeeded, as in *Les Iles d'Or*, in achieving an abstract monumentality, the harmony of his compositions stemming from a musical style.

Dado
Miodrag Djuric, *known as*
Cetinje, Montenegro, 1933

CP - *Le Massacre des Innocents [The Massacre of the Innocents]*, 1958-1959
Oil on canvas. 194 x 259.5 cm / Gift of the Scaler Foundation, 1979 / AM 1978-744

After training at art schools in Belgrade and Hercegnovi, in 1956 Dado settled in Paris where Jean Dubuffet was the first to appreciate the originality of his art. A meticulous craftsman and masterly technician, Dado finds his subjects in the museum: paintings of plump little putti for the *Massacre of the Innocents* or *Les Toiles des Bébés*, infants who die unbaptised to wander in Limbo where they wait to be turned into angels. An adept of Dürer's and Martin Schongauer's engravings, Dado's drawing style is sometimes of Ingres-like exactitude. Oblivious to contemporary trends yet gifted with a huge visual culture, Dado follows a path as complex and as idiosyncratic as the Balkan region of his roots.

Dalí, Salvador
Figueras, Catalonia, 1904 - *ibid.*, 1989

CP - *William Tell*, 1930
Oil and collage on canvas. 113 x 87 cm / Acquired in 2002 / EC-2002-1-AP

A consummate technician who underwent a classical training at the Academy of Fine Arts in Madrid, Dalí discovered his true self thanks to his encounter with psychoanalysis. Interpreting his dreams through his pictures, he made use of obsessive themes — from the grand piano in the family house to the celebrated 'soft watches' — that together compose an internally coherent dreamworld. One time friend of Breton and Picasso, he cited as his precursors both Vermeer and Ernest Messonier, though his style was also close to Tanguy, Max Ernst and De Chirico. His masterpiece was perhaps his stellar public persona that for decades embodied in the eyes of the international press the image of unhinged, attention-seeking Surrealism. Having set up a museum of his work in Figueras that opened in 1974, honoured by exhibitions the world over, and named Marquès de Pubol by the king of Spain in 1982, Dalí died at the summit of his glory.

David, Jacques Louis
Paris, 1748 - Brusels, 1825

ML - *Le Serment des Horaces [The Oath of the Horatii]*, 1785 Salon
Canvas. 331 x 425 cm / Commissioned by Louis XVI / Inv. 3692

ML - *Les Sabines [The Sabine Women or The Intervention of the Sabine Women]*, 1799
Canvas. 385 x 522 cm / Acquired in 1819 / Inv. 3691

ML - *Madame Récamier*, begun in 1800
Canvas. 174 x 244 cm / Acquired at the sale of David's studio, 1826 / Inv. 3708

ML - *Sacre de Napoléon 1er et couronnement de l'impératrice Joséphine dans la cathédrale Notre-Dame de Paris, le 2 décembre 1804 [Consecration of Emperor Napoleon I and Coronation of the Empress Josephine in the Cathedral of Notre-Dame, Paris, 2nd December 1804]*, 1806-1807
Canvas. 621 x 979 cm / Commissioned by Napoleon I / Inv. 3699

The creator of French Neoclassical style, David paid homage to the peerless grandeur of the Ancient Romans of the Republic. He celebrated the reconciliation of the French in his *Sabine Women*, which, under the pretence of recounting ancient history, is addressed to contemporaries of the recently completed Revolution. With pupils from all over Europe, he was promoted 'first painter' to an emperor he had already depicted as the all-conquering hero when he was still known simply as Bonaparte. Portraitist of a liberal elite, David never abandoned the cultivated and intelligent clientele to which Mme Récamier belonged. The Spartan theatricality of these 'virtuous examples' corresponded perfectly to the heroic-cum-sentimental expectations of the public of his time.

De Chirico, Giorgio
Volos, Greece, 1888 - Rome, 1978

CP - *Portrait prémonitoire de Guillaume Apollinaire [Premonitory Portrait of Guillaume Apollinaire]*, 1914
Oil on canvas. 81.5 x 65 cm / Purchase, 1975 / AM 1975-52

An Italian born in Greece, Giorgio De Chirico trained at Munich in a Symbolist milieu marked by the art of Arnold Böcklin and Max Klinger. His meeting in Paris with Apollinaire and the Surrealists was crucial: after 1914, his Pittura Metafisica, with its deserted squares, its disturbing mannequins and otherworldly titles, had a striking effect on many artists, from Dali to Tanguy, from Otto Dix to Max Ernst. After 1920, he reverted to a style and to subjects conforming to the most conventional figuration. Jettisoned by an avant-garde that stigmatised him as a 'traitor', none could see the irony and profundity of a second *maniera* that has only recently been re-evaluated.

Degas, Edgar
Hilaire Germain Edgar de Gas, *known as*
Paris, 1834 - *ibid.*, 1917

MO - *Portrait de famille* or *La famille Bellelli* [*The Bellelli Family*], c. 1860-1867
Oil on canvas. 200 x 250 cm / Acquired in 1918 through the good offices of René Degas, with the assistance of the Comte and Comtesse de Fels / R.F.2210

MO - *L'Orchestre de l'Opéra* [*The Orchestra of the Paris Opera*], c. 1870
Oil on canvas. 56.5 x 46 cm / Lifetime enjoyment gift of Mlle Marie Dihau, sister of Désiré Dihau, 1923. Entered in 1935 / R.F. 2417

MO - *L'Absinthe* [*Absinthe* or *In the Café*], c. 1876
Oil on canvas. 92 x 68 cm / Isaac de Camondo bequest, 1911 / R.F. 1984

Degas occupies a place apart in the Impressionist group. A dandy of good family, the son of a banker, he disparaged Monet's rustic style. Very much the recluse, throughout his life Degas returned to the same obsessions: horses and the turf, the female body and ballet. Modern life, sometimes even lowlife, as in *L'Absinthe*, provides him with the lion's share of his subjects. The Musée d'Orsay does possess two historical paintings by his hand, *Semiramis Building Babylon* and *Scene of War in the Middle Ages*, which demonstrate his initial ambition to carve a path to the museum as a history painter. A great collector who had amassed the kernel of a veritable museum that was dispersed on his death, he adored Ingres (as an early piece like *The Bellelli Family* betrays), whom he met in his youth. *The Orchestra of the Paris Opera*, by its daring construction, by the 'modern' way it is framed, is one of the summits of his oeuvre, where music, theatre, dance and portraiture fuse.

Delacroix, Eugène
Charenton-Saint-Maurice, then Saint-Maurice, 1798 - Paris, 1863

ML - *Mort de Sardanapale* [*The Death of Sardanapalus*], 1827 Salon
Canvas. 392 x 496 cm / Acquired from the residue of the Maurice Audéoud bequest, 1912 / R.F. 2346

ML - *Le 28 juillet : La Liberté guidant le peuple* [*Liberty at the Barricades* or *Liberty Leading the People*], 1830
Canvas. 260 x 325 cm / Acquired at the 1831 Salon / Transferred from the Musée du Luxembourg to the Louvre, 1874 / R.F. 129

ML - *Femmes d'Alger dans leur appartement* [*Algerian Women in their Apartment*], 1834
Canvas. 180 x 229 cm / Acquired at the 1834 Salon / Inv. 3824

ML - *Apollon vainqueur du Serpent Python* [*Apollo Vanquishing the Serpent Python*], 1850-1851
Canvas. 800 x 750 cm / (Painting in the central section of the ceiling of the Galerie d'Apollon) / Commissioned in 1850 / Inv. 3818

Writing in his *Journal*, Delacroix declined the role of leader of the Romantics, which he might well have claimed in opposition to Ingres. With no pupils and no teaching studio, he differed from his rival who amassed official honours and wanted to leave a school worthy of succeeding him. 'Passionately in love with passion' (Baudelaire), Delacroix painted his grand compositions with loaded brushstrokes, whose ardour evinces his admiration for Rubens and for artists closer to him in time, Gros and Géricault. He experienced 'living antiquity' during a 1832 voyage to Algeria and Morocco, encountering there colours, lighting and subjects to which he returned throughout his career. In Paris, he executed major decorative ensembles at the Luxembourg and Bourbon palaces (the Senate and National Assembly, respectively), for which he devised an iconographical programme that trumpets the triumph of civilisation and the arts over barbarism. An avid reader, a lion who walked alone, Delacroix retired to the country to undertake a dictionary of painting he was never to complete.

Delaunay, Robert
Paris, 1885 - Montpellier, 1941

CP - *Formes circulaires, soleil, n° 2* [*Circular Forms - Sun, n° 2*], 1912-1913
Tempera on canvas. 100 x 68.5 cm / Gift of the Société des Amis du Musée National d'Art Moderne, 1961 / AM 3910 P

From Impressionism to abstraction, Robert and Sonia (1885-1979) Delaunay together traversed a crucial period in the history of painting. Initially a Cubist and, like Braque and Picasso, an admirer of Cézanne, Robert Delaunay divides space up into simple forms, rebuilding it with pure colours impelled by dynamic values, as in the series of *Circular Forms* (1912-1913). Delaunay did not for all that abandon figurative work in which he achieved a highly individual, rhythmical grandeur that met with clamorous public success after his death.

Derain, André
Chatou, 1880 - Chambourcy, 1954

CP - *Les Deux Péniches* [*The Two Barges*], 1906
Oil on canvas. 80 x 97.5 cm / Purchase, 1972 / AM 1972-1

CP - *Nu devant un rideau vert* [*Nude in front of a Green Curtain*], 1923
Oil on canvas. 92 x 73 cm / Purchase, 1936 / AM 2101 P

In the legendary studio at Chatou, which he shared with Maurice de Vlaminck, the young Derain was first a Fauvist, who joined his friend Matisse in Collioure during the glorious summer of 1904 when they painted easel by easel. At the Bateau-Lavoir in Montmartre, he cemented friendships with Picasso and Braque, and with Apollinaire and Max Jacob, poets whose works he was to illustrate. Bypassing Cubism, he turned back to the familiar masters in the Louvre whom he had already amply copied: Ingres, whose influence is patent in *Nude in front of a Green Curtain*, but also Courbet, Corot and the Barbizon painters. Today Derain still suffers from his reputation as a cultured painter with literary tastes, and from having been hailed by inter-war critics as the greatest French artist of the 20th century, whereas it is perhaps more accurate to call him the most intelligent.

198

Detaille, Edouard
Paris, 1848 - *ibid.*, 1912

MO - *Le Rêve [The Dream]*, 1888
Oil on canvas, 300 x 400 cm / Acquired in 1888 / R.F.524

Like Ernest Meissonnier (an exponent of military subjects and a master of the small format), in his time Detaille was a famous and sought-after painter. Unlike Meissonnier, however, Detaille delighted in large spaces, producing several circular panoramas after the defeat of 1870 that verge on what we would now call 'installations'. Since they allowed the public to feel they were at the epicentre of a battle, these strikingly realistic works were hugely popular. Resembling some grand historical procession, by its dimensions *The Dream* is not far removed from this peculiar genre. Difficult to imagine today, these structures go some way to explaining the 'wraparound' effect of Monet's last series, the *Waterlilies* at the Musée de l'Orangerie, a 'panorama' that concludes and commemorates the 'victory' of Impressionism.

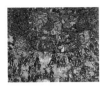

Dubuffet, Jean
Le Havre, 1901 - Paris, 1985

CP - *Rue passagère*, 1961
Oil on canvas. 129.3 x 161.7 cm / Purchase, 1983 /AM 1983-3

Rejecting the entire history of painting en bloc, Dubuffet turned to artlessness, appropriating, for his own ends, the way of looking of the mad, the savage and the child. Making use of materials until then considered unworthy of art, such as gravel or sump oil, or, on the contrary, sumptuously coloured butterfly wings, Dubuffet composed mind pictures, creating a personal imagery that makes occasional allusions to the figurative. The burlesque, pulsing 'human cells' in *Rue Passagère* seem derived from puppetry; it is a human comedy, which cleared the way for his later abstracts (blue and red on a white ground) painted before the final *Non-Lieux* on a black ground.

Dürer, Albrecht
Nuremberg, 1471 - *ibid.*, 1528

ML - *Autoportrait [Self-portrait]*, 1493
Parchment glued to canvas. 56.5 x 44.5 cm / Acquired in 1922 / R.F. 2382

A universal painter who synthesised medieval philosophy and the humanist spirit, Dürer was as talented with the brush as with pen or burin, open to Italy as well as to cities on the banks of the Rhine. In his earliest self-portrait known as 'with a thistle', Dürer shows himself as a totally assured artist. Though he has not yet encountered Italy nor received any major commissions, he already masters the art of illusion. This majestic enterprise of introspection deepened in a 1498 work (Prado, Madrid) and culminated in 1500 with the self-portrait 'in fur' (Alte Pinakothek, Munich), where he chose the pose and attitude of Christ against a dark-hued background, identifying the painter — considered at the time merely as a craftsman marginally more gifted than another — with the Creator of the universe.

Dix, Otto
Untermhaus, 1891 - Hemmenhofen, 1969

CP - *The Journalist Sylvia von Harden*, 1926
Oil and tempera on wood. 121 x 89 cm / Purchase, 1961 / AM 3899 P

CP - *Erinnerung an die Spiegelsäle von Brüssel [Souvenir of the Cristal Palace in Brussels]*, 1930
Oil and glaze over a silver ground on canvas. 124 x 80.4 cm / Purchase in memory of Siegfried Poppe, 1999 / AM 1999-178

During his studies Dix encountered the work of the great masters of the German School, especially Cranach and Dürer. Deeply scarred by the horrors of the First World War, this Expressionist attracted by Dada trudged through a modern cityscape haunted by maimed ex-serviceman, haggard prostitutes and disturbing figures, intellectuals, circus artistes, quacks... A major exponent of Neue Sachlichkeit ('New Objectivity'), he was given pride of place in the infamous exhibition of 'Degenerate Art' organised by the Nazis in 1937.

Duchamp, Marcel
Blainville-Crevon, Seine-Maritime, 1887 - Neuilly-sur-Seine, 1968

CP - *Les Joueurs d'échecs [The Chess Players]*, 1911
Oil on canvas. 50 x 61 cm / Purchase, 1954 / AM 3329 P

The man who was to contest the traditional system of art started out as a painter. Like *Nude Descending a Staircase* (1911, Museum of Art, Philadelphia), *The Chess Players* (the game was a lifelong passion that he also taught) is an attempt to forge a synthesis between static Cubist still life and the representation of movement. In 1913, he began the series of readymades that overlaps with the 'appropriation' of the *Mona Lisa*, *L.H.O.O.Q.* (1919, private collection). There then began Duchamp's prolonged, ironic, scientific, metaphysical phase, in the form of works that remain indispensable for an understanding of a 20th-century art scene in which painting no longer occupies centre stage: *The Bride Stripped Bare by her Bachelors, Even* (1915-1923, Museum of Art, Philadelphia) and the opus ultimum, *Étant donnés : 1° la chute d'eau, 2° le gaz d'éclairage* (1966, *ibid.*).

El Greco
Domenikos Theotokopoulos, *known as*
Candia, Crete, 1541 - Toledo, 1614

ML - *Le Christ en croix adoré par deux donateurs [Christ on the Cross Adored by Two Donors]*, c. 1585-1590
Canvas. 260 x 171 cm / From Louis-Philippe's 'Spanish Gallery' / Acquired in 1908 / R.F. 1713

Born in one of Venice's Greek possessions, the painter who was to become known as 'El Greco' trained in the Serenissima herself, where he surely seized the opportunity of admiring works by Titian and Tintoretto. His career unfolded predominantly in Spain; in Toledo, he executed many masterpieces, the most famous being *The Burial of Count d'Orgaz* (1586, Santo Tomé, Toledo). Forgotten for centuries, he was rediscovered by the 'Generation of 1898' in Spain, and by Maurice Barrès in France and Sacheverell Sitwell in England.

Ernst, Max
Brühl, Rhineland, 1891 - Paris, 1976

CP - *Ubu Imperator*, 1923
Oil on canvas. 81 x 65 cm / Gift of the Fondation pour la Recherche Médicale, 1984 / AM 1984-281

A Surrealist, the creator of an imaginary kingdom governed by its own rules, Ernst nonetheless continued to follow the tradition of the 'métier', using the classic techniques of painting to delve into the Unconscious. In paintings, collages, photomontages and drawings, he engineered 'fortuitous' encounters, gateways to parallel universes with which poets, such as Breton, Eluard and Desnos, readily identified. After 1941, breaking with the Surrealist group, he settled in the United States where his influence was immeasurable, especially on artists like Pollock.

Fantin-Latour, Henri
Grenoble, 1836 - Buré, Orne, 1904

MO - *Hommage à Delacroix [Homage to Delacroix]*, 1864
Oil on canvas. 160 x 250 cm / Gift of Étienne Moreau-Nélaton, 1906 / R.F. 1664

Fantin-Latour learned everything he knew in the Louvre. An exhibitor at the 1863 Salon des Refusés, he made his mark as the finest portraitist of the up-and-coming generation (*Manet*, 1867, Art Institute, Chicago), giving a new lease of life to group portraiture. Several paintings of these friendly gatherings appear at the Musée d'Orsay: *Homage to Delacroix* (1864), *Studio in the Batignolles* (1870), *Around the Table* (where Verlaine and Rimbaud pose on the left, 1872) and *Around the Piano* (1885), lively tributes to painting, literature and music. A friend of the Impressionists, he nonetheless stood outside the group: the classic craftsmanship of still lifes reminiscent of Chardin, his mythological pictures that recall Prud'hon, and his illustrations of Wagner place him in separate category, closer to the Symbolists and to *intimiste* painters like Vuillard.

Flandrin, Hippolyte
Lyon, 1809 - Rome, 1864

ML - *Jeune Homme nu assis au bord de la mer [A Young Man beside the Sea]*, 1836
Canvas. 98 x 124 cm / Acquired through the Civil List of Napoleon III in 1857 and presented by the Emperor / M.I. 171

Winner of the Prix de Rome in 1832, Flandrin was, with Chassériau, one of Ingres's star pupils. Where his master had failed, Flandrin excelled in large mural decorations. The apostle of a return to the Italian primitives and to the monumentality of the mosaics of Ravenna, and the focus of a group that was the French equivalent of the German Nazarenes, Flandrin's subjects were primarily religious, though his finest piece, the nave of the church of St-Germain-des-Prés in Paris, was once threatened with destruction so as to lay bare the 'purity' of the medieval stonework beneath. Two easel paintings in the Louvre testify to his sensitivity and extraordinary technical control: the portrait *Mme Flandrin* (1846) and *A Young Man beside the Sea*, of which there is a second version in the Musée Bonnat in Bayonne.

Eyck, Jan van
Maaseyck, vers 1390/1400 - Bruges, 1441

ML - *La Vierge du chancelier Rolin [The Madonna of the Chancellor Rolin]*, c. 1434
Wood. 66 x 62 cm / Originally from the collegial church of Notre-Dame at Autun / Entered the Louvre in 1800 / Inv. 1271

An illuminator who bore the title of valet to Philippe the Good, Duke of Burgundy, Jan van Eyck was the creator (perhaps with his brother Hubert, who died in Ghent in 1426) of the *Polyptych of the Mystic Lamb* (Saint-Bavo Cathedral, Ghent, 1432), the *Portrait of the Arnolfini Couple* (1434, National Gallery, London) and the famous picture in the Louvre depicting festivities at the Burgundian court. Painted for the chancellor to the duke, Nicolas Rolin, the altar painting was originally in the collegial church of Notre-Dame at Autun. It demonstrates the extraordinary technique of Jan van Eyck who, according to a tradition born in the 16th century, was acclaimed as the inventor of oil painting.

Fautrier, Jean
Paris, 1898 - Châtenay-Malabry, 1964

CP - *L'Ecorché, corps d'otage*, 1945
Oil on paper glue-mounted on canvas. 80 x 115 cm / Allocated in lieu of death duties, 1997 / AM 1997-93

Educated in England and schooled in watercolour, drawing and traditional engraving techniques (at fourteen he was already following courses at the Royal Academy), Fautrier suffered greatly in the 1914-1918 War during which he was gassed. Like Derain, he worked independently of Cubism, remaining closer to Soutine in large-scale, sombre works rich in matiere that vie explicitly with Rembrandt, *The Flayed Boar* (1926, Centre Pompidou). The series of *Otages* [Hostages], produced in 1943 and exhibited in 1945, promoted him into one of France's foremost post-war painters and a great Resistance artist. The whole series is characterised by a thick layer that is worked up with transparency effects in pastel or watercolour, the brutality of the paste as it builds up contrasting with the harmonious, bright palette.

Fontana, Lucio
Rosario de Santa Fe, Argentina, 1899 - Varese, Italy, 1968

CP - *La Fine di Dio*, 1963-1964
Oil on canvas, perforations and line drawing. 178 x 123 cm / Allocated in lieu of death duties, 1997 / AM 1997-94

Following an early figurative period, the painter and sculptor Fontana founded Movimento spaziale. His 'spatial concepts' are monochrome, stretched canvases that are notched, sliced or perforated. The gesture of painting no longer consists in applying paint but in modifying the physical surface of the work, opening it, traversing it in a way previously unthinkable in every convention of picture-making.

Fragonard, Jean-Honoré
Grasse, 1732 - Paris, 1806

ML - *L'Abbé de Saint-Non*, c. 1769
Canvas. 80 x 65 cm / Dr Louis La Caze bequest, 1869 / M.I. 1061

ML - *Le Verrou [The Bolt]*, before 1784
Canvas. 73 x 93 cm / Acquired in 1974 / R.F. 1974-2

A favourite pupil of Boucher, Fragonard was strongly marked by his stay in Italy as well as by his discovery of Rembrandt's work in Paris. He learned to paint rapidly with visible brushstrokes. Fragonard's *Coresus and Callirhoe* (Louvre), his *morceau d'agrément* for the Academy, was exhibited at the 1765 Salon. He steered clear of historical and mythological painting, and excelled in small formats, in cabinet pictures, such as *La Chemise Enlevée* (*ibid.*) and *The Bolt*, a libertine piece whose pendant is the eminently Catholic *Adoration of the Shepherds* (*ibid.*). There survive about fifteen portraits by him, the so-called 'fantasy figures' that include a portrait of Diderot and another of his friend the Abbé de Saint-Non, art lover and wit who accompanied the painter on his first Italian journey. Fragonard managed as it were to outlive himself: powerless in the face of David's meteoric rise, he could only look on as the world he had depicted evaporated.

Francis, Sam
San Mateo, California, 1923 - Santa Monica, 1994

CP - *In Lovely Blueness*, 1955-1957
Oil on canvas. 300 x 700 cm / Gift of the Scaler Foundation with the contribution of Sylvie and Eric Boissonnas, 1977 / AM 1977-207

Initially active in the Parisian arena, in the 1950s Sam Francis entered an American art scene overshadowed by the figure of Pollock. Fascinated by late Monet as well as by decorative aspects of the art of Matisse, Francis concentrated on large formats that he animated with bright spots of colour, leaving the whites and blues characteristic of his production in the years 1960-1965 to compete with each other. His art is particularly well represented in Japan (Idemitsu Museum, Tokyo) and in American collections.

Friedrich, Caspar David
Greifswald, 1774 - Dresden, 1840

ML - *Krähenbaum [The Tree of Crows or Raven Tree]*, c. 1822
Canvas. 59 x 73.7 cm / Acquired in 1975 / R.F. 1975-20

Romantic, religious, Realist, Friedrich created a world that transformed a scrupulously observed Nature into a meditation on destiny and divine power. A painter of feelings of the sublime experienced before the sea, mountains, the sunlit morning or the wonder of clouds, Friedrich treats pictorial practice as giving an account of the Great Book penned by the hand of God. For Friedrich painting is revelation, but he was acknowledged as a major talent only in the 20th century.

Füssli, Johann Heinrich
also known as Henry Fuseli
Zurich, 1741 - London, 1825

ML - *Lady Macbeth somnambule [Lady Macbeth Sleepwalking]*, 1784
Canvas. 221 x 160 cm / Acquired in 1970 / R.F. 1970-29

A voracious reader in his youth, enthused by Milton and Shakespeare, Füssli trained in Switzerland and during stays in London and Rome. The idea of a cycle of paintings in homage to the author of *Macbeth* came to him while contemplating the Sistine Chapel ceiling; back in London in the 1780s, he produced a number of paintings based on Shakespeare's histories and tragedies, a major source of British Romanticism. These sombre scenes from which surge forth dreams and fantasies (*The Nightmare*, 1790-1791, Goethemuseum, Frankfurt) relate to the etchings of Goya and the visionary drawings of his friend William Blake.

Gauguin, Paul
Paris, 1848 - Atuana, Marquesas Islands, 1903

MO - *Femmes de Tahiti* or *Sur la plage [Tahitian Women]*, 1891
Oil on canvas. 69 x 91.5 cm / Guy de Cholet bequest, 1923 / R.F. 2765

MO - *Le Cheval blanc [The White Horse]*, 1898
Oil on canvas. 140 x 91.5 cm / Acquired in 1927 / R.F. 2616

Though he made a clamorous appearance at the eighth Impressionist exhibition in 1886, Gauguin was not in truth an heir to the new plein air painting or to the colour revolution. Instead Gauguin strove for symbols, for powerful compositions in the style of Puvis de Chavannes and for the exoticism so loved by the Romantics. All stages in his career are reflected in the Musée d'Orsay: his sojourns at Pont-Aven and Arles, his doomed friendship with Van Gogh, his journeys to Tahiti. His reflection on fate culminates in the last paintings, classic and grave, and in the sculptures of his *Maison du Jouir* (Musée d'Orsay).

Gérard, François, Baron
Rome, 1770 - Paris, 1837

ML - *Psyché et l'Amour [Amor and Psyche or Psyche Receiving the First Kiss of Love]*, 1798 Salon
Canvas. 186 x 132 cm / Acquired in 1822 / Inv. 4739

Unlike his peers for whom Italy was the great revelation, Gérard, of Franco-Italian birth, joined David's Parisian studio at the age of sixteen. As well as *Amor and Psyche*, exhibited at 1798 Salon, evocative both of profiles on Greek vases and of the marmoreal grace of Canova's sculpture groups, the Louvre contains a portrait of the miniature painter Isabey and his daughter (1795), a tender homage of father to daughter captured in the intimate surroundings of a country house. Gérard could compete with David in tackling great historical subjects (*The Victory at Austerlitz*, Galerie des Batailles, Versailles), as well as portraits of high society (*Mme Récamier*, Musée Carnavalet, Paris). Official painter to the king and elevated to a baronage on the Restoration, he once more pitted himself against David even after his master's death with a *Coronation of Charles X* (1829, Versailles), and carried out the decoration of the cupola of the Panthéon (1829-1836).

Géricault, Théodore
Rouen, 1791 - Paris, 1824

ML - *Le Radeau de la Méduse [The Raft of The Medusa]*, 1819 Salon
Canvas. 491 x 716 cm / Acquired at the sale of Géricault's estate through a friend of the artist, Pierre-Joseph Dedreux-Dorcy, 1824 / Inv. 4884

ML - *La Folle monomane du jeu [Madwoman with Gambling Mania]*, c. 1822
Canvas. 77 x 64.5 cm / Gift of the Société des Amis du Louvre, 1938 / R.F. 1938-51

Studying first under Carle Vernet then with Guérin, Géricault, painter of soldiers and horses, built his own private museum from the copies he made of Old Masters in the Louvre. After a resounding debut at the Salon of 1812 with an *Officer of the Imperial Horse Guards Charging*, two years later his *Wounded Dragoon* (Louvre) symbolised the decline of the Empire. *The Raft of The Medusa* of 1819 was a call to arms for a young school of painters determined to shake off David's Neoclassical rules, in line with what Gros had begun doing a few years earlier. With a style that recalls Manet, his series of portraits of the insane corresponds to a final 'Realist' phase *ante litteram* (*The Plaster Kiln, ibid.*), which Géricault would have surely developed had he not prematurely been laid low by disease — thus becoming a kind of demigod of Romanticism.

Ghirlandaio, Domenico
Domenico Bigordi, *known as*
Florence, 1449 - *ibid.*, 1494

ML - *Vieillard avec un enfant [Old Man and a Child or Old Man with his Grandson]*, c. 1488
Wood. 62.7 x 46.3 cm / Acquired in 1886 / R.F. 266

His name means 'maker of garlands'. Like his father, Ghirlandaio started out as a goldsmith and it might be easy to think of him simply as the decorative painter who lined the walls of the choir of Santa Maria Novella in Florence with sumptuous narrative frescoes. His easel pictures, such as the portrait of *Giovanna Tornabuoni* (Museo Thyssen-Bornemisza, Madrid), the portrait of *Francesco Sassetti with his Son* (Metropolitan Museum of Art, New York) or the unnamed old man in the Louvre, reveal another side: a realistic observer of tiny details, yet simultaneously receptive to emotion and feeling.

Giacometti, Alberto
Stampa, Switzerland, 1901 - Coire, Switzerland, 1966

CP - *Jean Genet*, 1954-1955
Oil on canvas. 73 x 60 cm / Purchase, 1980 / AM 1980-35

Sculptor and painter, Giacometti initially essayed Post-Impressionism, Cubism and Surrealism, before devoting himself almost exclusively to sculpture, the most enduringly popular facet of his work. He returned to two dimensions after 1945, illustrating texts by André Breton, Georges Bataille, Genet,... though he focused more particularly on portraiture, of his artist brother Diego, or else of friends as here, in 1955, with Jean Genet (1910-1986), the controversial author of *Notre-Dame des Fleurs* (1946) and *The Maids* (1947). Like Genet's texts themselves, these portraits plumb the individual's depths, extracting elements of traditional figuration from a grey and white space scored with dark lines: in the middle hovers the sitter's minute face and piercing eyes.

Giotto di Bondone, *or* Giotto
Colle di Vespignano, 1266/1267 ? - Florence, 1337

ML - *Saint François d'Assise recevant les stigmates [St Francis of Assisi Receiving the Stigmata]*, c. 1300
Wood and gold ground. 313 x 163 cm / Originally from San Francesco, Pisa, 1811
Entered the Louvre in 1813 / Inv. 309

According to Vasari, Giotto was the first to paint figures that seemed real, with real shadows and volumes, their feet anchored on the ground, their faces expressing genuine emotions. In collaboration with the studio he headed, Giotto frescoed buildings in Assisi, Padua and Florence, totally renewing the art of painting, the composition of space and iconography. The three small-sized scenes running beneath the signed altarpiece in the Louvre return to subjects he had previously tackled in Assisi: *The Dream of Pope Innocent III*, *The Confirmation of the Franciscan Rule* and *Preaching to the Birds*.

Girodet, Anne-Louis
Girodet de Roussy-Trioson, *known as*
Montargis, 1767 - Paris, 1824

ML - *Endymion. Effet de lune [Endymion. Moon Effect*, or *Sleeping Endymion]*, 1793 Salon
Canvas. 198 x 261 cm / Acquired in 1818 / Inv. 4935

ML - *Atala au tombeau [The Burial of Atala]*, 1808 Salon
Canvas. 207 x 267 cm / Acquired in 1819 / Inv. 4958

A highly literary artist, Girodet affirmed himself as an original personality while still in David's studio. Girodet introduced the *sfumato* of Leonardo and Correggio within a style of Neoclassical rigour, *Endymion* being a case in point. Won over by Romanticism, he made a portrait of a swarthy Chateaubriand recently returned from his voyage to the East (1809, Musée de Saint-Malo), and illustrated his most popular novel. His reading of Ossian, the 'fake' ancient Gaelic poet concocted by the Scot James MacPherson, inspired one of the strangest and most alluring of all early 19th-century pictures: *The Apotheosis of French Heroes* (1802, Musée Nationale de Malmaison), which Bruno Foucart has dubbed the 'Demoiselles d'Avignon of Romanticism'.

Goncharova, Natalia Sergeyevna
Nagaevo, Russia, 1881 - Paris, 1962

CP - *Espace [Space]*, 1958
Oil on canvas. 55 x 46 cm / Gift from the Soviet State, 1988 / AM 1988-885

By the time she painted the series of works to which *Space* belongs, the artist whom Guillaume Apollinaire had called 'the head of the Russian Futurists' was a grand dame — but she could still be fascinated by the new *Sputnik*. Together with Mikhail Larionov (1881-1964), from 1912 she incarnated the Russian avant-garde, and was associated with both Futurism and Rayonism. After settling in Paris she remained deeply attached to her native land, designing sets for ballets by Diaghilev, as well as for many other productions and concerts. The result of years of research on light, Goncharova's late 'cosmic compositions' reverberate to a modern-day 'music of the spheres'.

Goya y Lucientes, Francisco de
Fuendetodos, Aragon, 1746 - Bordeaux, 1828

ML - *The Countess del Carpio, Marquise de la Solana*, c. 1794-1795
Canvas. 183 x 124 cm / Carlos de Besteigui bequest, 1942 / Entered the Louvre in 1953 / RF 1942B23

The Louvre possesses a number of fine pictures by Goya, including the *Portrait of Ferdinand Guillemardet*, a French ambassador, a *Still Life with a Sheep's Head* and a small religious painting, *Christ on the Mount of Olives*. The artist's most important works, however, hang in the Prado in Madrid: the youthful tapestry cartoons, the cycle of paintings known as of the 'House of the Deaf Man', the strangest group devoted to the myth Saturn, his 'black paintings'. The portrait of the Marquise de la Solana offers a splendid example of the master's brushwork: over a loosely laid-in ground and free of all superfluous detail, the contrast between the black dress and the white veil of the mantilla emphasises a severe expression that is brightened by a magnificent pair of eyes.

Greuze, Jean-Baptiste
Tournus, 1725 - Paris, 1805

ML - *La Cruche cassée [The Broken Jug]*, 1772 or 1773
Canvas, oval. 108.5 x 86.5 cm / Seized during the Revolution from the Collection of the Comtesse du Barry at Louveciennes / Inv. 5036

ML - *La Malédiction paternelle [The Father's Curse: the Ungrateful Son]*, 1777
Canvas. 130 x 162 cm / Acquired in 1820 / Inv. 5038

A sensitive spirit, a moralist, a *philosophe* (in the 18th-century acceptation of the term), Greuze is also a master of the genre scene, endowing anecdotes from middle-class life with a grandeur worthy of Poussin's scenes from antiquity. The pendant to *The Father's Curse* was entitled *The Son Punished* (1778, Louvre), combining to form a 'drama in two pictures' whose immediate success was furthered by its popularity with engravers. Diderot hailed Greuze for his originality. Without any particular concern with antiquity himself — the inspiration, nonetheless, behind *Emperor Septimus Severus Reproaching his Son Caracalla* (1769, *ibid.*) — the painter manages to translate into a contemporary idiom those 'examples of virtue' that provided so many subjects for David and his Neoclassical entourage.

Gros, Antoine-Jean, Baron
Paris, 1771 - Meudon, 1835

ML - *Bonaparte visitant les pestiférés de Jaffa [Napoleon Bonaparte in the Pesthouse at Jaffa or Napoleon Bonaparte Visiting the Plague-Stricken in Jaffa]*, 1804
Canvas. 523 x 715 cm / Commissioned and purchased from the artist, 1804 / Inv. 5064

Though working deep in Neoclassicism's heartland, the most spontaneous of David's pupils was one of the creators of French Romanticism. Receptive to the East, to the fury of battle and to the superb of the providential Bonaparte, he captured the face of the young hero of Arcole in a sketch (Louvre), while his talent as a colourist in *The Pesthouse at Jaffa* was a revelation at the 1804 Salon. The humanist grandeur of *The Battle of Eylau* (1808, *ibid.*) touched the younger artistic generation. However, after 1815, just as his ideas were in the ascendant, Gros reverted to the most classical academic painting; on the failure of his call to an anachronistic 'return to order' in the form of an *Hercules and Diomedes* (1835, Musée des Augustins, Toulouse), this artist who always seemed to be swimming against the current took his own life.

Guérin, Pierre Narcisse, Baron
Paris, 1774 - Rome, 1833

ML - *Énée racontant à Didon les malheurs de la ville de Troie [Aeneas Relating to Dido the Disaster of Troy]*, 1815
Canvas. 292 x 390 cm / Acquired in 1818 / Inv. 5184

Before discovering Italy, Guérin, a painter much in vogue, triumphed successively with *The Return of Marcus Sextus* (1799, Louvre) and *Phaedra and Hippolytus* (1802, *ibid.*). At the Restoration, he proved his loyalty to the monarchy with portraits of the generals of the Vendée, the finest of which is of *Henri de La Rochejacquelein* (1817, Musée d'Art et d'Histoire, Cholet). The painting of *Dido and Aeneas*, of which the Louvre also possesses the composition sketch, marks the summit of his career. The Romantics gleaned much from this original and inspirational lover of a living, radiant antiquity, who is sadly neglected today, Géricault, Delacroix, Cogniet and Scheffer all passing through his dynamic studio.

Hals, Frans
Antwerp, c. 1581/1585 - Haarlem, 1666

ML - *La Bohémienne [The Gypsy Girl]*, c. 1628-1630
Wood. 58 x 52 cm / Dr Louis La Caze bequest, 1869 / M.I. 926

A portraitist specialising in the portrayal of groups, Hals was already immensely fashionable in his own lifetime. His greatest masterpieces are his last pictures, painted when more than eighty years old: the Regents and the Regentesses of the Old Men's Alms House (1664, Frans Halsmuseum, Haarlem). 'Objectivity' and 'Expressionism before its time' have been mentioned in connection with Hals' work, but what fascinated contemporaries was the freedom of his brushwork, bursting forth in portraits of 'characters': *The Bohemian Girl, Malle-Babbe* (Gemäldegalerie, Berlin) and the *Merry Drinker* (Rijksmuseum, Amsterdam). In the 19th century, Manet was bewitched by his vigour, the richness of his blacks and the naturalism of his subjects.

Guardi, Francesco
Venise, 1712 - *ibid.*, 1792

ML - *Le Doge de Venise assiste aux fêtes du jeudi gras sur la Piazzetta [The Doge of Venice Takes Part in the Festivities on the Piazzetta on Shrove Thursday]*, between 1766 and 1770
Canvas. 67 x 100 cm / Seized during the Revolution from the collection of the Comte de Pestre-Senef / Inv. 321

Along with Canaletto (1697-1768), Guardi is the most famous of the Venetian *vedutista* ('view painters'), producing quantities of 'souvenirs' of the Serene Republic, its palaces and festivals for educated foreign patrons. Around 1770, he painted a series of Ducal Festivals commemorating in twelve pictures the accession of Doge Alvise IV Mocenigo (ten in the Louvre; one each at the Musées Royaux des Beaux-Arts, Brussels, and the Musée de Grenoble). Where Canaletto is 'architectural', Guardi favours colour, effects of gleam and shimmer and the imaginative transcription of reality.

Hains, Raymond (Saint-Brieuc, 1926) *et* Villeglé, Jacques
Jacques Mahé de la Villeglé, *known as*
(Quimper, 1926)

CP - *Ach Alma Manetro*, 1949
Torn posters glued to paper on canvas. 58 x 256 cm / Purchase, 1987 / AM 1987-938

Hains and Villeglé became friends at the fine arts school at Rennes, but it was only in 1949 that they discovered the techniques of 'ripping' and 'tearing' posters plastered on walls and 'framing' the images exposed. The *feuilleté* effect of these layered posters, these samples from the real world, telescopes different time-frames, jumbling up word and image. In 1957, their first great Parisian exhibition was entitled 'Law of July 29, 1881', referring to the law against flyposters. They were to continue this application of the Duchamp readymade to street life, becoming instrumental in the birth of Nouveau Réalisme.

Hantaï, Simon
Bia, Hungary, 1922

CP - *Peinture (Ecriture rose)*, 1958-1959
Coloured ink, gold-leaf on linen canvas. 329.5 x 424.5 cm / Gift of the artist, 1985 / AM 1984-783

After training in Budapest, Hantaï arrived in Paris in 1949 where his debut exhibition in 1953 was hailed by André Breton. *Ecriture rose* is a breakthrough work in which he explores paths opened up by Pollock. Later he adopted the technique of *pliage*, folding and painting over large stretches of screwed up and, then, unfolded canvas only later mounted on a stretcher. In addition to the radical change this has visually on the end result, such a practice simultaneously transforms both the artistic act and one's understanding of space.

Holbein the Younger, Hans
Augsbourg, c. 1497/1498 - London, 1543

ML - *Erasmus*, after 1523
Wood. 42 x 32 cm / Collection of Louis XIV / Inv. 1345

Son of Hans Holbein the Elder (c. 1460/1465-1524), he first settled in Basle where he was much in demand among the trading classes. In 1533-1536, during his second stay in London, he joined the service of Henry VIII, so becoming one of the most prominent artists in all Europe. He painted three portraits of Erasmus (National Gallery, London, on deposit from the Radnor Collection; and the Kunstmuseum, Basle, for the two others) that date from before his first journey to England; the philosopher probably recommended him to Thomas More. A master of line, Holbein was equally famous for now vanished, large-scale works in which the portraitist gave ample display of his talents as a decorator. At the acme of his fame, he fell victim to the plague in London in 1543.

Homer, Winslow
Boston, 1836 - Prout's Neck, Maine, 1910

MO - *Summer Night*, 1890
Oil on canvas. 76.7 x 102 cm / Acquired in 1900 / R.F.1977-427

Excelling as a draughtsman, Homer started out as an illustrator before devoting his talents to open-air subjects, in particular following a Parisian visit in 1866-1867. The sea lies at the centre of his work. Though rendered with realistic touches, the art of this great traveller bewitched by uncharted horizons never forsook its lyricism.

Ingres, Jean Auguste Dominique
Montauban, 1780 - Paris, 1867

ML - *Mademoiselle Caroline Rivière*, 1806 Salon
Canvas. 100 x 70 cm / Bequest of Mme Paul Rivière, sister-in-law of the sitter, 1870 / M.I. 1447

ML - *La Grande Odalisque*, 1814
Canvas. 91 x 162 cm / Acquired in 1899 / R.F. 1158

ML - *L'Apothéose d'Homère* [The Apotheosis of Homer], 1827
Canvas. 386 x 512 cm / Formerly the ceiling of the Salle Clarac. Removed in 1855 and replaced by a replica / Inv. 5417

ML - *Portrait de Louis-François Bertin*, 1832
Canvas. 116 x 95 cm / Acquired from the descendants of the sitter, 1897 / R.F. 1071

MO - *La Vierge à la hostie* [The Virgin of the Host], 1854
Canvas. Diameter 113 cm / Acquired in 1851. On deposit from the Louvre, 1986 / Inv. 20088

ML - *Le Bain turc* [Le Bain turc or The Turkish Bath], 1862
Canvas stuck on wood. 110 x 110 cm; diameter 108 cm / Gift of the Société des Amis du Louvre, with the assistance of Maurice Fenaille, 1911 / R.F. 1934

A musician who throughout his life liked to play the violin with friends, Ingres' interest focused predominantly on the harmony of bodies, on a 'style' that would transcend the imitation of nature, on what he termed 'the right note'. Contemporaries criticised the way he seemed to deform his models: the 'overlarge' head of Caroline Rivière, the 'elongated' back of the Odalisque, the rotundities of *Le Bain turc* and Mary's face in *The Virgin of the Host*. Obsessed by form, Ingres modifies reality to make it fit into the mould of ideal beauty as he understands it, persisting in his allotted task with unwavering constancy, from his earliest pictures to the magnificent triumphs of his old age.

Jacquet, Alain
Neuilly-sur-Seine, 1939

CP - *Le Déjeuner sur l'herbe*, 1964
Acrylic and screen-printing on canvas. 172.5 x 196 cm / Purchase, 1996 / AM 1996-428

Reacting against the art of the 1950s and Abstract Expressionism, since 1960 Alain Jacquet has been developing a style based on enlarged images and on quotation (series with titles like *Jeux de Jacquet*, *Cylindres*, *Camouflages Images d'Epinal*), sometimes letting a raster of dots show through. He reworks not only Botticelli, Michelangelo and Bronzino, but also De Chirico, Matisse, Picasso, Mondrian... Close in spirit to Martial Raysse, as well as to American Pop artists like Andy Warhol and Roy Lichtenstein, Jacquet quit that road in 1964, because, as he explained to critic Philippe Dagen (*Le Monde*, 9 May 2002, p. 27): 'At that time, American Pop had stagnated; it was an image of American society, whereas I was already looking for something else — a dialectic between the abstract and the figurative through enlarged images.'

Kandinsky, Wassily
Moscow, 1866 - Neuilly-sur-Seine, 1944

CP - *Bild mit rotem Fleck* [Painting with Red Dot], 1914
Oil on canvas. 130 x 130 cm / Gift of Nina Kandinsky, 1976 / AM 1976-853

With his first abstract watercolour (c. 1910, Centre Pompidou), Kandinsky achieved the 'leap into abstraction' that he had been edging towards since 1908. A theoretician of the avant-garde in his *On the Spiritual in Art*, and joining Klee in the Weimar Bauhaus where he taught 'science of art', Kandinsky founded a new aesthetics that was determinant for the future history of 20th-century art. On the 17th of February 1914, Kandinsky wrote to Franz Marc: 'My head is like a beehive or, worse still, a Futurist manifesto, full to bursting and horrendously muddled'. The process of distillation that followed these upheavals resulted in his finest works whose repercussions were enormous, particularly after his death.

Klee, Paul
Münchenbuchsee, Switzerland, 1879 - Locarno, Switzerland, 1940

CP - *Pfeil im Garten [Arrow in a Garden]*, 1929
Oil and tempera on linen canvas. 70 x 50.2 cm / Gift of Louise and Michel Leiris, 1984 / AM 1984-557

A violinist like Ingres, the young Klee worshipped Cézanne, became acquainted with Kandinsky, Franz Marc and Jawlensky, and translated Robert Delaunay's *Essay on Light*. From 1921, he held a teaching post at the Bauhaus. Klee's visual vocabulary was highly personal: arrows, fruit, snakes, trees and windows abbreviated to a few significant features in the way of an alphabet, sometimes legible, sometimes indecipherable, Runic, Glagolitic or Cretan. 'Primitive' yet erudite, it is a mathematical language that provides the key to a space whose true dimension only the artist knows. From this diversity arose an art to which he was committed heart and soul, in particular in his last years when his energies were sapped by disease: 'Art does not give an account of the visible, it renders visible.'

Klein, Yves
Nice, 1928 - Paris, 1962

CP - *Grande Anthropophagie bleue. Hommage à Tennessee Williams (ANT 76)*, 1960
Pure pigment and synthetic resins on paper glue-mounted on canvas. 275 x 407 cm / Purchase, 2000 / AM 2000-154

Like the good judoka he was, Klein used the strength of colour to throw over traditional painting and reduce it to submission. I.K.B. ('International Klein Blue') became a distinctive and publicly visible trademark. The Centre Pompidou possesses works characteristic of his evolution: monochromes (the most familiar part of his oeuvre), 'anthropometries' (impressions left by naked models daubed in blue paint), and the *Portrait-relief of Arman*, a bronze painted in blue on a gold ground. In 1958 at the Iris Clert gallery in Paris, Klein organised an 'Exposition du Vide', where 2,000 visitors were subjects in an artistic experiment of looking at the blank walls of a room — the work itself, in which they were also participants.

Klimt, Gustave
Vienna, 1862 - *ibid.*, 1918

MO - *Rosiers sous les arbres [Roses Under the Trees]*, c. 1905
Oil`on canvas, 110 x 110 cm / Acquired in 1980 / R.F.1980-195

A decorative artist trained in the tradition of history painting, Klimt's first apprenticeship was to collaborate on the ceiling of the Burgtheater in Vienna. Subjected to the influence of Puvis de Chavannes and his vast murals, as well as of French Impressionism — a style at odds with the art he was beginning to practise at that time — Klimt developed an extraordinary synthesis, in particular in his landscapes, where employing Pointillist technique, he built up a natural yet almost abstract architecture that did not jettison the symbolic dimension of his highly individual transcription of nature.

Lagrenée (the Younger), Jean-Jacques
Paris, 1739 - *ibid.*, 1821

ML - *Allégorie relative à l'établissement du Muséum [Allegory Regarding the Establishment of the Museum]*, 1783
Canvas. 52 x 68 cm / Acquired in 1998 / R.F. 1998-6

This allegory produced by the talented decorative painter Lagrenée 'the Younger' — to distinguish him from his brother painter, Louis-Jean-François (1725-1805) — seems to give the lie to the oft-repeated idea that the Louvre museum arose solely from the democratic will of the Revolution of 1789. Exhibited at the 1783 Salon, the picture was accompanied by the following commentary: 'Close to the pedestal on which can be seen the bust of the king [Louis XVI], Immortality receives the portrait of M. le comte d'Angiviller [the first to have proposed opening the royal collections to the public] from the hands of Painting, Justice and Benevolence so as to place it within his temple. Behind the figure of Immortality, the Genius of the Arts raises a curtain and one glimpses part of the great gallery where several smaller geniuses are shown fetching and carrying the king's pictures.'

La Tour, Georges de
Vic-sur-Seille, Lorraine, 1593 - Lunéville, 1652

ML - *Le Tricheur [The Card Cheat]*, c. 1635
Canvas. 106 x 146 cm / Acquired in 1972 / R.F. 1972-8

ML - *Madeleine à la veilleuse [The Magdalene with the Nightlight or The Penitent Magdalene]*, between 1630 and 1635
Canvas. 128 x 94 cm / Acquired in 1949 / R.F. 1949-11

Although rediscovered only around 1915, in his lifetime the great 17th-century Lorraine painter achieved considerable fame, and was known even at the court of Louis XIII, who granted him the title of Painter in Ordinary. Some thirty-five works by his brush are known, religious subjects as well as genre scenes, day as well as nighttime subjects. The popularity of this meditative, mysterious art is attested by the many early replicas. Another version of *The Card Cheat* is housed in the Kimbell Museum (Fort Worth, Texas), while other *Magdalenes* by this artist feature in the National Gallery, Washington, the Metropolitan, New York, and in the County Museum, Los Angeles.

Le Brun, Charles
Paris, 1619 - *ibid.*, 1690

ML - *Le Passage du Granique [The Passage of the Granicus]*, 1665
Canvas. 470 x 120.9 cm / Collection of Louis XIV / Inv. 2894

A pupil of Simon Vouet, who discovered Rome with Poussin, Le Brun started out in grand-style portraiture (*The Chancelier Séguier on a Horse*, about 1655, Louvre), before laying down the principles of French classicism in *The Tent of Darius* (1660-1661, Versailles) executed for Louis XIV. Premier Peintre du Roi, he continued his series of history paintings with four immense canvases for the Louvre recounting the deeds of Alexander the Great (*The Passage of the Granicus*, *The Battle of Arbela*, *Alexander and Porus*, *Entry to Babylon*), before carrying out decorations for the since destroyed Staircase of the Ambassadors and for the Galerie des Glaces (Versailles), whose iconographic programme glorifies the triumph of absolute monarchy.

Léger, Fernand
Argentan, 1881 - Gif-sur-Yvette, 1955

CP - *La Couseuse [Woman Sewing]*, 1909-1910
Oil on canvas. 73 x 54 cm / Gift of Louise and Michel Leiris, 1984 / AM 1984-578

CP - *La Noce*, c. 1911
Oil on canvas. 257 x 206 cm / Gift of Alfred Flechtheim, 1937 / AM 2146 P

Like Veronese and David, Léger revelled in expansive subjects and generous surfaces. As he wrote to the dealer D. H. Kahnweiler in 1919: 'I have used many [...] mechanical components in my pictures. [...] Modern life is full of elements for us; we just have to learn how to use them.' His constructions of tubes and scaffolding, his figures with massive feet and broad hands, are heroes from a mechanical world rising up into an urban, industrial light, representatives of a new collective and productive history.

Le Nain, Antoine *or* Louis, *also known as* The Brothers Le Nain
Laon, between 1597 and 1610 - Paris, 1648

ML - *Peasant Family in the Home*, c. 1642
Canvas. 113 x 159 cm / Arthur Pernolet bequest, 1915 / R.F. 2081

The brothers Le Nain (together with a third brother Mathieu [Laon, c. 1607 - Paris, 1677]) have posed many an art-historical quandary as regards attribution, so much so that it is sometimes still hard to differentiate between the various family members. Their work was long disregarded, until rediscovered in the slipstream of 19th-century Realism. Of peasant stock, the Le Nains' career nonetheless unfolded in Paris. Though they also painted a few portraits and mythological works (*Bacchus and Ariadne* in the museum at Orléans), they specialised in genre scenes depicting the life of humble folk in an amalgam of the Flemish and Caravaggesque traditions, placed in the service of extraordinary psychological penetration.

Leonardo da Vinci, Leonardo di ser Piero da Vinci, *known as*
Vinci, Tuscany, 1452 - Amboise, France, 1519

ML - *Portrait d'une dame de la cour de Milan* or *La Belle Ferronnière [Portrait of a Lady of the Court at Milan]*, c. 1495-1499
Wood. 63 x 45 cm / Collection of François I, then of Louis XIV / Inv. 778

ML - *La Gioconda [Mona Lisa]*, between 1503 and 1506
Wood. 77 x 53 cm / (The circumstances under which the picture entered the royal collections have never been adequately determined.) / Inv. 779

ML - *Saint-Jean Baptiste [St John the Baptist]*, 1513-1516
Wood. 69 x 57 cm / Collection of Louis XIV (Acquired in 1661 from the heirs of Cardinal Mazarin) / Inv. 775

The Louvre houses a fine collection of pictures by Leonardo as well as some extraordinary drawings, including the portrait of *Isabella d'Este* (1500). In addition to the *Mona Lisa*, which has been in the royal collections since François I invited the artist to France (it is perhaps a portrait of the wife of Francesco del Giocondo, though it is not even known whether her name actually was 'Monna Lisa'), there is the *Virgin of the Rocks*, a masterpiece from his Milan period, *La Belle Ferronnière*, one of his most beautiful portraits, and his last work, *St John the Baptist*. Theoretician, engineer, philosopher: it was Leonardo's avowed intent to 'become universal'.

Le Sueur, Eustache
Paris, 1616 - *ibid.*, 1655

ML - *La Dédicace d'une église des Chartreux [Dedication of a Carthusian Church]*, c. 1645-1648
Wood. 191 x 287 cm / Seized during the Revolution / Inv. 8049

A pupil of Vouet and an architectural painter of great refinement, Le Sueur is a master of subtle chromatic harmonies, of balanced and euphonious compositions, qualities that earned him the sobriquet 'the French Raphael'. With their lofty spirituality and formal perfection, the pictures composing the *Cycle of the Life of St Bruno*, produced between 1645 and 1648, show a more austere yet also more original aspect of his oeuvre. The most important works were presented to Louis XVI in 1776 by the Carthusian monks of Paris. The entire cycle was got together later, testimony to the fact that these works were regarded as one of the finest achievements of French painting and religious art alike.

Liotard, Jean-Etienne
Geneva, 1702 - *ibid.*, 1789

ML - *Mr Levett et Mlle Glavany en costumes turcs [Mr Levett and Mlle Glavany in Turkish Costume]*, c. 1740
Board. 24.7 x 36.4 cm / Acquired in 1995 with the participation of the Fonds du Patrimoine / R.F. 1995-14

Nicknamed the 'peintre turc', this artist from Geneva who spent the years 1738 to 1742 in Constantinople, lived his life as if on the stage, affecting to wear the very Oriental garb for which his oeuvre is best known. No less than twenty self-portraits by his hand are preserved. In spite of all the characteristics of the artist's later work — concision, refinement, clarity of line, an imperceptible facture — it is possible that this small picture, which entered the Louvre only in 1995, was actually painted when in Turkey. His illusionism culminates in his most celebrated work, *La Belle Chocolatière* (Gemäldegalerie, Dresden), and in pastels, such as the portrait of *Madame d'Epinay* (c. 1759, Musée d'Art et d'Histoire, Geneva), which was much admired by Ingres.

Magritte, René
Lessines, Belgium, 1898 - Brussels, 1967

CP - *Le Viol [The Rape]*, 1945
Oil on canvas. 63.3 x 50.4 cm / Georgette Magritte bequest, 1987 / AM 1987-1097

As a friend of André Breton and of the Surrealist circle, Magritte's art is based on the unlikely encounter and on condensation, creating surprise effects that can be tinged with black humour or arouse feelings of anguish. His technique aims at a neutral perfection subordinated to the subject, even though, from 1943 to 1947, fleeting memories of Renoir's more fluid paint substance can occasionally ruffle the smooth surface. *The Rape*, a very famous piece, illustrated the cover of the catalogue to the 1945 Surrealist Exhibition at the Galerie La Boétie.

Malevich, Kasimir
Kiev, Ukraine, 1878 - Leningrad, today St-Petersburg, 1935

CP - *Croix [noire] [Black Cross or Cross]*, 1915
Oil on canvas. 80 x 79.5 cm / Gift of the Scaler Foundation and the Beaubourg Foundation, 1980 / AM 1980-1

With Kandinsky and Mondrian, Malevich was one of the first painters to completely abandon the subject. Associated with the Russian avant-garde of Larionov and Goncharova, as well as with Kandinsky, he was attracted for a time by Cubism. In 1915, he exhibited his first great statement: *Black Square on a White Ground*, and developed the theory of 'Suprematism'. In 1918, he painted the *White Square on a White Ground* (MoMA, New York), before publishing *The Non-Objective World* (*Die gegenstandslose Welt*) thanks to the Bauhaus. The five *arkhitektony* (architectural models) preserved at the Centre Pompidou transpose Suprematism into the three dimensions of architecture. Unfolding back in Soviet Russia, his last period is characterised by a return to the figure.

Manet, Edouard
Paris, 1832 - *ibid.*, 1883

MO - *Olympia*, 1863
Oil on canvas. 130.5 x 190 cm / Donated to the State through public subscription initiated by Claude Monet, 1890 / R.F. 644

MO - *Le Déjeuner sur l'herbe*, 1863
Oil on canvas. 208 x 264.5 cm / Gift of Etienne Moreau-Nélaton, 1906 / R.F. 1668

MO - *Portrait de Emile Zola*, 1868
Oil on canvas. 146 x 114 cm / Lifetime Enjoyment Gift of Mme Emile Zola in 1918; entered the Louvre on her death in 1925 / R.F. 2205

Modernity in painting is played out in these three key pictures: *Olympia* is often contrasted with Alexandre Cabanel's *Birth of Venus* (Musée d'Orsay), a mythological painting that triumphed at the Salon of 1863. *Le Déjeuner sur l'herbe* illustrates the famous dictum: 'Only one thing is true: to paint what you see without a moment's thought'. Manet left off mythology to celebrate modernity, fulfilling Baudelaire's wish for a painter 'who could show us how great we are in our neckties and shiny boots'. Zola was the first to give Manet his rightful place, playing the same role of enlightened critic that Baudelaire had fulfilled for Delacroix.

Masson, André
Balagny-sur-Thérain, 1896 - Paris, 1987

CP - *Le Labyrinthe*, 1938
Oil on canvas. 120 x 61 cm / Gift of Basil and Elisa Goulandris, 1982 / AM 1982-46

Initially tempted by Cubism, a friend of Gris, Derain, Miró and André Breton, Masson invented sand-painting, practised automatic drawing and was a committed Surrealist, though he was briefly excluded from Breton's group in 1929. A highly literate artist, he illustrated the great myths of antiquity as well as the Marquis de Sade. In 1965, he decorated the ceiling of the Théâtre de l'Odéon in Paris. A reviver of legends and a first-rate draughtsman, Masson has not yet attained the status he deserves in the 20th-century canon.

Mathieu, Georges
Boulogne-sur-Mer, 1921

CP - *Les Capétiens partout*, 1954
Oil on canvas. 295 x 600 cm / Gift of the Galerie Lacarde, 1956 / AM 3447 P

Spiritualist, lyrical, fascinated by the Far East and by calligraphy, Mathieu had links with Wols, Hans Hartung and Atlan. The focal point of the 'Lyrical Abstraction' movement, he single-handedly orchestrated a return to history painting (*Homage to the Maréchal de Turenne*, 1952) whose ironic distance has not always been correctly understood. He painted in public, at great speed and on large formats, with an audacity and a facility that can be a source of wonder or of irritation. A monarchist in politics — hence *Les Capétiens partout*, a vibrant homage to the dynasty that at one time reigned over territories from Europe to Brazil — he gave himself the air of a gentleman artist who would have liked to have inherited Le Brun's or Boucher's title of 'Painter to the King'. Active in the porcelain factory of Sèvres and at the Gobelins tapestry factory, in 1974 Mathieu signed a 10-franc coin for the Mint of which the French long remained fond.

Matisse, Henri
Le Cateau-Cambrésis, 1869 - Nice, 1954

MO - *Luxe, calme et volupté*, 1904
Oil on canvas. 98.5 x 118.5 cm / Allocated in lieu of death duties, 1982 / AM 1982-96

CP - *Figure décorative sur fond ornemental [Decorative figure Against an Ornamental Background]*, 1925-1926
Oil on canvas. 130 x 98 cm / Purchase, 1938 / AM 2149 P

CP - *Le Rêve [The Dream]*, 1935
Oil on canvas. 81 x 65 cm / Purchase, 1979 / AM 1979-106

In 1904, in Signac's house at St-Tropez, Matisse even tried his hand at Divisionism, *Luxe, calme et volupté* providing ample evidence of the master's hesitations. His subsequent career is well documented in the collections of the Centre Pompidou: the disconcerting *Porte-fenêtre à Collioure* (1914), an almost abstract piece that was recognised as a major achievement only at a much later date, shows an opening walled up with a coat of black paint; *La Blouse roumaine* (1940), a work of absolute purity whose popularity with the public has never waned; the *Grand Intérieur Rouge* (1948), the culmination of the last years; and the most successful work in gouache-painted cut-out paper, *La Tristesse du Roi*.

Matta, Roberto,
Roberto Sebastian Matta Echaurren, *known as*
Chiloé, Santiago de Chili, 1911 - Civita Vecchia, 2002

CP - *Xpace and the Ego*, 1945
Oil on canvas. 202.2 x 457.2 cm / Purchase, 1983 / AM 1983-94

Matta settled in Europe in 1930 where he was influenced by Magritte, and then by Dalí, Picasso and André Breton. In the United States during the Second World War, he participated in the activities of the Surrealist group, from which he was eventually excluded in 1948. He then worked between Europe and the Americas, producing large-format works that were sometimes grouped into cycles for which he conceived political (against the conflict in Algeria or the Vietnam War...) or literary subjects ('illustrating' Shakespeare and Cervantes) with deliberately enigmatic titles. In 1956, with a vast mural painting, Matta participated in the decoration of one of least-liked and least-known 20th-century monuments in all Paris, the head offices of UNESCO.

Metsys, Quentin
Louvain, c. 1465/1466 - Antwerp, 1530

ML - *Le Prêteur et sa femme [The Moneylender and his Wife]*, 1514
Wood. 70.5 x 67 cm / Acquired in 1806 / Inv. 1444

Very popular in his lifetime, Metsys forged a synthesis between the lessons of 15th-century Flemish art and the contemporary Italian tradition. Remaining close to Van Eyck in the trompe-l'oeil rendering of fabric and in allusions such as the convex looking-glass, Metsys handled perspective with rigour, detailing every last accessory with illusionistic precision. The subject chosen, frequent enough in a world in which patrons were no longer ashamed to show their wealth, had already been treated by Petrus Christus (*St Egidius*, 1449, Metropolitan Museum, New York), and gave rise to many versions by various Flemish masters.

Millet, Jean-François
Gruchy, Manche, 1814 - Barbizon, 1875

MO - *Le Printemps [Spring]*, 1868-1873
Oil on canvas. 86 x 111 cm / Gift of Mme Frédéric Hartmann, 1887 / R.F. 509

Though he died at Barbizon, Millet remained on the margins of the group of artists who gathered in this village near Fontainebleau. His true homeland was the Cotentin around Cherbourg on the Channel, whose peasants he portrayed with a Biblical grandeur that fascinated Van Gogh. *L'Angélus* (Musée d'Orsay) has been so frequently reproduced in chromolithographs, on petit-point tapestries and on chocolate box lids that today it is difficult to look at afresh. The irksome fame of this deeply nostalgic, even reactionary, rural scene that appeared in the middle of the Industrial Revolution masks the fact that Millet is one of the most interesting Realist artists, with a Realism which regularly resorts to symbols, able to create sublime landscapes imbued with the awesome power of Nature.

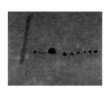

Miró, Joan
Barcelona, 1893 - Palma de Majorca, 1983

CP - *Bleu II [Blue II]*, 1961
Oil on canvas. 270 x 355 cm / Gift of the Menil Foundation, 1984 / AM 1984-357

The vastness of Miró's *Blues*, in which the eye can easily get lost, goes hand in hand with canvases in which smaller forms appear comparable to the fly that settles on the vast *Bull* by Paulus Potter, a Dutch artist of the 17th century (Mauritshuis, The Hague): 'I was entranced by the capacity of Dutch painters to emphasise tiny points like grains of dust, to attract one's attention to a minute spark amid the darkness.' Miró's work does not in fact aim so much at recapturing the supposed spontaneity of children's drawings as in furthering the history of representation.

Mondrian, Piet,
Pieter Cornelis Mondriaan, *known as*
Amersfoort, Netherlands, 1872 - New York, 1944

CP - *Composition II avec rouge et bleu [Composition II with Red and Blue]*, 1937
Oil on canvas. 75 x 60.5 cm / Purchase, 1975 / AM 1975-53

A founder of abstraction like Kandinsky and Malevich, Mondrian started out with figurative landscapes caressed by memories of the Barbizon School and Impressionism, before making the lessons of Cubism his own. Painted in Paris in 1937, *Composition II with Red and Blue* is an example of his 'grid' period as it stood shortly before his departure for New York where he settled in 1940. The Manhattan cityscape resulted in new works from which black was excluded (*New York City I*, 1941-1942, Centre Pompidou). Immediately after his death, Mondrian's oeuvre was acclaimed as truly revolutionary, while in France, following his first posthumous exhibition of 1957, his influence was enormous.

Monet, Claude
Paris, 1840 - Giverny, 1926

MO - *Coquelicots[Poppies or Field Poppies]*, 1873
Oil on canvas. 50 x 65 cm / Gift of Étienne Moreau-Nélaton, 1906 / R.F. 1676

MO - *La Gare Saint-Lazare*, 1877
Oil on canvas. 75.5 x 104 cm / Gustave Caillebotte bequest, 1894 / R.F. 2775

MO - *Essai de figure en plein air*, known as *Femme à l'ombrelle tournée vers la gauche [Study of a Figure in the Open Air, known as Woman with a Parasol Turning to the Left]*, 1886
Oil on canvas. 131 x 88 cm / Gift of Michel Monet, the artist's son, 1927 / R.F. 2621

MO - *La Cathédrale de Rouen. Le Portail, soleil matinal. Harmonie bleue [Rouen Cathedral. Harmony in Blue]*, 1893
Oil on canvas. 91 x 63 cm / Isaac de Camondo bequest, 1911 / R.F. 2000

MO - *Le Bassin aux nymphéas: harmonie rose [Waterlily Pond: Harmony in Pink]*, 1900
Oil on canvas. 89.5 x 100 cm / Isaac de Camondo bequest, 1911 / R.F. 2005

MO - *Nymphéas bleus [Blue Waterlilies]*, c. 1916-1919
Oil on canvas. 200 x 200 cm / Acquired in 1981 / R.F. 1981-40

MO - *Le Déjeuner sur l'herbe*, 1865
Oil on canvas. Cutted by Monet in 1884.
Left section : 418 x 150 cm / Gift of Wildenstein, 1957 / R.F. 1957.7
Central section : 248 x 217 cm / Allocated in lieu of death duties, 1987 / R.F. 1987.12

The aged master of the *Waterlilies* in the Orangery remains the most popular of all French painters — the creator of a 'total work of art' that paves the way for the 20th century, for Matisse, Pollock, Rothko. The Musée d'Orsay possesses a number of masterpieces, including *Le Déjeuner sur l'herbe*, an 'open-air' riposte to Manet that long languished in Monet's studio and that survives today in a fragmentary state. From the vilified figure at whose 1874 *Impression, Sunrise* (1872, Musée Marmottan, Paris) critics famously scoffed, to the artist who in his own lifetime witnessed fourteen of his pictures enter the Louvre in 1914 through the Camondo bequest, Monet's path, marked by the long line of 'series', such as the Cathedrals, the Poplars, the Haystacks, the Waterlilies, was that of one of the very last painters to have begun by taking reality as the model, yet who ended by transfiguring it in the crucible of a personal vision — a path that recalls that of Wagner from the episodic *Rienzi* to the leitmotifs of *Parsifal*…

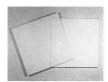

Morellet, François
Cholet, France, 1926

CP - *Superposition et transparence, carré derrière 0°90°-carré devant, 20°-110° [Superposition and Transparency, Square Behind 0°90° B Square in Front, 20°B110°]*, 1980
Acrylic on two superposed canvases. 256.5 x 363 cm / Gift of the artist, 1987 / AM 1987-945

Humorist and purist at one and the same time, influenced by Mondrian as much as by the Conceptual art in which he was a pioneer, Morellet is determined to demystify the image of the artistic demiurge, creative heir to the great Renaissance masters. Since 1950, Morellet has been a practitioner of an abstraction whose formal rigour does not preclude wordplay or puns nor appeals to randomness (*Aleatory Repartition of Triangles in accordance with the Odd and Even Numbers from a Telephone Directory*, 1958, Musée de Grenoble). Of a scientific bent, interested in Kinetic art, working with neon tubes, his pieces are always integrated into the architecture of the exhibition space. As often with Morellet, the title of the work is here a description that details, to a limited extent at least, the rules of the game.

Murillo, Bartolomé Esteban
Seville, 1618 - *ibid.*, 1682

ML - *Le Jeune Mendiant [The Young Beggar or The Beggar Boy]*, c. 1645-1650
Canvas. 134 x 100 cm / Collection of Louis XVI (Acquired in 1782) / Inv. 933

In the line of Ribera and Zurbarán, Murillo was responsible for some of the greatest works of religious painting of the Spanish Golden Age. To the chromatic rigour and Baroque gloom of the Spanish school, he brought a new sensitivity verging on sentimentality that thrived in portraits and in genre scenes showing the common people. Greatly admired in the 19th century, in our time his place in the gallery of great Spanish painters has receded, and he still awaits rehabilitation.

Nemours, Aurélie
Paris, 1910

CP - *Sans titre (Ligne) [Untitled (Line)]*, 1988-1990
Acrylic on canvas. 80 x 720 cm / Gift of the Scaler Foundation in memory of Sylvie Boissonnas, 2001 / AM 2001-55

Before discovering Mondrian, Nemours — as her debut one-woman show in 1953 attests — had already started assembling squares of pure colour that divide the picture space with mathematical exactness. Through a long line of series (*Dwellings*, *Cornerstones*, *Chessboards* and *Crosses*), her work led to vividly coloured monochromes, though her palette can limit itself to black and white. With dogged determination, her latest paintings and prints continue her research with rigour and an unwillingness to compromise.

Noland, Kenneth
Asheville, North Carolina, 1924

CP - *First*, 1958
Acrylic on canvas. 149.5 x 150.5 cm / Purchase, 1976 / AM 1976-590

An advocate of pure colour and opponent of Abstract Expressionism, Noland's very large canvases often present concentric circles painted in acrylic with a roller. His work on optics lead him to apply stripes and diamond shapes on to spaces left blank, it being often impossible to differentiate the ground from what might be termed the 'motif' or 'form'.

Panini, Giovanni Paolo
Piacenza, c. 1691/1692 - Rome, 1765

ML - *Fête musicale donnée par le cardinal de la Rochefoucauld au theatre Argentina de Rome le 15 juillet 1747 à l'occasion du marriage du Dauphin de France, Louis; fils de Louis XV avec Marie-Josèphe de Saxe [Musical Performance Given by Cardinal de la Rochefoucauld at the Teatro Argentina in Rome on July 15th 1747 on the Occasion of the Wedding of the French Dauphin, Louis, Son of Louis XV with Marie-Josephe of Saxony]*
Canvas. 204 x 247 cm / Collection of Louis-Philippe (probably acquired before March 1832) / Inv. 414

Panini's is a set-painter's talent, an observer of aristocratic society in Rome, whose works were produced for an international clientele. A painter of *vedute* ('views'), he favoured large compositions, such as the recreation of the musical festival given on the occasion of the Dauphin's wedding, where the details and the picturesque attitudes of the figures are finely observed. He also created large-format works, which show imaginary museums or combine in a single canvas different views of Roman monuments (*Ancient Rome and Modern Rome*, Louvre).

Parmentier, Michel
Paris, 1938 - *ibid.*, 2000

CP - *Rouge [Red]*, 1968
Oil on waxed canvas. 233.5 x 240 cm / Purchase, 1986 / AM 1986-158

In December 1966, Daniel Buren, Olivier Mosset, Michel Parmentier and Niele Toroni founded the group BMPT — the initials of their surnames. Its aim was to free painting from any purpose other than itself. Buren's work derives solely from vertical stripes, Mosset's from the circle, Parmentier's from the horizontal line, while Toroni opted for the mark left by the paint-brush. A year later, Parmentier left the quartet and, from 1968 to 1983, stopped making paintings entirely — without, however, ceasing 'to be a painter', as his silence is to be interpreted as an artistic act. After 1983, he resumed his work based on horizontal stripes.

Picabia, Francis,
François Marie Martinez-Picabia, *known as*
Paris, 1879 - *ibid.*, 1953

CP - *L'Œil cacodylate*, 1921
Oil on canvas and collages. 148.6 x 117.4 cm / Purchase, 1967 / AM 4408 P

Before his meeting with Duchamp, Picabia had tried his hand somewhat tardily at Impressionism, Fauvism and abstraction: after a first trip to the United States, he embarked on large canvases that impressed Apollinaire. Captivated by the work of Tristan Tzara and by the Dada movement generally, this unclassifiable artist went on to totally reject this period, exhibiting *Transparences* of which the Centre Pompidou possesses a fine collection. For a long time critics were interested only in his Surrealist phase: his complex and multiform corpus is in the process of being re-evaluated today.

Picasso, Pablo
Pablo Ruiz y Picasso, *known as*
Málaga, 1881 - Mougins, 1973

CP - *Arlequin [Harlequin]*, 1923
Oil on canvas. 130 x 97 cm / Baronne Eva Gourgaud bequest, 1965 / AM 4313 P

CP - *Stage curtain for the ballet Mercure*, 1924
Tempera on canvas. 392 x 501 cm Purchase, 1955 / AM 3377 P

CP - *Confidences*, 1934
Tempera and papiers collés on canvas. 194 x 170 cm / Gift of Marie Cuttoli, 1963 / AM 4210 P

CP - *La Muse*, 1935
Oil on canvas. 130 x 162 cm / Gift of the artist, 1947 / AM 2726 P

In 1985, the Picasso Museum opened in Paris with more than two hundred paintings and almost as many sculptures, not counting graphic works, relief-paintings, *papiers collés*, and part of the private collection of the greatest artist of the 20th century. The Centre Pompidou, however, possesses many significant works by the creator of *Les Demoiselles d'Avignon* (1906-1907, MoMA, New York) and of *Guernica* (1937, Museo Reina Sofia, Madrid). The collections contain works from the period of the invention of Cubism, of the post-1918 return to the figure, from the rivalry-cum-emulation in which he was involved with Surrealists and with Matisse, as well as powerful works from his later years, that together allow one to obtain an overall grasp of the main strands of his life and work.

Piero della Francesca
Borgo San Sepolcro, Arezzo, vers 1422 - *ibid.*, 1492

ML - *Portrait of Sigismondo Pandolfe Malatesta*, c. 1450-1451
Wood. 44 x 34 cm / Acquired in 1978 / R.F. 1978-1

Dying on the day America was 'discovered', Piero, who in his own time had been a significant influence on Perugino and Signorelli, was almost totally neglected until the 20th century. The cycle of frescoes for the church of San Francesco in Arezzo, the *Flagellation* at Urbino (Galleria Nazionale delle Marche), the *Sacra Conversazione* in Milan (Brera) number today among the most famous works of the Quattrocento. In 1451, Piero painted a fresco of *St Sigismund and Sigismondo Pandolfe Malatesta* (Tempio Malatestiano, Rimini); the work in the Louvre portraying Malatesta to the same dimensions is perhaps a complete study or a derivation from that portrait.

Pissarro, Camille
St-Thomas, West Indies, 1830 - Paris, 1903

MO - *Gelée blanche [Hoar Frost]*, 1873
Oil on canvas. 65 x 93 cm / Enriqueta Alsop bequest, 1972 / R.F. 1972-27

Discovering painting through Corot, Courbet and Ingres at the 1855 World Fair, Pissarro then grew close to Monet and to the group that was to found the Impressionist movement in 1874. Though Pissarro's compositions are rigorous, this did not prevent him from observing landscapes directly, and his discoveries were heeded by Gauguin and Cézanne, Seurat and Signac. It was not one-way traffic, however: under Seurat's influence, Pissarro passed through a 'Divisionist' phase, before returning to his earlier manner, executing a famous series of views of Paris that capture 'modern' life in a capital which, in the end of the 19th century, was in the midst of a process of urban renewal.

Pollock, Jackson
Cody, Wyoming, 1912 - Springs, Long Island NY, 1956

CP - *Number 26 A, Black and White*, 1948
Glycerophtalic paint on canvas. 205 x 121.7 cm / Allocated in lieu of death duties, 1984 / AM 1984-312

Action Painting: Pollock lays the canvas on the ground, bores holes in his paint-pots, squeezes tubes over the surface. Standing over the picture as he paints, he maps out the space, keeping his body in constant motion. A projection of the self, and therefore of the Unconscious, on to the surface, the work is a record of the artist at a precise moment of his existence. Pollock absorbed the lessons of Surrealism and paved the way for a new American painting. Dying tragically in a car accident, his life was transformed into a modern art-historical legend.

Poussin, Nicolas
Les Andelys, 1594 - Rome, 1665

ML - *Echo and Narcissus*, c. 1640
Canvas. 74 x 100 cm / Collection of Louis XIV (acquired in 1682) / Inv. 7297

ML - *Les Bergers d'Arcadie [The Shepherds of Arcadia]*, c. 1640
Canvas. 85 x 121 cm / Collection of Louis XIV (acquired in 1685) / Inv. 7300

The undisputed master of French classicism is particularly well represented in the Louvre, with the near totality of his major pictures, except notably for the celebrated *Death of Germanicus* (1628, Institute of Arts, Minneapolis). Punctuated by two Roman sojourns, he spent his career working for a group of collectors and committed amateurs keen on erudite or intellectual subjects. He drew themes from poetry and myth (*The Inspiration of the Poet*, Louvre; *Echo and Narcissus*, an illustration after Ovid's *Metamorphoses*, ibid.) and from the Bible (the four pictures of the Seasons, ibid.), though he also worked on the (lost) decoration of the gallery of the Louvre Palace. His final *Self-portrait* (ibid.) embodies his spirit of rigour and intelligence. It was only with David and Neoclassicism that painting began to draw lessons from Poussin, from his sensitivity to poetic geometry, and a searing austerity, especially in his landscapes, which also marked Cézanne.

Puvis de Chavannes, Pierre
Lyon, 1824 - Paris, 1898

MO - *L'Espérance [Hope]*, 1872
Oil on canvas. 70.5 x 82 cm

MO - *Les Jeunes filles au bord de la mer [The Girls on the Seashore]*, 1879
Oil on canvas. 61 x 47 cm / Isaac de Camondo bequest, 1911 / R.F. 2015

MO - *Le Pauvre Pêcheur [The Poor Fisherman]*, 1881
Oil on canvas. 155 x 192 cm / Acquired in 1887 / R.F. 506

MO - *Le Rêve [The Dream]*, 1883
Oil on canvas. 82 x 102 cm / Gift of Étienne Moreau-Nélaton, 1906 / R.F. 1685

In the history of French literature, if one wants to understand how Flaubert led to Proust, one needs to re-evaluate an underrated novelist such as Anatole France, who, though famous in his time, is hardly read today. Similarly, in painting, a once-venerated turn-of-the-20th-century master like Puvis de Chavannes provides the 'missing link' between Ingres and Picasso, and was a guiding light for Gauguin, the Fauvists, and, outside France, for Segantini, Pellizza da Volpedo, Sargent and Hammershøi. It is through Puvis that one can trace the shift from Impressionism to Cubism — or, rather, see why Cubism did not emerge from Impressionism. Long the subject of opprobrium, the role of Puvis, decorator of the great amphitheatre at the Sorbonne, was crucial and his influence considerable, but he vanished from the place of honour in major museums; only *The Poor Fisherman* resisted this tidal wave of historical neglect. Today, however, in the Musée d'Orsay, *The Dream* and *Girls on the Seashore* now appear as two of the finest pictures of their era.

Quarton, Enguerrand
Originally from the diocese of Laon; recorded in Provence between 1444 and 1466

ML - *Pietà de Villeneuve-lès-Avignon*, c. 1455
Originally from the Church of Villeneuve-lès-Avignon / Gift of the Société des Amis du Louvre, 1905 / R.F. 1569

In all likelihood Quarton had seen Van Eyck, Van der Weyden and the Master of Flémalle (Robert Campin), and perhaps also Tuscan artists contemporary with Matteo Giovanetti da Viterbo and Simone Martini, active at the Papal Palace in Avignon. A major figure and the creator of *The Coronation of the Virgin* now in the museum at Villeneuve-lès-Avignon, Quarton's masterpiece is the Louvre *Pietà*. As the stream of blood from Christ's wounds dries, St John removes the Crown of Thorns, while the Virgin is portrayed in the traditional pose of a carved *pietà*. Dressed as a canon, the donor appears in a position of prayer and the same size as other the figures. The landscape shows an imaginary Jerusalem, an earthly counterpart of the celestial city. The rugged arrangement of the rocks recalls a later master who lived at Aix-en-Provence: Paul Cézanne.

Raphaël
Raffaello Santi *or* Sanzio, *known as*
Urbino, 1483 - Rome, 1520

ML - *Baldassare Castiglione*, 1516
Canvas. 82 x 67 cm / Collection of Louis XIV (acquired from the heirs of Cardinal Mazarin, 1661) / Inv. 611

ML - *The Virgin with the Veil*, c. 1518
Wood. 68 x 48.7 cm / Collection of Louis XV (acquired in 1743 from the collection of the Prince of Carignano) / Inv. 603

Raphael was particularly well represented in the collections of the French monarchy. The large *Holy Family* and the *Great St Michael [St Michael Archangel Slaying the Dragon]* are two paintings upon which the identity of the royal collections is based. But taste for Raphael has changed. Over the past century, preference has shifted from the triumphal works to the precious, smaller altarpieces for private devotion and, above all, to the portraits. The small-sized *The Virgin with the Veil* can be likened to early pieces, such as the *St George* or the smaller *St Michael* (Louvre), that still bear the stamp of the sensitivity of Raphael's formative master, Perugino. For the portrait of Castiglione (1478-1529), author of the manual of courtly behaviour, *The Book of the Courtier*, Raphael was at the summit of his mastery of form and colour, capturing perfectly the face of an *honnête homme*, cultivated, elegant, self-possessed. Raphael himself is quoted in the *Courtier*, a veritable guide on to how to construct the self, on how to resemble one's ideal portrait.

Raysse, Martial
Golfe-Juan, 1936

CP - *Made in Japan-La Grande Odalisque*, 1964
Acrylic paint, glass, fly on photograph mounted on canvas. 130 x 97 cm / Gift of the Scaler Foundation, 1995 / AM 1995-213

Cofounder of the Nouveau Réaliste group, Martial Raysse's images betray an interest in consumer society, from fashion magazine to museum, from kitsch to advert, following a similar line to contemporary American Pop art. His view is that: 'Prisunic [department stores] are the museums of modern art.' Between 1963 and 1965, Raysse started co-opting to his own ends earlier masterpieces of art, such as Gérard's *Psyche Receiving the First Kiss of Love* or Ingres' *Bain Turc*. A video-art pioneer who later turned to traditional figuration and to the landscapes of Poussin and Ruisdael (*Ceux du Maquis*, 1992, Centre Pompidou), Raysse has always had a surprise up his sleeve.

Rebeyrolle, Paul
Eymoutiers, Haute-Vienne, 1926

CP - *Nude*, 1971
Oil on canvas. 190 x 275 cm / Purchase of the Fonds National d'Art Contemporain, 1979 / Deposit at the Musée National d'Art Moderne, 1983 / AM 1983-DEP 8

Between a realism invested by symbols and vast abstract, yet politically 'committed' canvases, in about 1955, Rebeyrolle, initially marked by Picasso, struck out for pastures new. Taking his inspiration from everyday life, he transcends it through an occasionally grandiose lyricism and a power reminiscent of Courbet's Realism, conveyed in a modern and personal idiom. Lyrical in execution, his large formats testify to an overriding ambition to obliterate the border between abstraction and the pictorial translation of the pulse of life.

Redon, Odilon
Bordeaux, 1840 - Paris, 1916

MO - *Le Char d'Apollon [The Chariot of Apollo]*, 1905-1914
Pastel on canvas. 91.5 x 77 cm / Allocated in lieu of death duties, 1978 / R.F. 36724

A draughtsman fascinated by the effects allowed by etching and pastel, inventing fantastic or Symbolist subjects in a dream-like, lyrical universe, Redon was the strangest artist of his generation, a solitary genius who was nonetheless perfectly attuned to the taste of his time, haunted by images whose only equivalents are to be found later among the Surrealists. The favourite painter of Des Esseintes, the rarefied hero of *A Rebours*, Huysmans' 1884 novel that best expresses the curiosities and experiments of the Symbolist movement, Redon's colours and saturated blacks were a formative influence on the Nabis, Paul Gauguin, Emile Bernard, Maurice Denis, Edouard Vuillard, and on another introspective recluse, Pierre Bonnard.

Regnault, Henri
Paris, 1843 - Buzenval, 1871

MO - *Exécution sans jugement sous les rois maures de Grenade [Execution without Trial under the Moorish Kings of Granada]*, 1870
Oil on canvas. 302 x 146 cm / Acquired in 1872 / R.F. 22

Dying all too young in a skirmish in the Franco-Prussian War of 1871, Regnault first shone in a Neo-Romantic style, before turning to Orientalism after a journey to Morocco during which he crisscrossed Spain. Memories of the Alhambra serve as a backdrop in an amalgam of extreme sophistication and violence. The expansive composition and the sheer power of the decapitation scene, inspired perhaps by Delacroix, readily explain how this canvas quickly came to be regarded as the artist's masterpiece.

Rembrandt
Rembrandt Harmenszoon van Rijn, *known as*
Leiden, 1606 - Amsterdam, 1669

ML - *Le Philosophe en méditation [The Meditating Philosopher]*, 1632
Wood. 28 x 34 cm / Collection of Louis XVI (Acquired in 1784) / Inv. 1740

ML - *Bethsabée au bain [Bathsheba or Bathsheba at the Bath]*, 1654
Canvas. 142 x 142 cm / Dr Louis La Caze bequest, 1869 / M.I. 957

ML - *Le Bœuf écorché [The Flayed Ox or The Carcass of Beef]*, 1655
Wood. 94 x 69 cm / Acquired in 1857 / M.I. 169

The Louvre possesses a remarkable series of Rembrandt's masterpieces — though at one time using allegedly scientific procedures, some mistakenly tried to contest the authenticity of the famous *Meditating Philosopher*. In truth, this is one of the artist's most beautiful works. The Louvre also contains *The Pilgrims at Emmaüs* (1648), as well as several canvases dating from the artist's prime in the 1650s. The opulent paint substance of the figure of Bathsheba and the young woman's extraordinary face make it one of his finest historico-religious pictures. Superficially a genre scene, *The Flayed Ox* in fact testifies to the absolute freedom of Rembrandt's handling of matière, a foretaste of the artist's final phase, of the ultimate self-portraits and *The Oath of Claudius Civilis* (Nationalmuseum, Stockholm).

Reni, Guido
Calvenzano, near Bologna, 1573/1575 - Bologna, 1642

ML - *L'Enlèvement d'Hélène [The Rape of Helen]*, 1631
Canvas. 253 x 265 cm / Seized during the Revolution from the collection of the Duc de Penthièvre at Paris / Inv. 539

Deeply affected by the innovations in painting brought about by Annibale and Ludovico Carracci in 1595, the discovery of Caravaggio eventually converted Reni to realism. The refined aestheticism of the figures and the harmonious rhythm of the settings bypasses the intervening Mannerist period to hark back instead to Raphael's sublime compositions. Reni delighted in the portrayal of heroic women: Cleopatra, Lucretia, Judith, Mary Magdalene, Semiramis, Salome. Led by Paris and flanked by servants, Helen, too, is figure from his gallery of illustrious females.

Renoir, Pierre-Auguste
Limoges, 1841 - Cagnes-sur-Mer, 1919

MO - *Etude or torse, effet de soleil [Study or Torso: Sun Effect]*,
c. 1875-1876
Oil on canvas. 81 x 65 cm / Gustave Caillebotte bequest, 1894 / R.F. 2740

MO - *Bal du Moulin de la Galette*, 1876
Oil on canvas. 131 x 175 cm / Gustave Caillebotte bequest, 1894 / R.F. 2739

MO - *Les Baigneuses [The Bathers]*, c. 1918-1919
Oil on canvas. 110 x 160 cm / Gift of the artist's son, 1923 / R.F. 2795

Renoir started out in Limoges as a porcelain painter. From this first calling he never lost his love for a delicate touch, fine craftsmanship, a pearly clarity of palette and even for a conventional 18th-century style rethought in line with late 19th-century bourgeois taste; rather than as essays in Impressionism, this is how Renoir himself saw his art, framing his paintings in lavish examples of Louis XV-style carving. An admirer of Ingres and of his bathers, of Raphael and the eyes of his Virgins, a lover of classical and mythological subjects, this did not preclude direct observation or a fondness for the kinds of festivities depicted in the *Bal du Moulin de la Galette*. Society portraitist and, at the same time, portraying the common people of his district of Montmartre, in his lifetime he remained the best-loved of all the Impressionists — the cause, perhaps, of his waning popularity today.

Richter, Gerhard
Dresden, 1932

CP - *1024 Farben, n° 350-3 [1024 Colours, n° 350-3]*, 1973
Lacquer on canvas. 254 x 478 cm / Gift of the artist, 1984 / AM 1984-285

Born in one of pre-war Europe's most important cultural centres (the Dresden art museum was lucky to survive the bombing of the city), Richter's oeuvre is a heterogeneous mix that ranges from the abstract to the figurative, monochromes (*Grau n° 349*, Centre Pompidou), as well as large-scale landscapes (*Chinon*, *ibid.*), not forgetting self-portraits taken from photographs whose blurred effect he painstakingly reconstitutes. A much-appreciated figure in the United States, Richter prefers to hang his pictures in a disorderly fashion so as to disorientate his audience and convey the sense that one artist can encapsulate every aspect of art. Arising from the upheaval and confusion resulting from the collapse of a personal Berlin Wall, his essentially multifaceted oeuvre is in fact a response to this unique, if immensely ambitious, goal.

Rigaud, Hyacinthe
Hyacinthe Rigau y Ros, *known as*
Perpignan, 1659 - Paris, 1743

ML - *Louis XIV*, 1701
Canvas. 277 x 194 cm / Collection of Louis XIV / Inv. 7492

In this 1701 portrayal of the Sun King, the greatest portraitist of French Classicism realises an image of regal majesty that has imprinted itself on the collective imagination. It succeeds in marrying the lesson of Van Dyck and Le Brun's typically French grandeur with the psychological penetration and personal vibrancy of which Largillière was the past master. Instead of a ceremonial portrait, in which the rendering of fabric, lace and gold counts as much as the figure depicted, it shows both man and sovereign, thereby creating a prototype that all Europe admired and strove to emulate. His portrait of Bossuet is another major piece in the Louvre, where the ornamental and 'elevated' idiom the painter adopted alludes to the sitter's mastery of oratory.

Robert, Hubert
Paris, 1733 - *ibid.*, 1808

ML - *Le Pont du Gard [The Pont du Gard]*, 1787 Salon
Canvas. 242 x 242 cm / Commissioned by Louis XVI / Inv. 7650

ML - *Project for the Grande Gallery of the Louvre*, 1796 Salon
Canvas. 114.5 x 146 cm / Acquired in 1975 / R.F. 1975-11

Strongly influenced by the light of Italy and by Panini's *capricci* in which ancient and modern architecture are combined, Robert asserted his personality first in Paris, then, from 1765, in all Europe (major Russian collectors quickly became devotees of his work). A painter of real and imaginary or half-imaginary views, he was just as inventive in his depictions of the gardens at Versailles during the reign of Louis XVI as he was for the storming of the Bastille or the official Revolutionary festivals. His *Pont du Gard* was a commission for the château at Fontainebleau, together with other 'Antiquities': *Interior of the Temple of Diana at Nîmes*; *The Maison Carrée at Nîmes, with the Arènes and the Tour Magne*; *The Triumphal Arch and Amphitheatre of Orange*. At the 1796 Salon, he exhibited two *Views of the Grande Gallery of the Louvre*, one roofed and intact, the other in ruins, a meditation on the destiny of museums.

Rothko, Mark
Dvinsk, Russia, 1903 - New York, 1970

CP - *N 14 (Browns over Dark)*, 1963
Oil and acrylic on canvas. 228.5 x 176 cm / Purchase, 1968 / AM 1976-1015

Of Baltic origin, emigrating to the United States in 1913, where he studied at Yale, Rothko began as a figurative artist attracted by Surrealism. In early works, a Matisse-like taste in colour and an interest in geometrical composition provide a foretaste of what was to follow: large formats on which appear luminous rectangles with blurred outlines that, in a later more sombre period, are supplanted by a black, maroon and grey palette. Truly Biblical in inspiration, without a single human figure or earthly subject, this is an art designed for prolonged contemplation, in the way of the great altarpieces of the Renaissance. His chapel of 1971 in Houston (Texas) is an ecumenical exercise that reconciles, beyond any specific religion, all meditation on Man and Creation. It naturally remains possible to view Rothko's pictures agnostically, and to be moved solely by their visual qualities. Rothko may be imagined listening to Bach. This is a mistake: his favourite composer was Mozart...

Rouault, Georges
Paris, 1871 - *ibid.*, 1958

CP - *Filles*, 1917
Oil on paper glue-mounted on canvas. 72 x 56 cm / Gift of Mme Rouault and her children, 1959 / AM 3637 P

These prostitutes would seem to undermine Rouault's reputation as an exclusively religious artist. Once apprenticed to a glass painter — as his life-long predilection for thick, black outlines betrays — Rouault used the language of stained-glass. The first conservator of the Musée Gustave Moreau in Paris, associating with both Symbolists and Fauvists, he developed an art at odds with that of his masters and friends. If his Christs derive from Rembrandt, his clowns and these loose women instead recall Daumier. He is a painter of outsiders, outcasts, of the disinherited, of all those to whom he proclaims a Gospel message in which he himself believed deeply and which remains the linchpin to his entire oeuvre.

Rousseau, Henri,
also known as Le Douanier Rousseau
Laval, 1844 - Paris, 1910

MO - *La Guerre or La chevauchée de la Discorde [War]*, 1894
Oil on canvas. 114 x 195 cm / Acquired in 1946 / R.F.1946-1

MO - *La Charmeuse de serpents [The Snake Charmer]*, 1907
Oil on canvas. 169 x 189.5 cm / Jacques Doucet bequest, 1936 / R.F. 1937-7

Throughout his life, this 'Sunday painter' and museum copyist, this unassuming employee of the Paris octroi, dreamed of remote lands and lions, of enigmatic women and legends. Cherished by figures such as Jarry, Apollinaire and Marie Laurencin, and hailed by the avant-garde, his true ambition seems to have been to emulate Ingres, Cabanel and Gérôme, and so to join the serried ranks of those academic 'masters' who would carry off the laurels at the yearly Salons. The paradox is that this artist blessed with a vast visual culture, yet with outmoded ambitions, was transformed into the ultimate modern, a reformer of the arts, his role comparable to the 'primitive' Italians of the early Renaissance. In the past, it was believed that he had seen nothing, which is false, and he had read nothing, which is less so. The long line of 20th-century 'Naive' painters claim descent from him, though they fail to grasp the disconcerting complexity of an oeuvre that appears original, fresh and novel, but which has its roots deep in the world of the museum.

Rubens, Peter Paul
Siegen, Westphalia, 1577 - Antwerp, 1640

ML - *Débarquement de Marie de Médicis au port de Marseille, [Marie de Medicis Landing at Marseille]*, between 1621 and 1625
Canvas. 394 x 295 cm / Collection of Louis XIV, 1693; transferred permanently from the Luxembourg Palace to the Louvre in 1816 / Inv. 1774

The greatest of them all? Yoked to a host of clichés (Balzac's description of the women he preferred as a 'heap of Flemish meat', the modern notion that his sketches are more interesting than his large-scale compositions, etc.), Rubens has always exerted considerable sway over the artistic imagination, with David, Géricault and Delacroix at the head, whereas today's public shows him little regard. His Baroque style, of fire and soaring flight, full of frenzy and ardour, bursts forth in the twenty-four canvases of the cycle of the *Life of Marie de Medicis*, wife of Henri IV, commissioned in 1621 and one of the most beautiful series in the entire Louvre. A truly European artist, he knew Italy as well as London and Madrid, enjoying a regal life style in his palace in Antwerp as chief of a prestigious studio. Negotiating on an equal footing with all the princes of Europe, Rubens transformed the social status of the painter, before this was changed in its turn by the Romantic image of the painter who is a genius *because* he is an outsider.

Ruisdael, Jacob van
Haarlem, vers 1628/1629 - *ibid.* ?, 1682

ML - *Le Coup de soleil, [The Ray of Sunlight, or The Burst of Sunshine]*, **after 1660**
Canvas. 83 x 99 cm / Collection of Louis XVI (acquired in 1784) / Inv. 1820

Son of the painter Isaack van Ruisdael (1599-1677) and nephew of Solomon van Ruysdael (c. 1600-1670, note the name spelt with a 'y'), Jacob is the most celebrated painter of this family of landscapists, primarily because the Romantic era imagined him as a painter *maudit* who died heartbroken and poverty-stricken. Undoubtedly this was far from the truth, but it remains significant that his works have always been surrounded by a dark yet glittering aura. For Ruisdael, landscape ought to be an ideal, a panoramic view elevated by contrasts of light. An early inclusion in most major European collections, Ruisdael devised many formal solutions, which were widely taken up right into the Romantic era, the Barbizon School and Millet.

Saenredam, Pieter Jansz
Assendelf, Pays-Bas, 1597 - Haarlem, 1665

ML - *Intérieur de l'église Saint-Bavon de Haarlem [Interior of the Church of St Bavo in Haarlem]*, **1630**
Wood. 41 x 37 cm / Acquired in 1983 / R.F. 1983-100

A rare painter by whom one can see only one other picture in Paris (in the collection of the Institut Néerlandais, Fondation Custodia), Saenredam is a painter of churches, of architectural rigour, of interiors in brown and white, of light shafts glimpsed between stonework. Close inspection of his pictures often reveals an inscription, a graffito on a pillar, or a signature. Near monochrome architectural painting, a genre fashionable in 17th-century Holland (Emmanuel de Witte is another prime example), aroused the interest of many 20th-century abstract artists who strove for balance, economy and interiority.

Samba, Chéri
Samba Wa Mbiumba N'Zuiga Nurimasi Ndombasi, *known as*
Kinto-M'Vuila, Zaire (Congo), 1956

CP - *Marche de soutien à la campagne sur le sida [March in Support of the Campaign Against AIDS]*, **1988**
Oil and spangles on prepared canvas. 134.5 x 200 cm / Purchase, 1990 / AM 1990-36

A painter of the people, much influenced by the imagery of local advertising and sign-painters' puns, Chéri Samba excels in a bitter-sweet mix of comedy and tragedy, of everyday life and universal messages. His studio on Kosa-Vubu Avenue, Kinshasa, has become the focal point for a whole school of politically committed artists who, while reviling contemporary mores, are still in love with the African sky, painting scenes featuring people typical of those who throng the city streets.

Sassetta
Stefano di Giovanni, *known as*
Siena or Cortona, 1392/1400 - Siena, 1450

ML - *Le bienheureux Ranieri Rasini délivre les pauvres d'une prison de Florence [The Blessed Ranieri Rasini Freeing the Poor from the Prison in Florence]*, **1444**
Wood and gold ground. 43.4 x 63.3 cm / Gift of the Société des Amis du Louvre, 1965 / R.F. 1965-2

Until the art historian Bernard Berenson (1865-1959) attributed to him a corpus of works that had lain dormant or was wrongly ascribed to other artists, the name of Sassetta (literally, 'little stone') had simply slipped out of the collective memory. Unlike the Florentine school of the Quattrocento, whose masters have never been forgotten, this rediscovery marked the reappearance of the most important figure of the Sienese school. Of Franciscan spirituality (whereas the Florentine Fra Angelico was a Dominican) and an elegant apostle of poverty, Sassetta wedded supreme refinement to a sometimes grim Gothic, though he was well aware of the breakthroughs of the Tuscan school in matters of perspective, as this predella panel makes obvious. Such a 'gothicising' response to Masaccio's revolution is neither backward-looking nor retrograde, but perpetuates a poetical and imaginative mode that had many followers, such as Sano di Pietro and the Master of the Observance, before Florentine principles took permanent hold of European painting.

Saytour, Patrick
Nice, 1935

CP - *Sans titre [Untitled]*, **1968**
Plastic-coated canvas and traces of folding. 354 x 136.5 cm / Purchase, 1983 / AM 1983-373

The distinguishing characteristic of Saytour's art is his use of *pliage* (folding): his raw material is the unstretched canvas, sometimes printed or coloured, then folded and retouched often in a near invisible manner. Saytour creates a palpable third dimension in relief, with real shadows that move and make the viewer want to touch the work. The divide between the industrial (patterns from mass-produced carpets and wallpapers...) and the creative act remains vague, dubious. Faced with the canvas hanging in the Centre Pompidou, one wonders: is this a 'painting' or an installation?

Seurat, Georges
1859, Paris - *ibid.*, 1891

MO - *Poseuse de face [Model, Frontal View]*, c. 1886-1887
Oil on panel. 25 x 16 cm / Acquired in 1947 / R.F. 1947-13

Initially an Impressionist, impressed by Ingres (his first professor was Henri Lehmann, himself a pupil of the master) and Puvis de Chavannes, Seurat revels in monumentality, as his pivotal 1886 work *Sunday Afternoon on the Ile de la Grande Jatte* testifies (Art Institute, Chicago). In the Divisionist technique he employed, tiny dots of paint are juxtaposed according to scientific principles. The three *Models* are characteristic of this Neo-Impressionist method that derives as much from theoretical reflection as from the observation of the model, and which calls for slow, meticulous working methods and careful organisation of the picture surface.

Soulages, Pierre
Rodez, 1919

CP - *Peinture, 202 x 453, 29 juin 1979*, 1979
Oil on canvas. 202 x 453 cm / Purchase, 1980 / AM 1980-45

Is black a colour? Soulages's almost exclusive means of expression — he describes the luminous reflections of his chosen medium by the word *outrenoir* ('ultrablack') — his black is actually the result of careful construction, crisscrossed with marks by brush, palette knife and scraper. In Soulages' work, black, a colour traditionally neglected in painting in spite of Matisse's use of it for contours, is employed to monumental effect, invested by palpable traces of the artistic act. Poorly served by reproduction, such paintings must be seen 'live', from near and far, taking time to dive deep within them.

Staël, Nicolas de
Nicolas de Staël-Holstein, *known as*
St-Petersburg, 1914 - Antibes, 1955

CP - *Les Toits*, or *Les Toits de Paris [Roofs]*, 1952
Oil on hardboard. 200 x 150 cm / Gift of the artist, 1952 / AM 3159 P

CP - *Les Musiciens, souvenir de Sidney Bechet [The Musicians. Souvenir of Sidney Bechet]*, 1953
Oil on canvas. 161.9 x 114.2 cm / Allocated in lieu of death duties, 1982 / AM 1982-263

A Baltic aristocrat whose family was driven out of Russia shortly after he was born, Nicolas de Staël trained initially in Brussels. An admirer of Cézanne and Braque, he nevertheless chose the path of abstraction. *Roofs* is a masterpiece of his first manner, recognisable in the powerfully constructed surfaces worked up with the palette knife. The title, however, conveys a figurative meaning. Together with still lifes and landscapes, De Staël, a great jazz lover, also produced spectacular set pieces inspired not only by football, the sea or boats, but also by music, where the improvisations he had heard on disc or at a concert are captured in paint. *The Musicians* was painted in memory of a concert he had been to: the work's title emphasises its quality as a 'transcription' from one artistic language into another.

Signac, Paul
Paris, 1863 - *ibid.*, 1935

MO - *La Bouée rouge [The Red Buoy]*, 1895
Oil on canvas. 81 x 65 cm / Gift of Dr. Pierre Hébert, 1957 / R.F. 1957-12

A disciple of Seurat, Signac exhibited at the eighth and last Impressionist exhibition in 1886. An adept of Divisionism, he painted a great deal in Normandy, Brittany and on the Mediterranean coast, particularly at St-Tropez where he lived for many years. Sensitive to rhythm and to architecture, his *D'Eugène Delacroix au Néo-impressionnisme* (1899) preached the absolute primacy of colour and artistic asceticism, marking a radical break with Impressionist observation of nature. Matisse, who worked with him closely, as well as the Cubists, Delaunay and Kandinsky, drew many of their essential principles from this cardinal text.

Spoerri, Daniel
Daniel Feinstein, *known as*
Galati, Romania, 1930

CP - *La Douche [The Shower]*, 1961
Oil on canvas, plumbing fittings, pipe, shower rose on wood. 70.2 x 96.8 x 18.5 cm
Purchase, 1991 / AM 1991-267

The *autothéâtre*, realised in tandem with the sculptor Jean Tinguely, shows that by 1959 Spoerri was already playing with the situation of the viewer before the artwork. Joining the Nouveaux Réalistes group in 1960, he transformed pre-existing works and objects into 'appropriated' artworks. In the 1960s, he invented the concept of the 'gallery-restaurant', in which works are made not only out of food (artists César and Ben 'cooked' for him), but also from cooking utensils and 'reliefs' of leftovers — and even perhaps by the viewer who 'consumes' this idiosyncratic means of consecrating the real.

Tanguy, Yves
Paris, 1900 - Woodbury, Conn., 1955

CP - *Jour de lenteur*, 1937
Oil on canvas. 92 x 73 cm / Purchase, 1938 / AM 2173 P

Tanguy, an ex-seaman, a Surrealist close to Giorgio De Chirico, Max Ernst and the poet Jacques Prévert, specialised in landscapes showing ill-defined plains reminiscent of the desert or the ocean. He replaces figures and animals with hazy 'biomorphic' forms gliding over a milky ground, the depths of a dreamworld. Employing the Surrealist technique of automatism, Tanguy freed himself from all extraneous rules, creating a distinctly personal body of work that he continued to develop in the United States when he moved there on the outbreak of the Second World War.

Tàpies, Antoni
Barcelona, 1923

CP - *Grand Blanc horizontal*, 1962
Mixed technique on canvas. 195 x 310 cm / Purchase, 1982 / AM 1982-17

After a 'Surrealist' period during which this Catalan artist showed his close links not only to Miró but also to Klee and Ernst, Tàpies then joined Wols, Fautrier and Dubuffet in Paris. Printmaker and sculptor, Tàpies rejoices in the 'handicraft' of artistic creation, in his contact with everyday things: his matière resembles an old wall riven by cracks, soiled, scraped, streaked with trickles and pierced with stitching. His works can be indirectly figurative and integrate real objects, such as string, nails or bits of wood.

Titian
Tiziano Vecellio, *known as*
Pieve di Cadore, Belluna c. 1488/1489 - Venice, 1576

ML - *Concert champêtre*, c. 1509
Canvas. 105 x 136.5 cm / Collection of Louis XIV / Inv. 71

ML - *L'Homme au gant [Man with a Glove]*, c. 1520-1523
Canvas. 100 x 89 cm / Collection of Louis XIV / Inv. 757

Spanning almost a century and continuing to create until his last years, Titian's long life meant he was necessarily a multifaceted artist. Few artists have gone through as many transformations: from being a pupil of Gentile Bellini's, he then espoused the manner of Giorgione (to whom the *Concert Champêtre* was long attributed) and became the creator of magnificent altarpieces, such as the *Assumption* in Santa Maria dei Frari, Venice, ending as the tormented genius who painted his final, tortured canvases with his fingers. His portraits, such as *Man with a Glove*, are characterised by a singular economy of means: the composition is sober, the palette frugal, but the eye sparkles and the gesture etches itself on the memory. In 1520s Venice, sheer, scented gloves like these were a sign of consummate elegance. Yet the name of the sitter remains as mysterious as the real subject of the Concert.

Toulouse-Lautrec, Henri de
Henri de Marie Raymond de Toulouse-Lautrec-Monfa, *known as*
Albi, 1864 - Château de Malromé, Gironde, 1901

MO - *La Toilette*, 1896
Oil on carton. 67 x 54 cm / Pierre Goujon bequest, 1914 / R.F. 2242

The legendary life story of this sickly, handicapped midget, ferocious yet amusing, friend to prostitutes and their madames, born into one of very few French aristocratic families whose origins genealogists can trace back to one of the twelve noble *pairs* in Emperor Charlemagne's retinue, is in the image of the bitter-sweet revels of the Impressionist myth. A hugely talented draughtsman — Degas is his only peer in the field — Toulouse-Lautrec turned the poster into an authentic art, while the models he made famous (La Goulue and other artistes) amount today almost to historical figures, turning the world he invented into a collection of family portraits.

Turner, Joseph Mallord William
London, 1775 - *ibid.*, 1851

ML - *Landscape with a River and a Bay in the Distance*, c. 1835
Canvas. 93.5 x 123.5 cm / Acquired in 1967 / R.F. 1967-2

Turner wanted to be a classical landscapist, the Claude Lorraine of his time. He visited Napoleon's Louvre and was well-acquainted with both Poussin and Italian painting. His many landscapes can be historical, literary or, even, modern (*Rain, Steam and Speed*, National Gallery, London). In a cosmic synthesis, he reduces the subject to accents of light in spiralling compositions much admired by the Romantic generation. Turner's path towards abstraction, towards a painting of ideas rather than of locale (of which the picture in the Louvre is a prime example) is also explained by the incomplete state — to what extent deliberately so is not known — of a good number of canvases from late in his career. Long scorned by critics who considered them awkward, they are today hailed as pioneering attempts to release painting from the figurative motif.

Uccello, Paolo di Dono, *known as*
Florence, 1397 - *ibid.*, 1475

ML - *La Bataille de San Romano [The Battle of San Romano]*, c. 1435-1440
Wood. 182 x 317 cm / Collection Campana, Rome. Acquired in 1861; Musée Napoleon III. Entered the Louvre in 1863 / M.I. 469

Vasari saw him as an ultimately minor painter, a curiosity of Quattrocento art history, driven mad by a remorseless study of perspective, but his oeuvre was rehabilitated by the Cubists and the Surrealists, who were both receptive to his mathematical approach. His corpus is a small one: in addition to the frescoes of Santa Maria Novella in Florence (the superb *Flood* in the Green Cloister) and the still 'Gothic' *St George* in the Musée Jacquemart-André in Paris, his finest works are the hunting scene in Oxford, the fresco representing Giovanni Acuto in the Duomo in Florence and the San Romano triptych, split between three major European museums (the Louvre, the Uffizi, and the National Gallery, London). For conservation reasons, these three very fragile panels will undoubtedly never be again united as they were in the Medici palace.

Van der Weyden, *see* Weyden, Rogier van der

Van Eyck, Jan, *see* Eyck, Jan van

Van Gogh, Vincent
Groot Zundert, Netherlands, 1853 - Auvers-sur-Oise, France, 1890

MO - *Portrait de l'artiste [Portrait of the Artist]*, 1889
Oil on canvas. 65 x 54.5 cm / Gift Paul and Marguerite Gachet, 1949 / R.F. 1949-17

MO - *La chambre de Van Gogh à Arles [Van Gogh's Room at Arles]*, 1889
Oil on canvas. 57.5 x 74 cm / Formerly Matsukata Collection. Entered the Louvre in 1959 in application of the peace treaty with Japan / R.F. 1959-2

MO - *Dr Paul Gachet*, 1890
Oil on canvas. 68 x 57 cm / Gift Paul and Marguerite Gachet, 1949 / R.F. 1949-16

An admirer of Millet, a consummate draughtsman, exalting the humble (peasants and potato eaters), Van Gogh fits into both the Dutch tradition and that of French masters — he met Toulouse-Lautrec in Fernand Cormon's studio in Paris. The violent clash between two searchers after the absolute during the period in Arles where Gauguin joined him in 1888 has become the stuff of legend. His tormented, sculptural self-portraits testify to the struggles of a man against the mental illness that dogged him. Nursed by Doctor Gachet at Auvers-sur-Oise, Van Gogh produced a long sequence of testamentary works where the principal subject is brushwork, thereby paving the way for Expressionism.

Vasarely, Victor
Viktor Vasarhelyi, *known as*
Pécs, Hungary, 1908 - Paris, 1997

CP - *Hommage à Georges Pompidou*, 1976
Aluminium. 500 x 400 x 6 cm / Gift of the artist, 1984 / AM 1976-1141

Much-vaunted by the public in the 1970s — the posthumous portrait of the President of the Republic is symptomatic of this glorious period — today Vasarely's oeuvre is passing through the kind of temporary purgatory without which no phoenix can arise from the ashes. Raised in the tottering Austro-Hungarian Empire and trained at Budapest, once he settled in Paris Vasarely explored the byways of an abstraction one might describe as post-Cubist, in the form of a crystallised, kinetic world. *Georges Pompidou* is not a 'painting', but a monumental metal sculpture designed to be suspended in mid-air. Though from the front it alludes to the idiom of painted portraiture, the form 'moves' depending on one's viewing angle. Seeing himself as a Renaissance artist, Vasarely has created a synthesis between painting, sculpture and architecture, which also encompasses photography and the *image-movement* of cinema.

Vermeer, Johannes
Delft, 1632 - *ibid.*, 1675

ML - *La Dentellière [The Lacemaker]*, c. 1670
Canvas transferred on to wood. 24 x 21 cm / Acquired in 1870 / M.I. 1448

ML - *L'Astronome [The Astronomer]*, c. 1668-1670
Canvas. 51 x 45 cm / Acquired in 1983 / R.F. 1983-28

For a long time, this artist who was to fascinate Pissarro, Proust and Dalí was practically unknown. The oeuvre of the 'recluse of Delft' is limited to no more than thirty-five pictures rediscovered in the wake of pioneering studies by the critic Thoré-Bürger (1866). With *The Procuress* (1656, Gemäldegalerie, Dresden), *The Astronomer* is the only picture to bear a date: 1668. *The Lacemaker* was presumably also executed during the artist's mature period. Devised by use of a camera obscura, his realistic compositions verge on illusionism in the way materials are rendered, though elsewhere their pointillism serves to capture the physical play of light. Probably influenced initially by a pupil of Rembrandt, Carel Fabritius (1622-1654), and close to Pieter de Hooch (1629-1684), the style he invented is immediately recognisable: the conquest of the absolute, a detailed vision of interiority as it appears in the middle-class 'interiors' in the United Provinces.

Veronese
Paolo Caliari, *known as*
Verona, 1528 - Venice, 1588

ML - *Les Noces de Cana [The Wedding Feast at Cana]*, 1562-1563
Canvas. 666 x 990 cm / Convent of San Giorgio Maggiore, Venice. Entered the Louvre, 1797 / Inv. 142

The splendid majesty of Venice: the artist his contemporaries placed as high as Titian and Tintoretto is regarded today as the greatest decorative painter, the most inspired orchestrator of the palaces, convents and churches of the 16th-century capital of the Mediterranean (*An Allegory of Venice and the Virtues*, 1575-1577, Doge's Palace, Venice; *The Triumph of Venice*, 1583, *ibid.*, the ceiling of the Great Council Chamber, *ibid.*). His Last Suppers, painted for monastery refectories, were already considered the acme of his art by the 17th century (*Wedding Feast at Cana*, Louvre; *Feast at the House of Levi*, Accademia, Venice; *Banquet of St Gregory the Great*, Museo Civico, Vicenza; *Feast in the House of Simon*, Musée National des Châteaux de Versailles et de Trianon).

Villeglé, Jacques Mahé de La Villeglé, *known as*
(Quimper, 1926), *see* Hains, Raymond

Vuillard, Edouard
Cuiseaux, Saône-et-Loire, 1868 - La Baule, 1940

MO - Five panels of the *Jardins publics [Public Parks]* series, 1894 :
La Conversation [The Conversation]
Oil on canvas. 213 x 154 cm / Acquired in 1929 / R.F. 1977-365

Les Nourrices [The Nursemaids]
Oil on canvas. 213.5 x 73 cm / Acquired in 1929 / R.F. 1977-365

L'Ombrelle rouge [The Red Parasol]
Oil on canvas. 214 x 81 cm / Acquired in 1929 / R.F. 1977-365

Fillettes jouant [Little Girls Playing]
Oil on canvas. 214.5 x 88 cm / Mme Alexandre Radot bequest, 1978 / R.F. 1978-46

L'Interrogatoire [The Examination]
Oil on canvas. 214.5 x 92 cm / Mme Alexandre Radot bequest, 1978 / R.F. 1978-47

Starting out among the Nabis with Maurice Denis, Paul Sérusier and his brother-in-law Kerr-Xavier Roussel, Vuillard adopted their technique of flat tints and cloisonné close to the style of the Japanese woodblock (*In bed*, Musée d'Orsay). He later specialised in painting intimate scenes beneath 'the desolate beams of a lamp', in which the figures are seated in highly decorated and crowded settings crammed with furniture. A painter of interiors, Vuillard also concerned himself with gardens, in particular in the series painted for Alexandre Natanson entitled *Public Parks* (other pictures are in the Musées Royaux des Beaux-Arts, Brussels, and at Cleveland and Houston).

Warhol, Andy
Andrew Warhola, *known as*
Pittsburg, 1928 - New York, 1987

CP - *Electric Chair*, 1967
Screen-print on canvas. 137.2 x 185.3 cm / Gift of the Menil Foundation in memory of Jean de Menil, 1976 / AM 1976-1232

It would be incorrect to reduce Warhol's genius to a talent for transposing the techniques and aesthetics of advertising into the field of art and to envisage him solely as a consummate manufacturer of modern myth. Of death, he said simply: 'I don't believe in death. I can't say anything about it because I'm not prepared for it'. The electric chair shows the brutality of an untimely end whereby legal judgement is translated into technological procedure, as modern as the movies and the car. After superstar 'series' that included figures such as *Liz Taylor* (Centre Pompidou), *Marilyn Monroe*, *Jackie Kennedy* and *Elvis Presley*, as well as the *Mona Lisa* and the dollar bill itself, Warhol here presents the idea that the electric chair, too, is a sacred cow of American culture.

Watteau, Jean-Antoine
Valenciennes, 1684 - Nogent-sur-Marne, 1721

ML - *L'Embarquement pour Cythère [The Embarkation for Cythera]*, 1717
Canvas. 129 x 194 cm
Collection of the Academy
Inv. 8525

ML - *Gilles*, c. 1718-1720
Canvas. 184.5 x 149.5 cm / Dr Louis La Caze bequest, 1869 / M.I. 1121

Disdained by Neoclassical artists, Watteau returned to popularity only in the second half of the 19th century, thanks especially to the brothers Edmond and Jules de Goncourt; prior to the Caze bequest in 1869 he had been represented in the Louvre only by the *Embarquement*. This late work had served as his reception piece for the Academy in 1717. In it one finds his supreme qualities as a draughtsman and as a master of luminous colours inspired by the Venetians, and the true spirit of his oeuvre, of *fêtes galantes* (a genre continued by Lancret and Pater) shot through with levity and melancholy. The Louvre also possesses a series of small-format works depicting country parks with lovers' trysts and gardens dotted with statues.

Weyden, Rogier van der
Tournai, c. 1400 - Brussels, 1464

ML - *L'Annonciation [The Annunciation]*, c. 1435
Wood. 86 x 93 cm / Collection of the dukes of Savoy; originally from the Royal Gallery in Turin, 1799 / Inv. 1982

ML - *Triptyque de la famille Braque [The Braque Triptych]*, before 1452
Central panel: *Christ the Redeemer between the Virgin and St John the Evangelist* / Wood. 41 x 68 cm
Left-hand wing : *St John the Baptist* / Reverse: Death's-head and the Braque coats-of-arms / Wood. 41 x 34 cm
Right-hand wing : *The Magdalene* / Reverse: Cross and the Braque-Brabant coats-of-arms / Wood. 41 x 34 cm / Acquired in 1913 / R.F. 2063

The Annunciation is perhaps the central panel of a triptych whose wings are in Turin (Galleria Sabauda). One can here sense the importance to this artist of the technique of Van Eyck, who belonged to the same Burgundian milieu — around 1445-1450, Chancellor Rolin commissioned Van der Weyden's masterpiece, *Last Judgement* (still in the Hospice at Beaune). If *The Annunciation* derives from a composition made popular by an artist close to him, Robert Campin, the *Braque Triptych* is, on the other hand, a success of a more original stamp. All is here: rigour of composition, perfection of line, finesse of detailing and rendering of distance; moreover, Van der Weyden shows himself as one of the finest portraitists of his time.

Whistler, James Abbott McNeill
Lowell, Mass., 1834 - London, 1903

MO - *Arrangement in Grey and Black n° 1*, or *The Mother of the Artist*, 1871
Oil on canvas. 144.3 x 162.5 cm / Acquired in 1891 / R.F. 699

Even before exhibiting at the Salon des Refusés in 1863, this Francophile American, close to Courbet and Fantin-Latour, was a master etcher — indeed in the background of the *Arrangement in Grey and Black n° 1* (known as *The Mother of the Artist*) the role played by engraving is paramount. The title 'Arrangement', like that of 'Harmony' for other works, refers to the language of music. The value of an arrangement derives not from the original composition to be re-scored: it is the skill of the arranger in transposing themes and chords from the source piece that is admired. A picture entitled *Arrangement in Grey and Black n° 2* (and subtitled *Portrait of Carlyle*) is in the Art Gallery of Glasgow. The subject, be it his friend Carlyle or even his own mother, is relegated to a subtitle: the true 'subject' of the work is the technique of the 'arranger'.

Wols, (Alfred)
Otto Wolfgang Schülze, *known as*
Berlin, 1913 - Paris, 1951

CP - *Aile de papillon [Butterfly Wing]*, 1947
Oil on canvas. 55 x 46 cm / Gift of René de Montaigu, 1979 / AM 1979-255

Deeply influenced by his use of watercolour and capable of handling the most vaporous pigments, Wols is the inventor of Tachism. After a Surrealist phase, he came into his own after settling in Paris in 1945 in works that parallel the efforts of Pollock on the other side of the Atlantic. A tormented and solitary individual, a poet profoundly impressed by the Far East, Wols' unique oeuvre forms a process in which his entire existence is involved. His line is as precise as Klee's, with transparency effects occasionally reminiscent of Fautrier.

Zurbarán, Francisco de
Fuente de Cantos, 1598 - Madrid, 1664

ML - *L'Exposition du corps de saint Bonaventure [St Bonaventura on his Deathbed]*, 1629
Canvas. 245 x 220 cm / Acquired in 1858 from the heirs of the Maréchal Soult / M.I. 205

Although a painter of transcendentally perfect still lifes and of everyday life in monasteries that can be theatres of miraculous events, Zurbarán did not shy away from violence or from conveying the modelling of contemporary sculpture in a strongly contrasting light. *The Death of St Bonaventura*, like *St Bonaventura at Prayer* (Gemäldegalerie, Dresden), numbers among his most powerful works. The theatricality which regulates the obsequies of the Seraphic Doctor — St Bonaventura (1221-1274) is the author of a *Journey of the Soul towards God* — is a spur to prayer and meditation. Zurbarán shows that painting is a road that can lead from the reality of things to the seemingly inconceivable representation of what cannot be seen. In the most celebrated definition of the art, Leonardo da Vinci called painting, a *cosa mentale*.

Index
of real names

Photo credits

© **CNAC/MNAM/DistRMN. Photographers : Jacques Faujour, Béatrice Hatala, Georges Meguerditchian, Philippe Migeat, Jean-Claude Planchet, Bertrand Prévost, Adam Rzepka.**
pp. 11 (left), 30, 59, 62 (right), 64, 68 (left), 83 (right), 91 (right), 117 (bot.), 127 (right), 136 (right), 138 (right), 139, 144 (right), 146 (left), 150, 164 (right), 168 (right), 172 (right).
Documents CGP : pp. 11, 13, 15, 19, 21, 25, 27, 42, 45 (right), 46, 49 (right), 55 (left), 56 (right), 67 (right), 72 (left), 75, 77, 79, 81, 85 (right), 87 (right), 93 (right), 95, 101, 105 (right), 107, 113, 114 (left), 120 (left), 123, 124 (right), 129, 135, 140, 142 (left), 143, 144 (left), 147, 149, 153, 154 (bot.), 157, 158, 159, 160, 174 (bot.), 179 (right), 181 (right), 184.

© **2002 Erich Lessing.**
pp. 12, 14, 17, 18, 20 (left), 26, 32, 38, 39 (left), 40, 44, 50, 52, 53, 54 (left), 55 (right), 56 (left, ctr.), 58, 60, 62 (left, ctr.), 67 (left), 68 (right), 69, 70, 71, 74, 78, 80, 82, 83 (left), 84, 85 (left), 86, 88, 92, 93 (left), 96, 97, 98 (left), 99 (left), 100 (left), 102, 104, 108, 109, 110, 111, 115, 116, 121, 122, 124 (left), 126, 128, 130, 131, 132, 133, 136 (left), 137, 138 (left, ctr.), 141, 151, 152, 154 (top), 161, 162 (left, right), 164 (left), 166, 168 (left), 170 (left), 172 (left, ctr.), 174 (right), 176, 185 (left)

© **Photos RMN. Photographers : Jean Schormans, Gérard Blot, Hervé Lewandowski, J.G. Berizzi, G. Blot/C. Jean, C. Jean, Franck Raux, R.G. Ojeda, Bellot/Blot, Arnaudet, P. Bernard, K. Ignatiadis.**
pp. 10, 20 (right), 22, 23, 24, 28, 33, 35, 36, 37, 39 (right), 43, 45 (left, ctr.), 47, 48, 49 (left), 54 (ctr., right), 67 (ctr.), 72 (right), 73, 76, 87 (left), 89, 90, 91 (left), 94, 98 (right), 99 (right), 100 (right), 103, 105 (left), 106, 112, 114 (right), 120 (right), 124 (ctr.), 127 (left), 134, 136 (ctr.), 142 (ctr., right), 145, 146 (right), 148, 156, 162 (ctr.), 167, 170 (right), 174 (left), 175, 178, 179 (left), 180, 181 (left), 182, 183, 185 (right).

The Centre national d'art et de culture Georges Pompidou is a national state institution under the responsability of the Minister of Culture (law n° 75-1, 3 January 1975).

Photolithography :
Arciel Graphic, Paris
Printing :
Printed in December 2002
by Artegrafica, in Verona, Italy